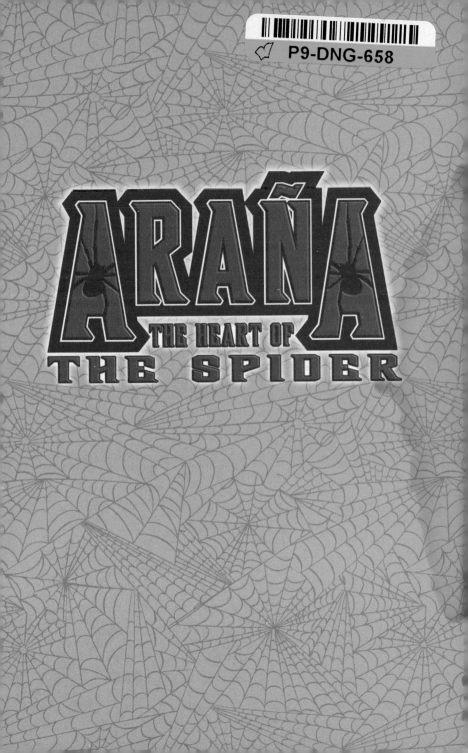

ARAÑA

THE HEART OF

THE SPIDER

ARAÑA
THE HEART OF THE SPIDER

writer
Fiona Avery

pencilers
Mark Brooks & Roger Cruz

inkers
Jaime Mendoza & Victor Olazaba

Colorist
UDON's Larry Molinar & Jeannie Lee

Letterers
Virtual Calligraphy's Rus Wooton
& Chris Eliopoulos

Cover Artist
Mark Brooks

Assistant Editor
Cory Sedlmeier

Editor
Jennifer Lee

Executive Editor
Axel Alonso

Creative Consultant
J. Michael Straczynski

Special Thanks to Larry Ewing

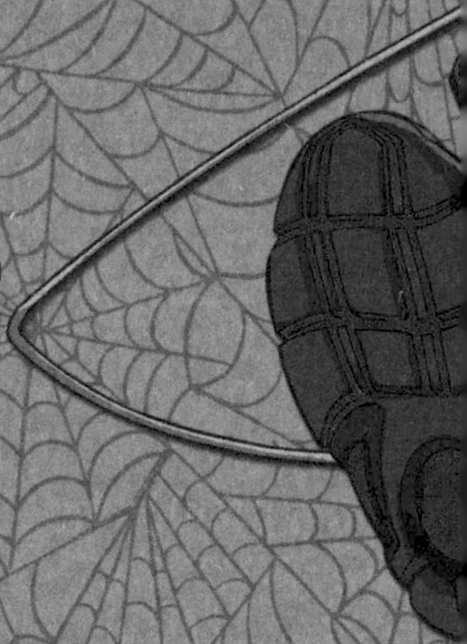

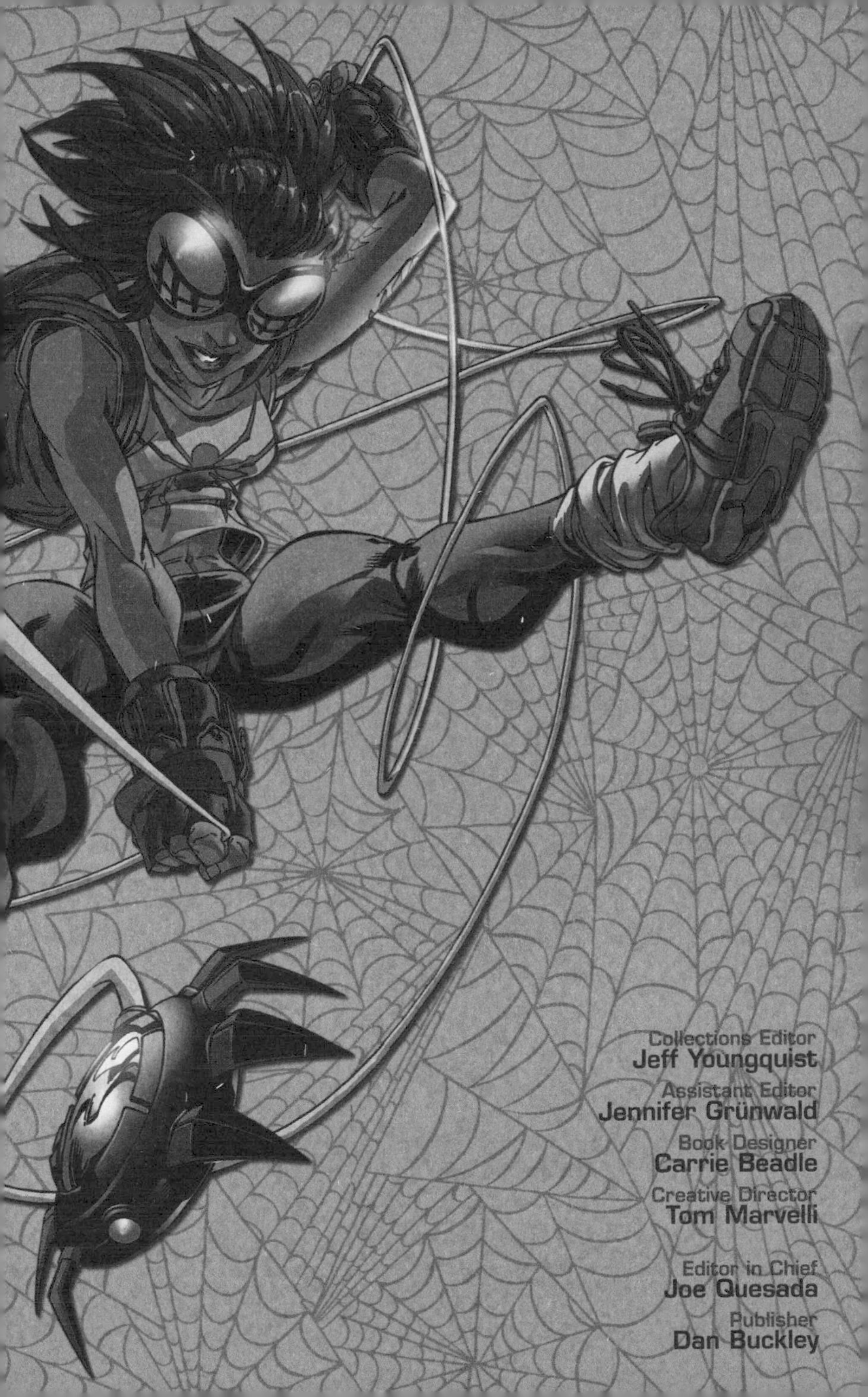

Collections Editor
Jeff Youngquist
Assistant Editor
Jennifer Grünwald
Book Designer
Carrie Beadle
Creative Director
Tom Marvelli

Editor in Chief
Joe Quesada
Publisher
Dan Buckley

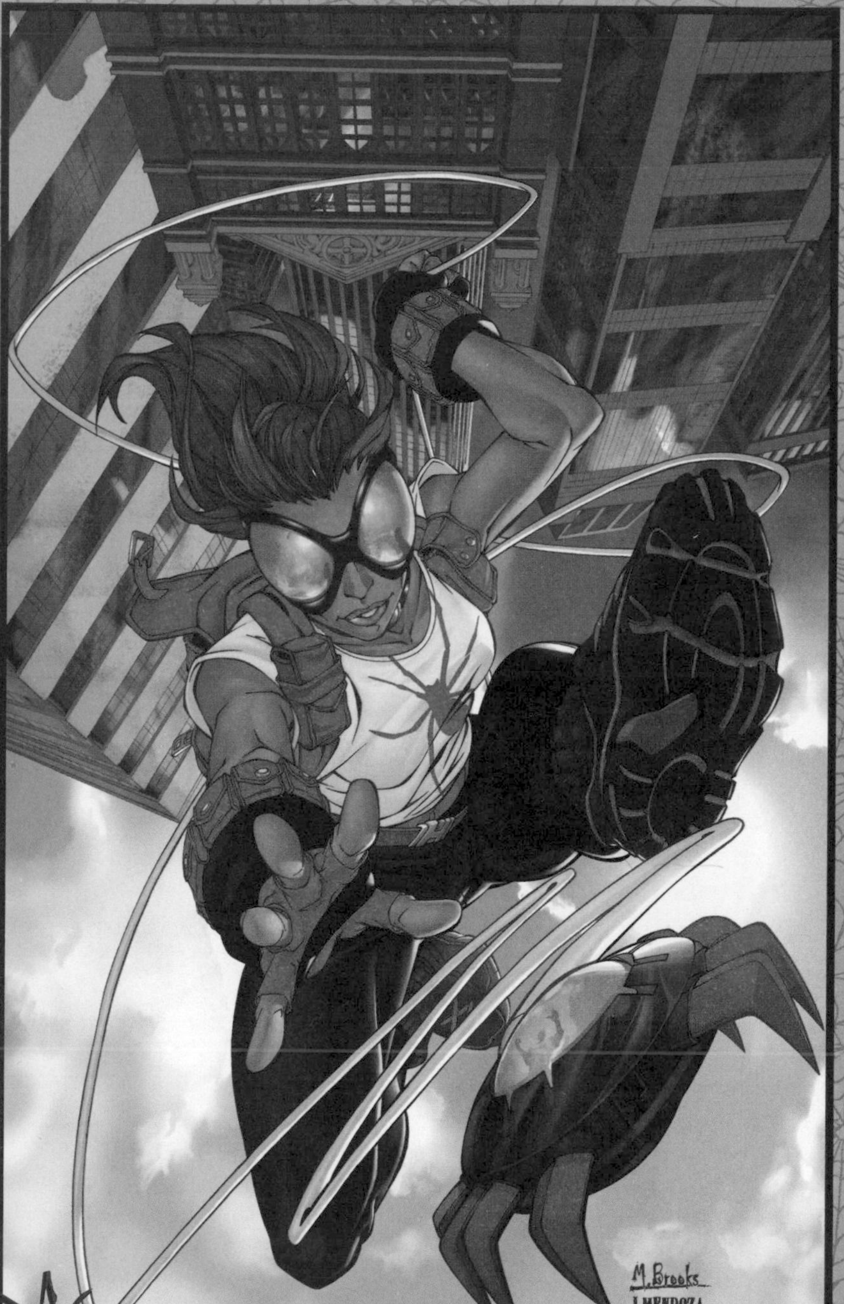
M. Brooks
J.MENDOZA

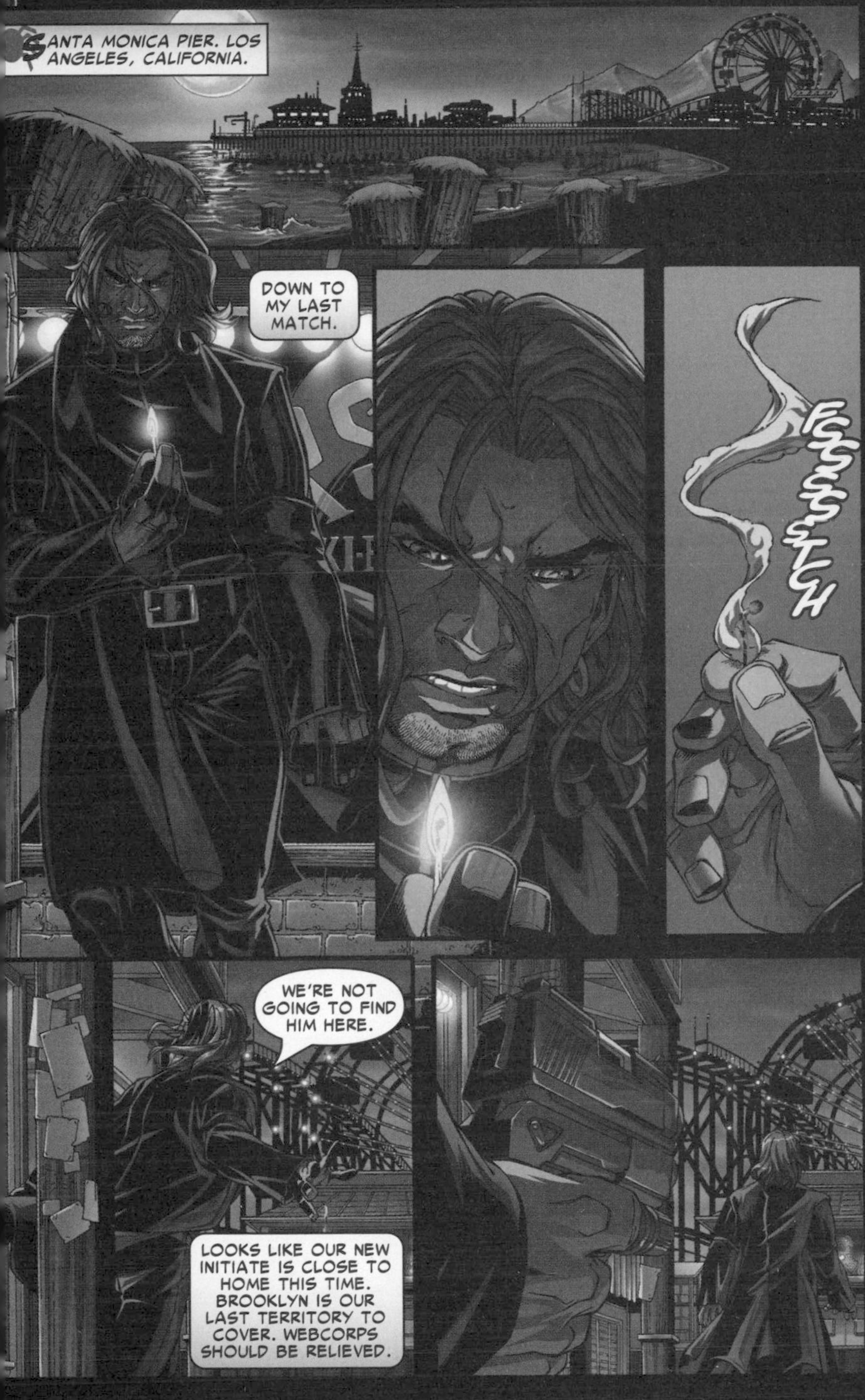
SANTA MONICA PIER. LOS ANGELES, CALIFORNIA.
DOWN TO MY LAST MATCH.
FSSSSSTCH
WE'RE NOT GOING TO FIND HIM HERE.
LOOKS LIKE OUR NEW INITIATE IS CLOSE TO HOME THIS TIME. BROOKLYN IS OUR LAST TERRITORY TO COVER. WEBCORPS SHOULD BE RELIEVED.

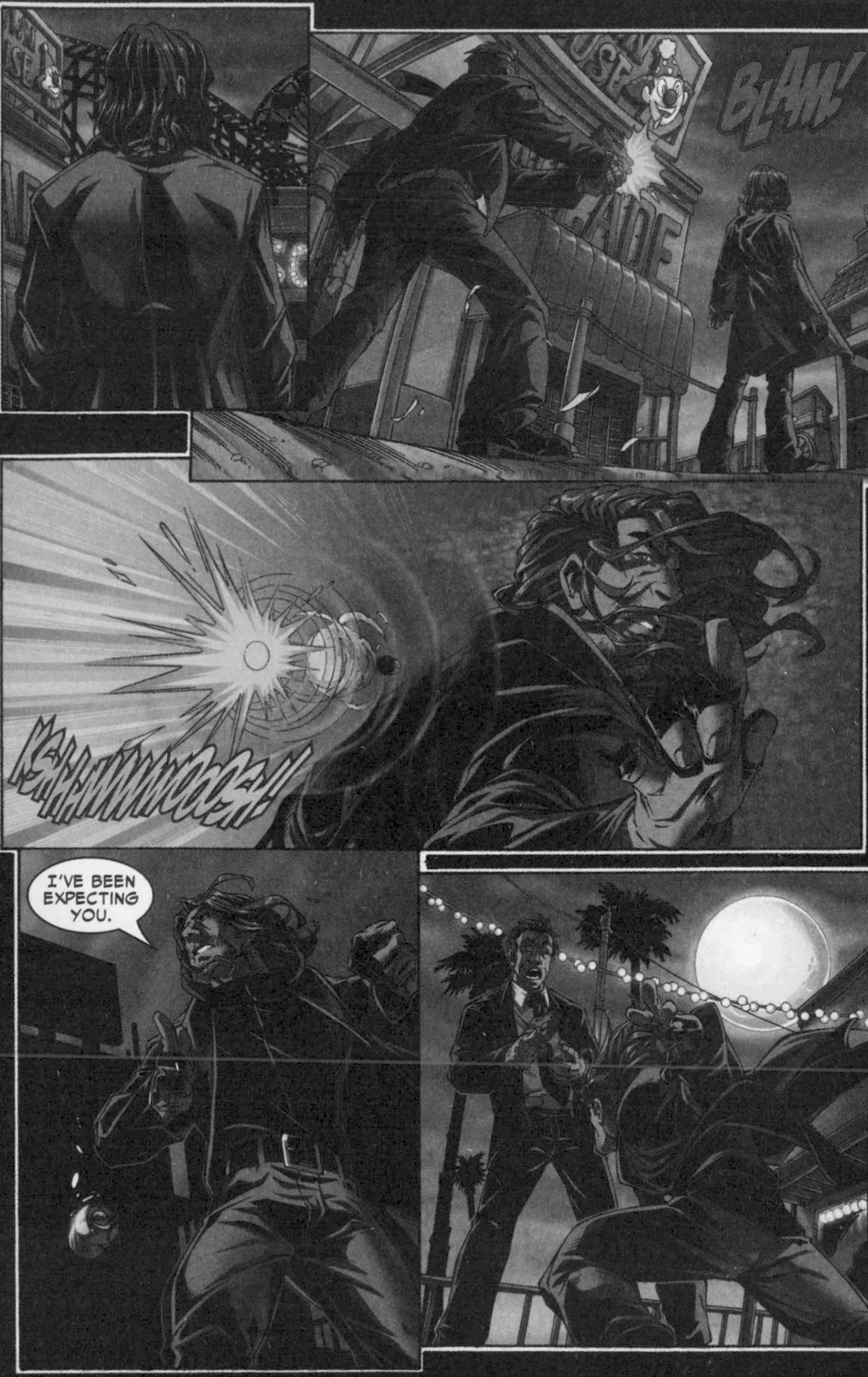
BLAM!
KSHHWWWOOOSH!!
I'VE BEEN EXPECTING YOU.

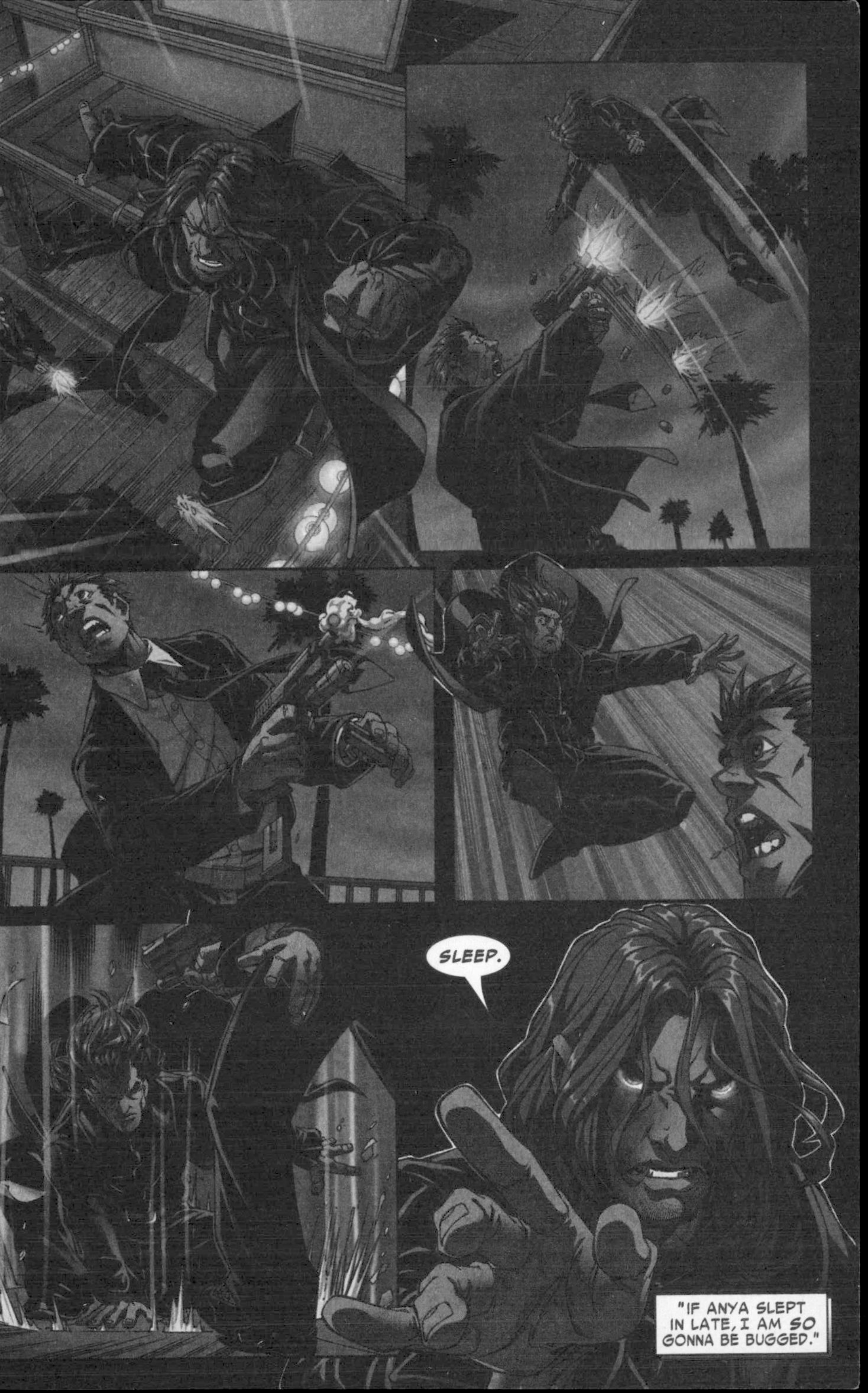
SLEEP.
"IF ANYA SLEPT IN LATE, I AM SO GONNA BE BUGGED."

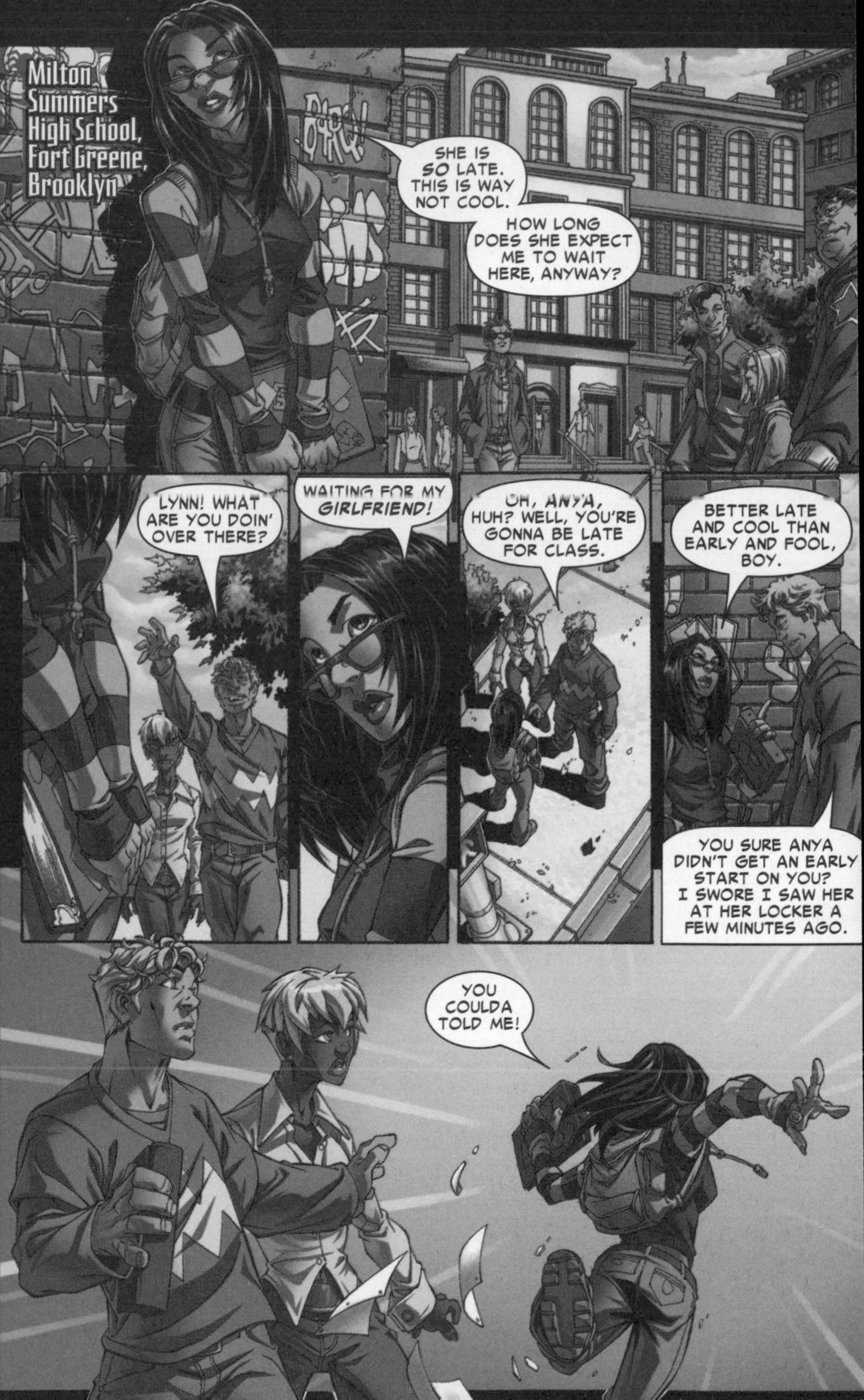

Milton Summers High School, Fort Greene, Brooklyn
SHE IS SO LATE. THIS IS WAY NOT COOL.
HOW LONG DOES SHE EXPECT ME TO WAIT HERE, ANYWAY?
LYNN! WHAT ARE YOU DOIN' OVER THERE?
WAITING FOR MY GIRLFRIEND!
OH, ANYA, HUH? WELL, YOU'RE GONNA BE LATE FOR CLASS.
BETTER LATE AND COOL THAN EARLY AND FOOL, BOY.
YOU SURE ANYA DIDN'T GET AN EARLY START ON YOU? I SWORE I SAW HER AT HER LOCKER A FEW MINUTES AGO.
YOU COULDA TOLD ME!

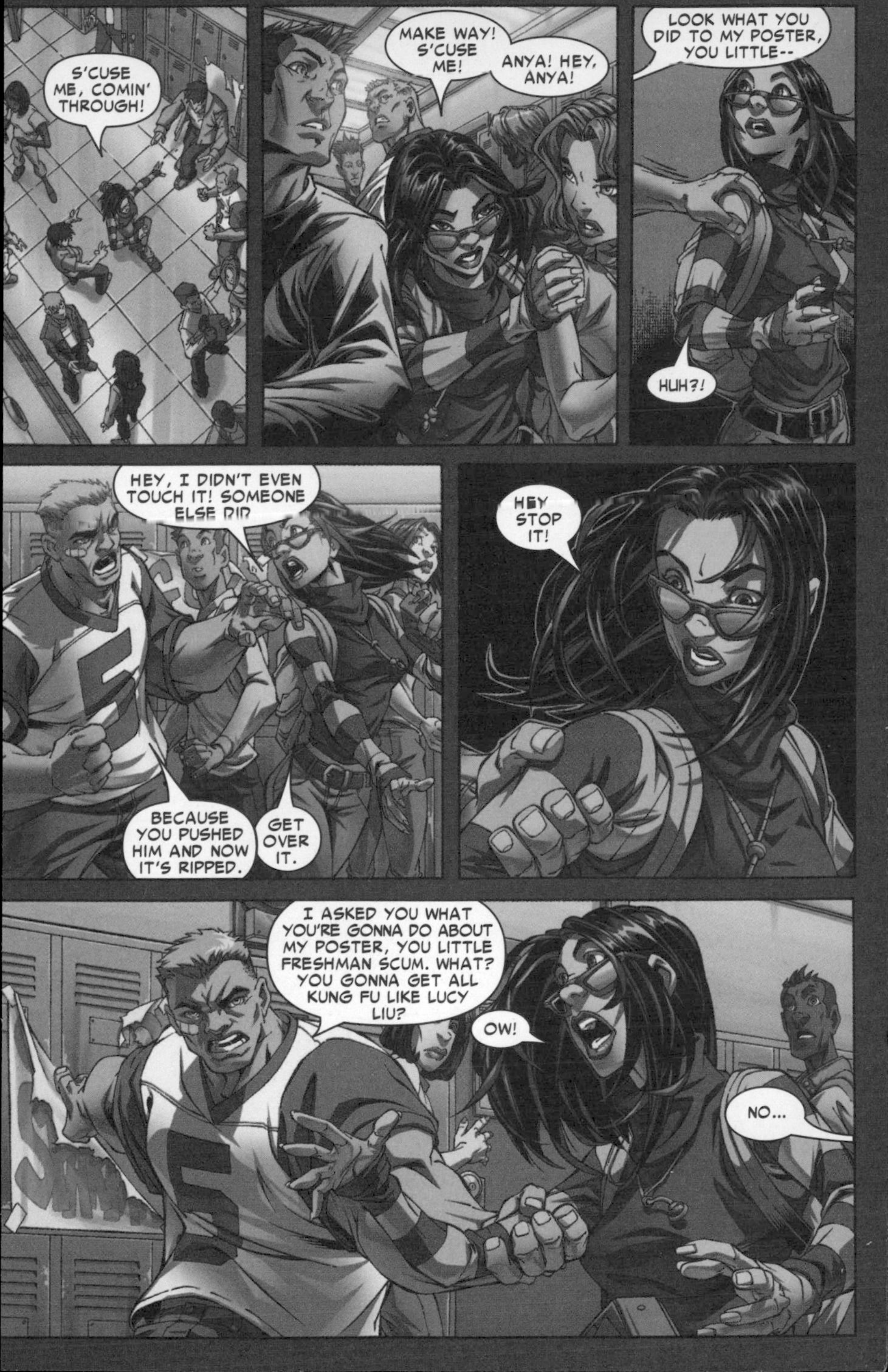
S'CUSE ME, COMIN' THROUGH!
MAKE WAY! S'CUSE ME!
ANYA! HEY, ANYA!
LOOK WHAT YOU DID TO MY POSTER, YOU LITTLE--
HUH?!
HEY, I DIDN'T EVEN TOUCH IT! SOMEONE ELSE DID
BECAUSE YOU PUSHED HIM AND NOW IT'S RIPPED.
GET OVER IT.
HEY STOP IT!
I ASKED YOU WHAT YOU'RE GONNA DO ABOUT MY POSTER, YOU LITTLE FRESHMAN SCUM. WHAT? YOU GONNA GET ALL KUNG FU LIKE LUCY LIU?
OW!
NO...

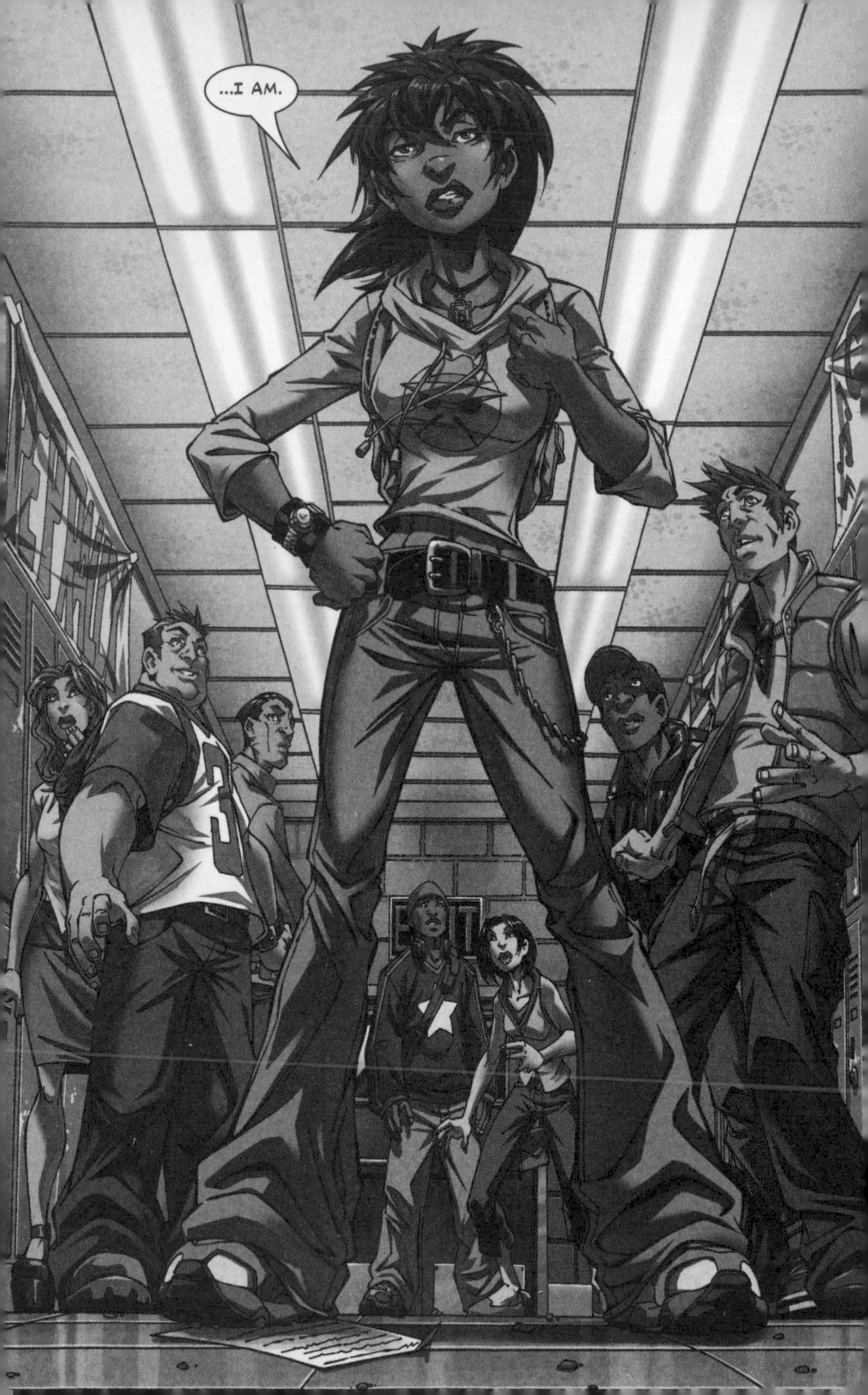
...I AM.

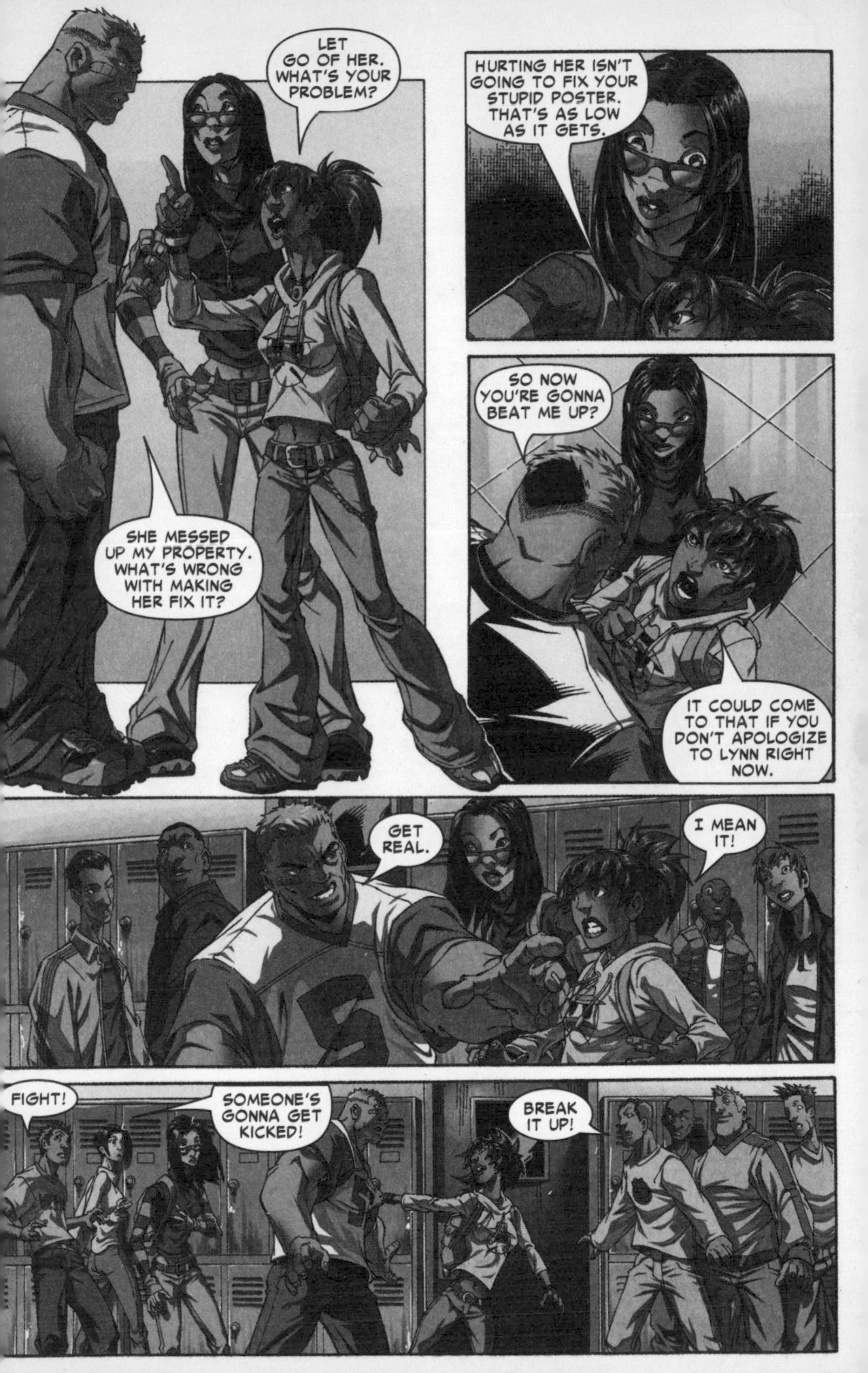
LET GO OF HER. WHAT'S YOUR PROBLEM?
SHE MESSED UP MY PROPERTY. WHAT'S WRONG WITH MAKING HER FIX IT?
HURTING HER ISN'T GOING TO FIX YOUR STUPID POSTER. THAT'S AS LOW AS IT GETS.
SO NOW YOU'RE GONNA BEAT ME UP?
IT COULD COME TO THAT IF YOU DON'T APOLOGIZE TO LYNN RIGHT NOW.
GET REAL.
I MEAN IT!
FIGHT!
SOMEONE'S GONNA GET KICKED!
BREAK IT UP!

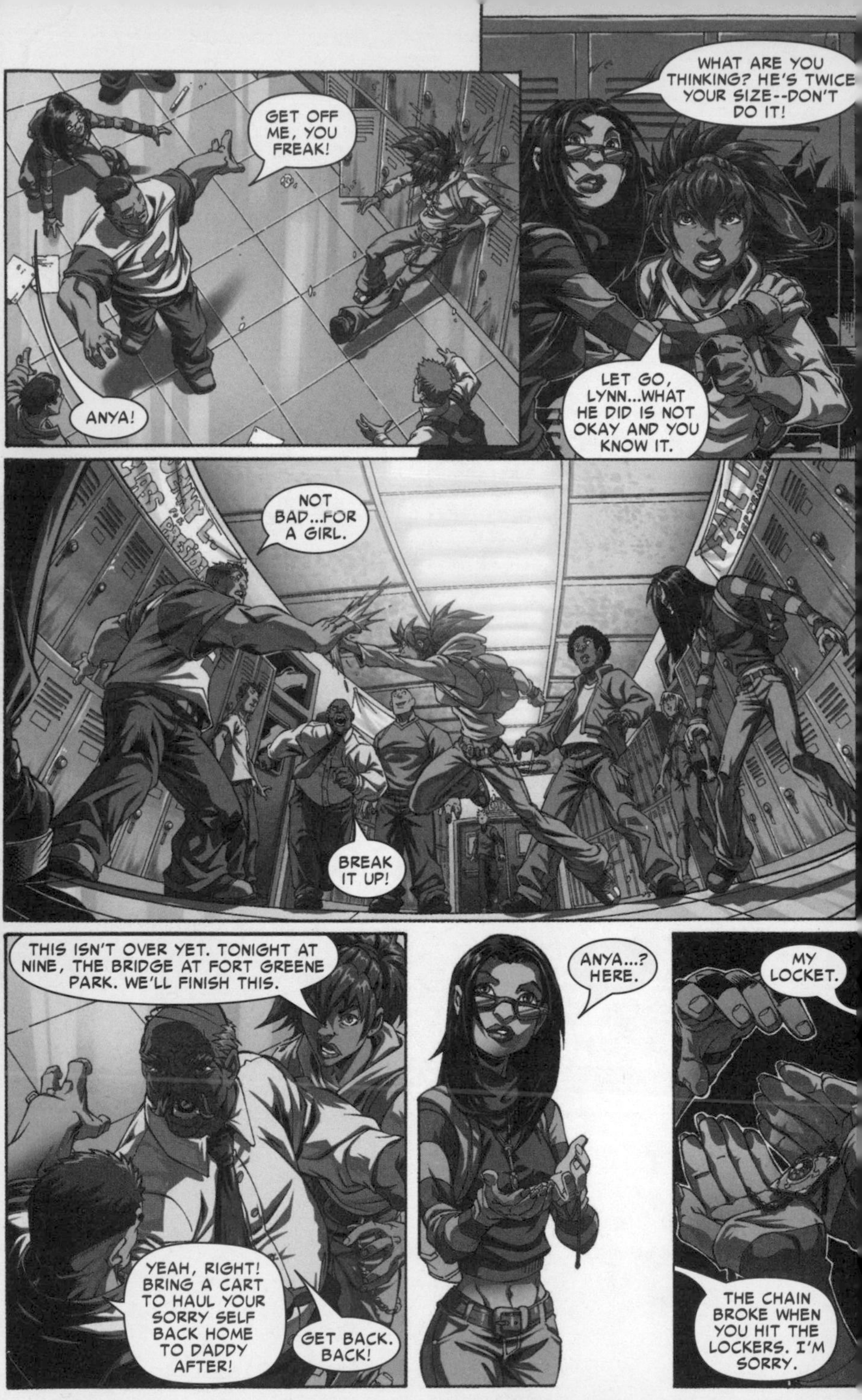
GET OFF ME, YOU FREAK!
ANYA!
WHAT ARE YOU THINKING? HE'S TWICE YOUR SIZE--DON'T DO IT!
LET GO, LYNN...WHAT HE DID IS NOT OKAY AND YOU KNOW IT.
NOT BAD...FOR A GIRL.
BREAK IT UP!
THIS ISN'T OVER YET. TONIGHT AT NINE, THE BRIDGE AT FORT GREENE PARK. WE'LL FINISH THIS.
YEAH, RIGHT! BRING A CART TO HAUL YOUR SORRY SELF BACK HOME TO DADDY AFTER!
GET BACK. BACK!
ANYA...? HERE.
MY LOCKET.
THE CHAIN BROKE WHEN YOU HIT THE LOCKERS. I'M SORRY.

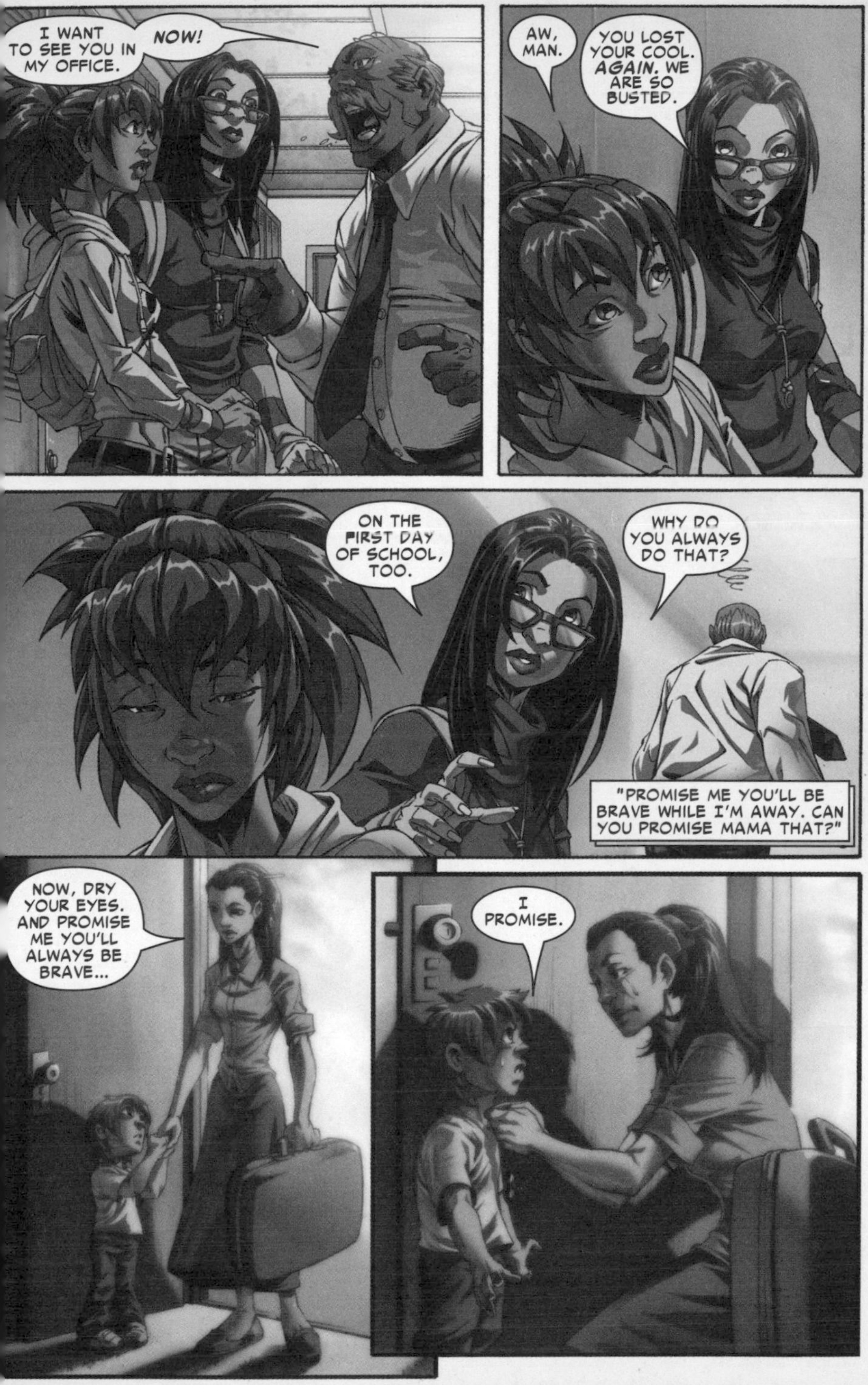
I WANT TO SEE YOU IN MY OFFICE.
NOW!
AW, MAN.
YOU LOST YOUR COOL. AGAIN. WE ARE SO BUSTED.
ON THE FIRST DAY OF SCHOOL, TOO.
WHY DO YOU ALWAYS DO THAT?
"PROMISE ME YOU'LL BE BRAVE WHILE I'M AWAY. CAN YOU PROMISE MAMA THAT?"
NOW, DRY YOUR EYES. AND PROMISE ME YOU'LL ALWAYS BE BRAVE...
I PROMISE.

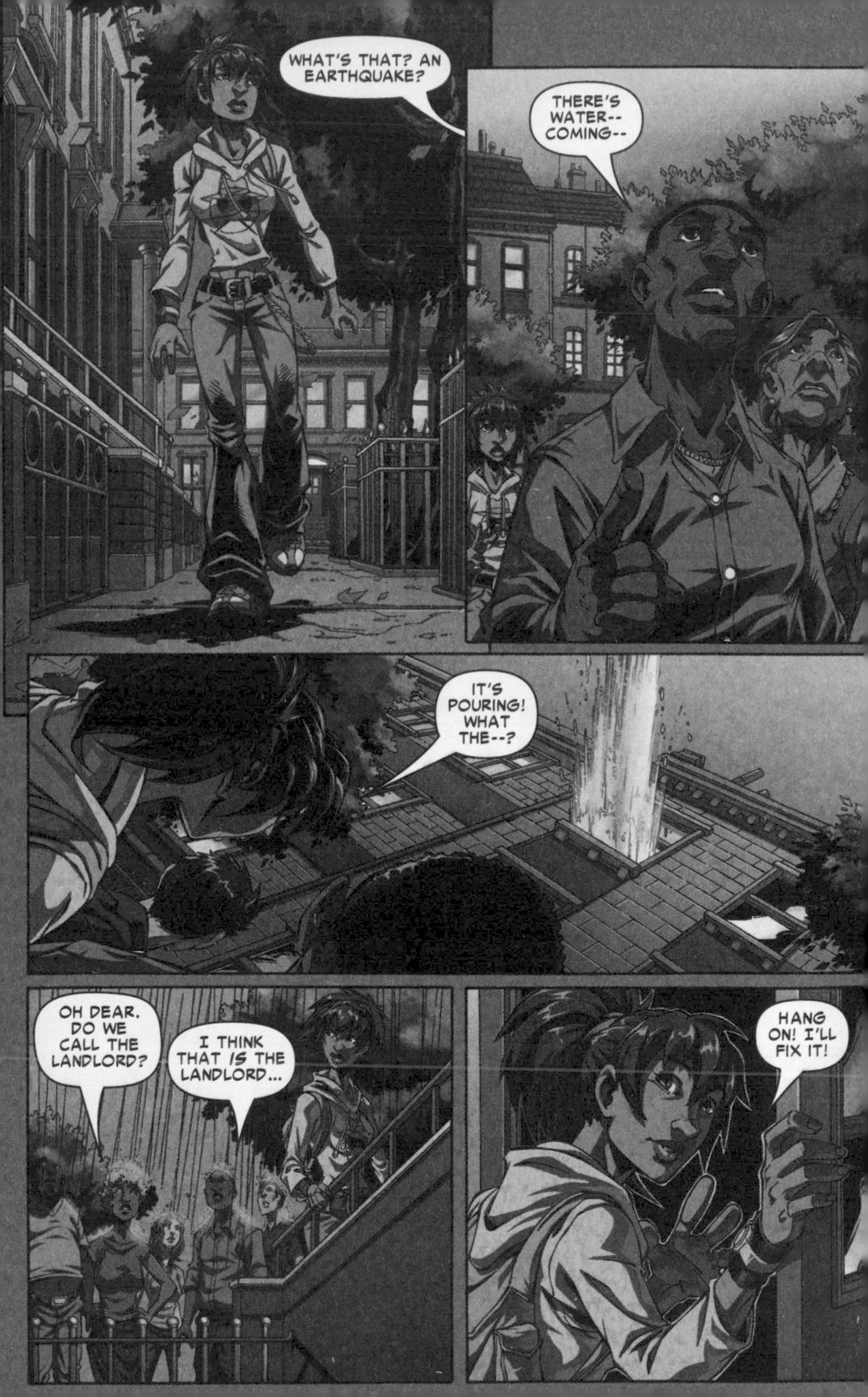
WHAT'S THAT? AN EARTHQUAKE?
THERE'S WATER-- COMING--
IT'S POURING! WHAT THE--?
OH DEAR. DO WE CALL THE LANDLORD?
I THINK THAT *IS* THE LANDLORD...
HANG ON! I'LL FIX IT!

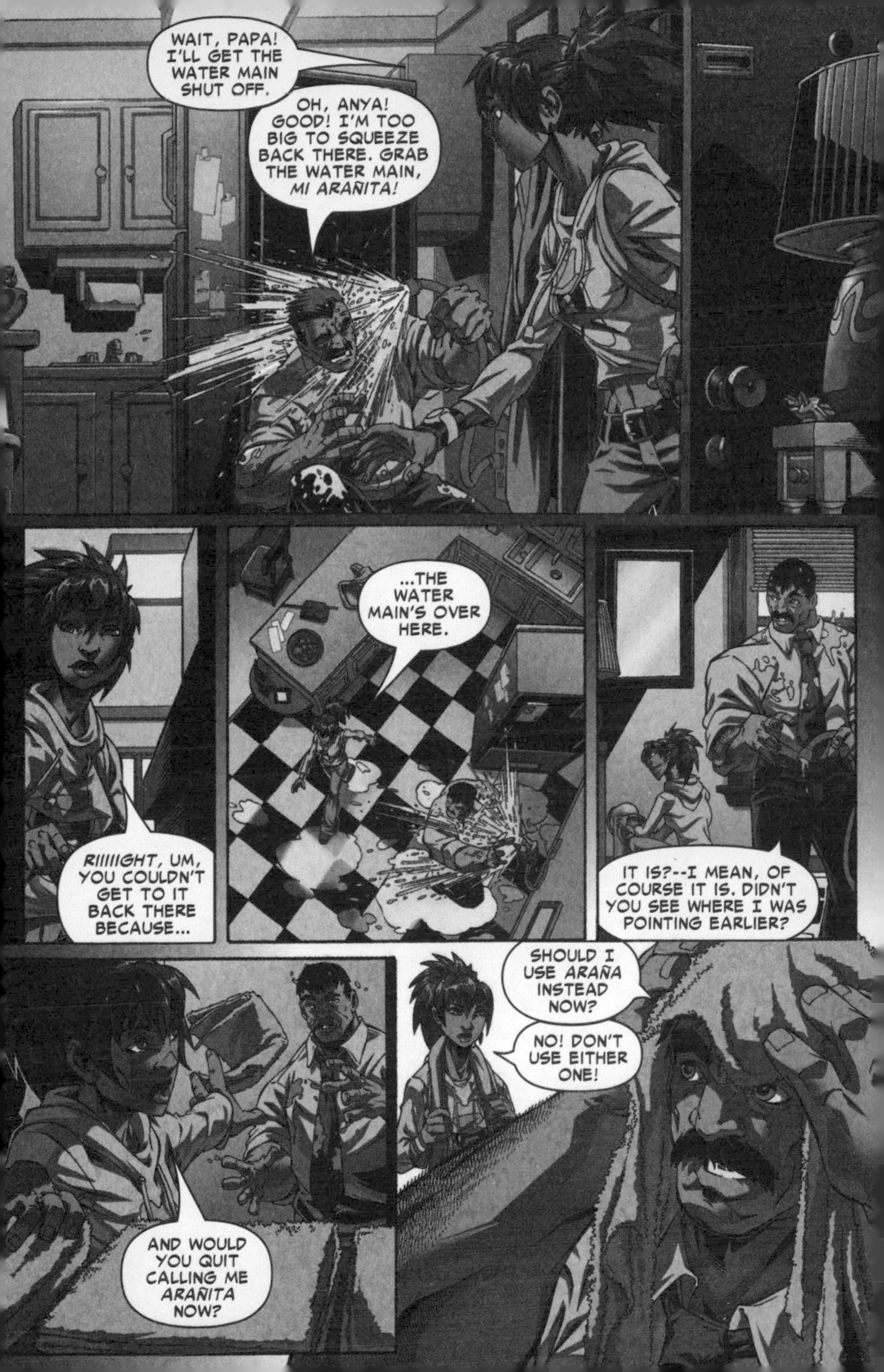
WAIT, PAPA! I'LL GET THE WATER MAIN SHUT OFF.
OH, ANYA! GOOD! I'M TOO BIG TO SQUEEZE BACK THERE. GRAB THE WATER MAIN, *MI ARAÑITA!*
RIIIIIGHT, UM, YOU COULDN'T GET TO IT BACK THERE BECAUSE...
...THE WATER MAIN'S OVER HERE.
IT IS?--I MEAN, OF COURSE IT IS. DIDN'T YOU SEE WHERE I WAS POINTING EARLIER?
AND WOULD YOU QUIT CALLING ME *ARAÑITA* NOW?
SHOULD I USE *ARAÑA* INSTEAD NOW?
NO! DON'T USE EITHER ONE!

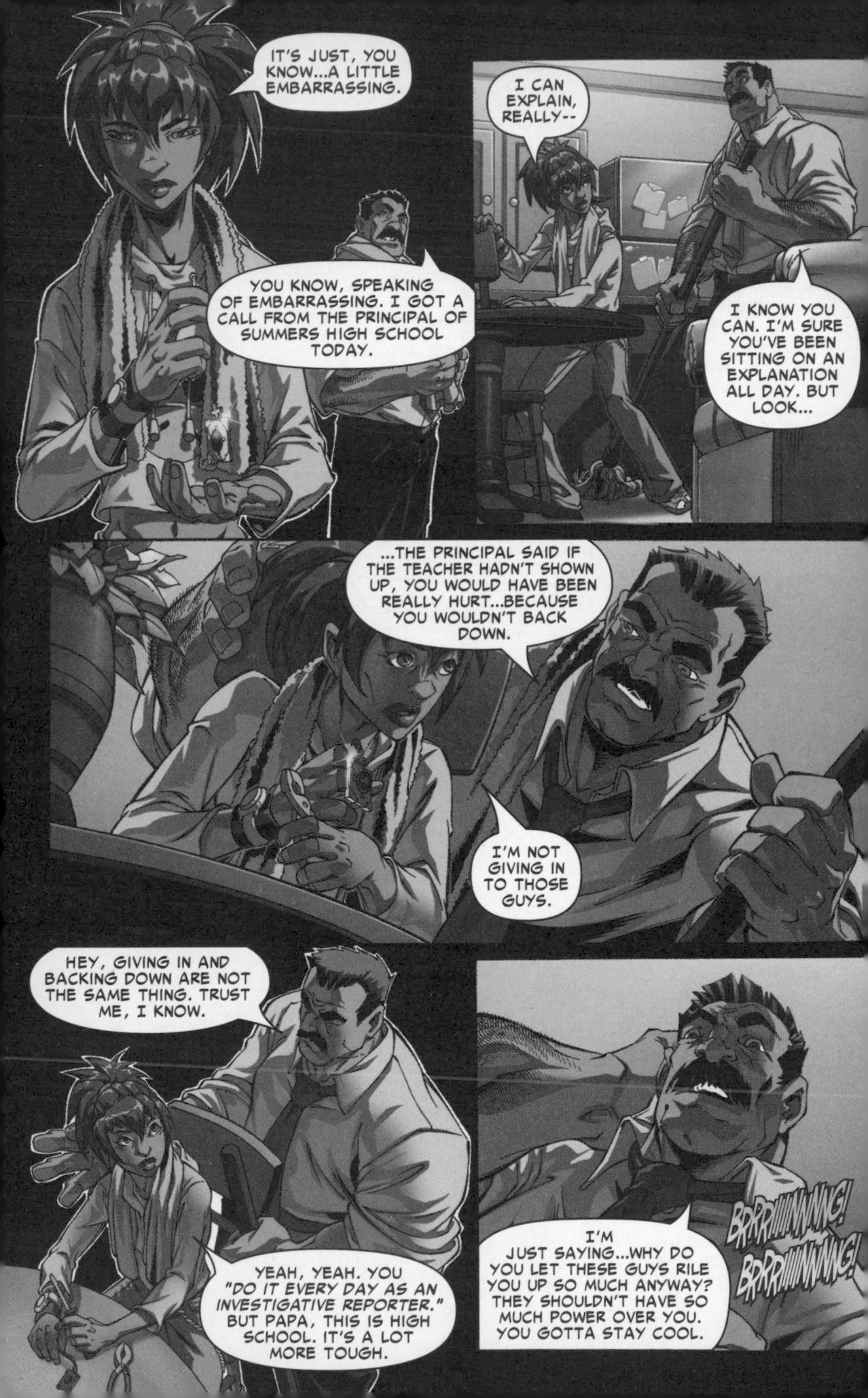
IT'S JUST, YOU KNOW...A LITTLE EMBARRASSING.
YOU KNOW, SPEAKING OF EMBARRASSING. I GOT A CALL FROM THE PRINCIPAL OF SUMMERS HIGH SCHOOL TODAY.
I CAN EXPLAIN, REALLY--
I KNOW YOU CAN. I'M SURE YOU'VE BEEN SITTING ON AN EXPLANATION ALL DAY. BUT LOOK...
...THE PRINCIPAL SAID IF THE TEACHER HADN'T SHOWN UP, YOU WOULD HAVE BEEN REALLY HURT...BECAUSE YOU WOULDN'T BACK DOWN.
I'M NOT GIVING IN TO THOSE GUYS.
HEY, GIVING IN AND BACKING DOWN ARE NOT THE SAME THING. TRUST ME, I KNOW.
YEAH, YEAH. YOU *"DO IT EVERY DAY AS AN INVESTIGATIVE REPORTER."* BUT PAPA, THIS IS HIGH SCHOOL. IT'S A LOT MORE TOUGH.
I'M JUST SAYING...WHY DO YOU LET THESE GUYS RILE YOU UP SO MUCH ANYWAY? THEY SHOULDN'T HAVE SO MUCH POWER OVER YOU. YOU GOTTA STAY COOL.
BRRRIIIIINNNNG!
BRRRIIIIINNNNG!

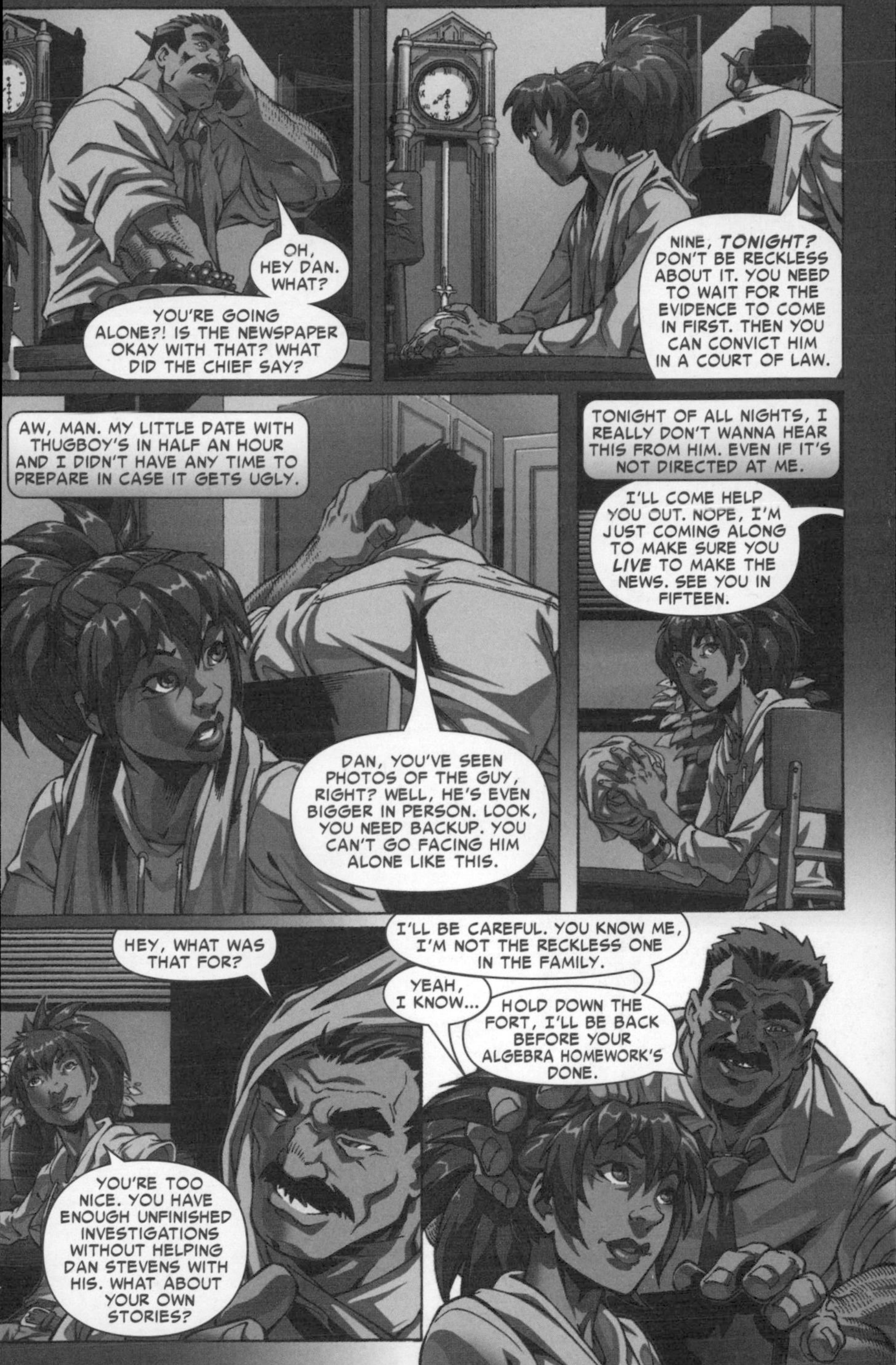
OH, HEY DAN. WHAT?
YOU'RE GOING ALONE?! IS THE NEWSPAPER OKAY WITH THAT? WHAT DID THE CHIEF SAY?
NINE, TONIGHT? DON'T BE RECKLESS ABOUT IT. YOU NEED TO WAIT FOR THE EVIDENCE TO COME IN FIRST. THEN YOU CAN CONVICT HIM IN A COURT OF LAW.
AW, MAN. MY LITTLE DATE WITH THUGBOY'S IN HALF AN HOUR AND I DIDN'T HAVE ANY TIME TO PREPARE IN CASE IT GETS UGLY.
DAN, YOU'VE SEEN PHOTOS OF THE GUY, RIGHT? WELL, HE'S EVEN BIGGER IN PERSON. LOOK, YOU NEED BACKUP. YOU CAN'T GO FACING HIM ALONE LIKE THIS.
TONIGHT OF ALL NIGHTS, I REALLY DON'T WANNA HEAR THIS FROM HIM. EVEN IF IT'S NOT DIRECTED AT ME.
I'LL COME HELP YOU OUT. NOPE, I'M JUST COMING ALONG TO MAKE SURE YOU LIVE TO MAKE THE NEWS. SEE YOU IN FIFTEEN.
HEY, WHAT WAS THAT FOR?
YOU'RE TOO NICE. YOU HAVE ENOUGH UNFINISHED INVESTIGATIONS WITHOUT HELPING DAN STEVENS WITH HIS. WHAT ABOUT YOUR OWN STORIES?
I'LL BE CAREFUL. YOU KNOW ME, I'M NOT THE RECKLESS ONE IN THE FAMILY.
YEAH, I KNOW...
HOLD DOWN THE FORT, I'LL BE BACK BEFORE YOUR ALGEBRA HOMEWORK'S DONE.

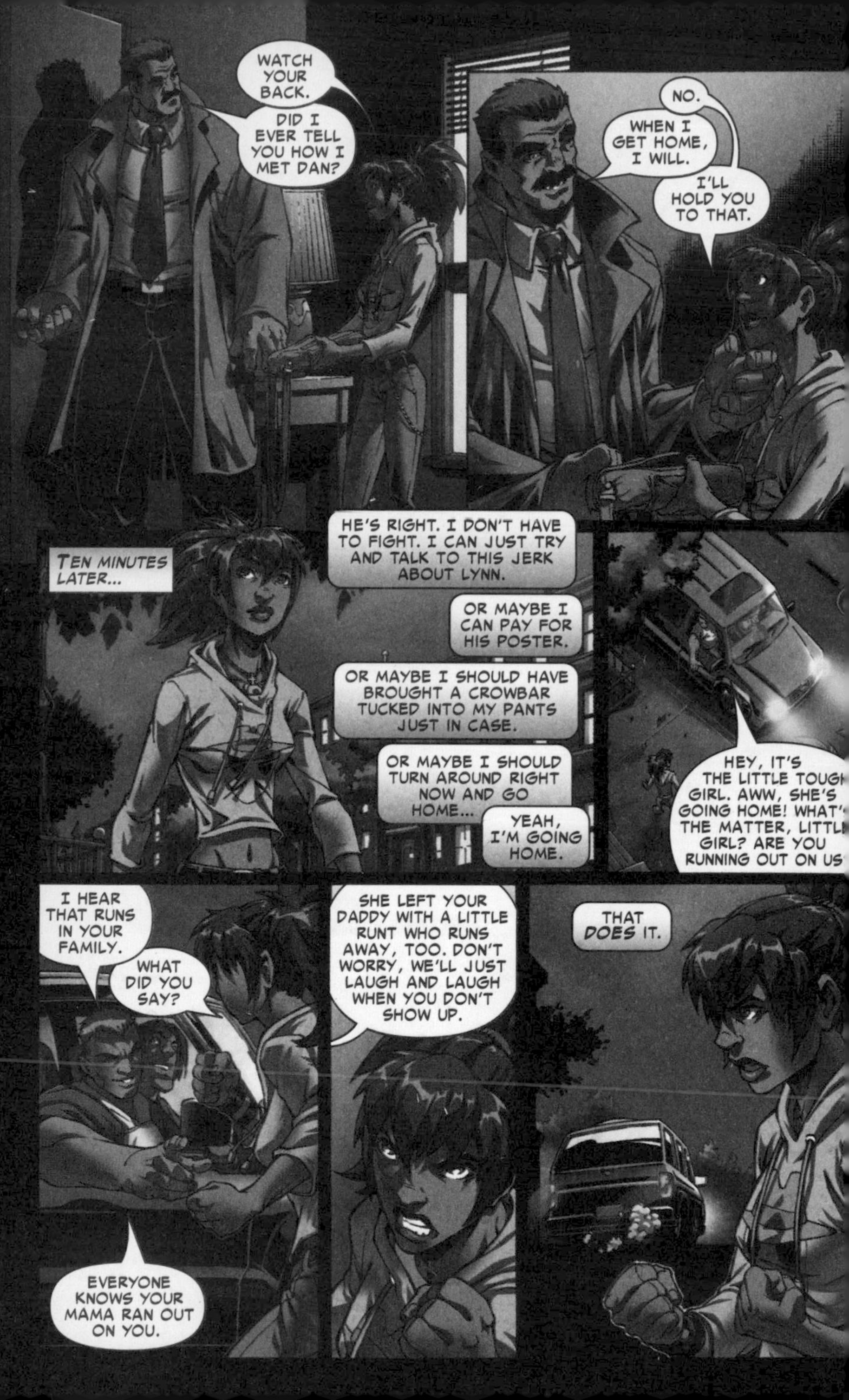
WATCH YOUR BACK.
DID I EVER TELL YOU HOW I MET DAN?
NO.
WHEN I GET HOME, I WILL.
I'LL HOLD YOU TO THAT.
TEN MINUTES LATER...
HE'S RIGHT. I DON'T HAVE TO FIGHT. I CAN JUST TRY AND TALK TO THIS JERK ABOUT LYNN.
OR MAYBE I CAN PAY FOR HIS POSTER.
OR MAYBE I SHOULD HAVE BROUGHT A CROWBAR TUCKED INTO MY PANTS JUST IN CASE.
OR MAYBE I SHOULD TURN AROUND RIGHT NOW AND GO HOME...
YEAH, I'M GOING HOME.
HEY, IT'S THE LITTLE TOUGH GIRL. AWW, SHE'S GOING HOME! WHAT'S THE MATTER, LITTLE GIRL? ARE YOU RUNNING OUT ON US
I HEAR THAT RUNS IN YOUR FAMILY.
WHAT DID YOU SAY?
EVERYONE KNOWS YOUR MAMA RAN OUT ON YOU.
SHE LEFT YOUR DADDY WITH A LITTLE RUNT WHO RUNS AWAY, TOO. DON'T WORRY, WE'LL JUST LAUGH AND LAUGH WHEN YOU DON'T SHOW UP.
THAT *DOES* IT.

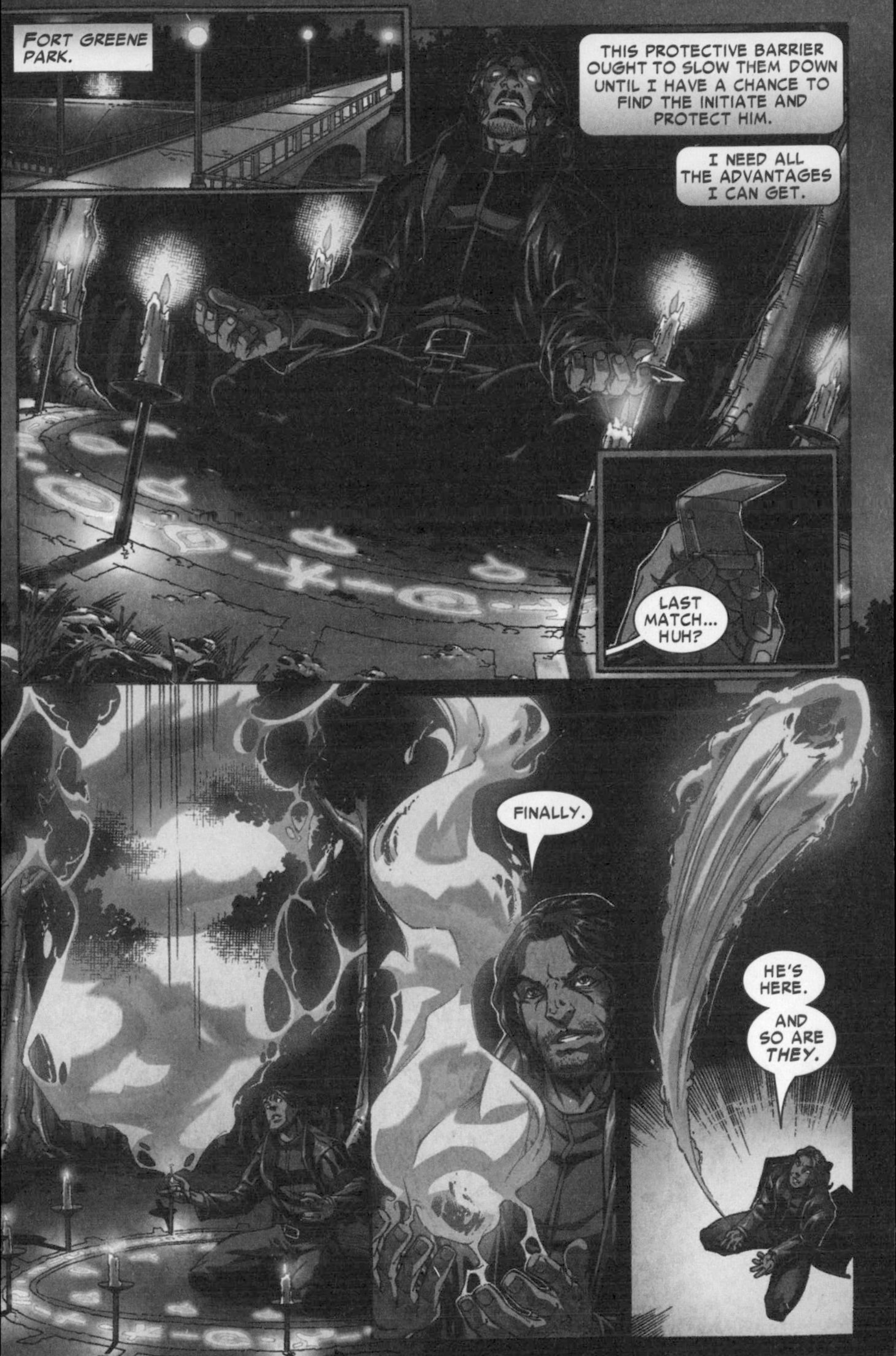
FORT GREENE PARK.
THIS PROTECTIVE BARRIER OUGHT TO SLOW THEM DOWN UNTIL I HAVE A CHANCE TO FIND THE INITIATE AND PROTECT HIM.
I NEED ALL THE ADVANTAGES I CAN GET.
LAST MATCH... HUH?
FINALLY.
HE'S HERE.
AND SO ARE THEY.

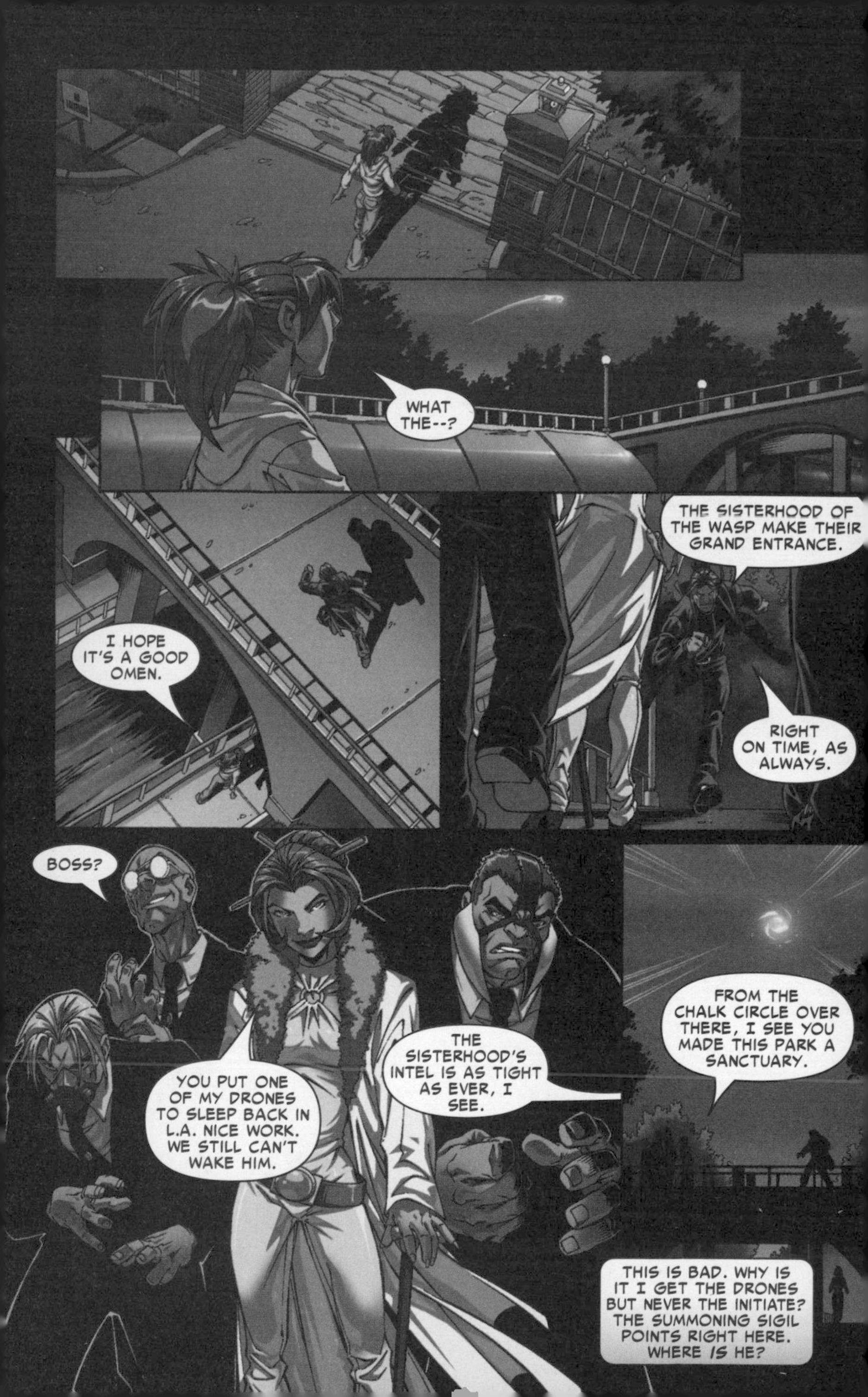
WHAT THE--?
I HOPE IT'S A GOOD OMEN.
THE SISTERHOOD OF THE WASP MAKE THEIR GRAND ENTRANCE.
RIGHT ON TIME, AS ALWAYS.
BOSS?
YOU PUT ONE OF MY DRONES TO SLEEP BACK IN L.A. NICE WORK. WE STILL CAN'T WAKE HIM.
THE SISTERHOOD'S INTEL IS AS TIGHT AS EVER, I SEE.
FROM THE CHALK CIRCLE OVER THERE, I SEE YOU MADE THIS PARK A SANCTUARY.
THIS IS BAD. WHY IS IT I GET THE DRONES BUT NEVER THE INITIATE? THE SUMMONING SIGIL POINTS RIGHT HERE. WHERE IS HE?

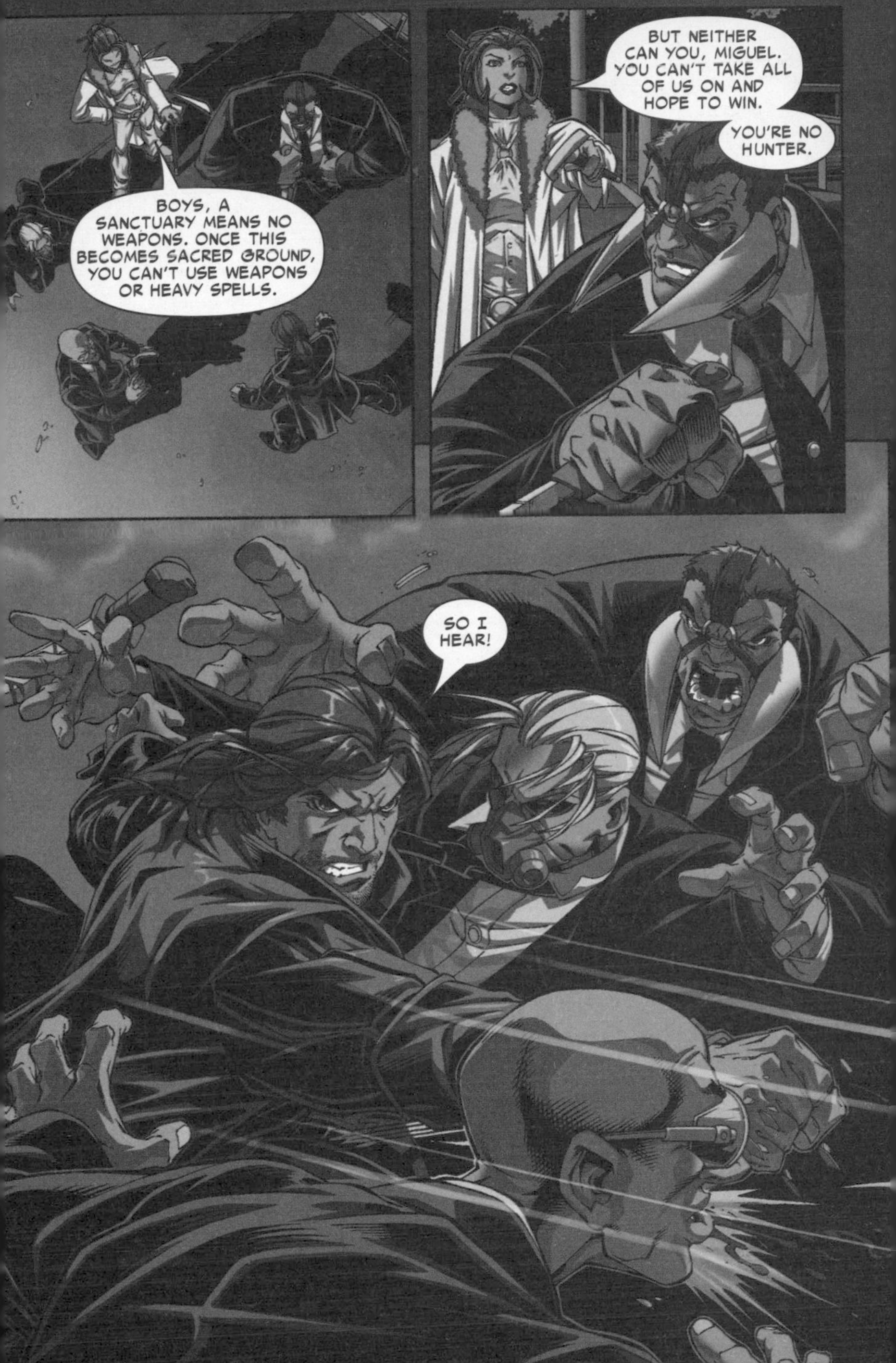

BOYS, A SANCTUARY MEANS NO WEAPONS. ONCE THIS BECOMES SACRED GROUND, YOU CAN'T USE WEAPONS OR HEAVY SPELLS.
BUT NEITHER CAN YOU, MIGUEL. YOU CAN'T TAKE ALL OF US ON AND HOPE TO WIN.
YOU'RE NO HUNTER.
SO I HEAR!

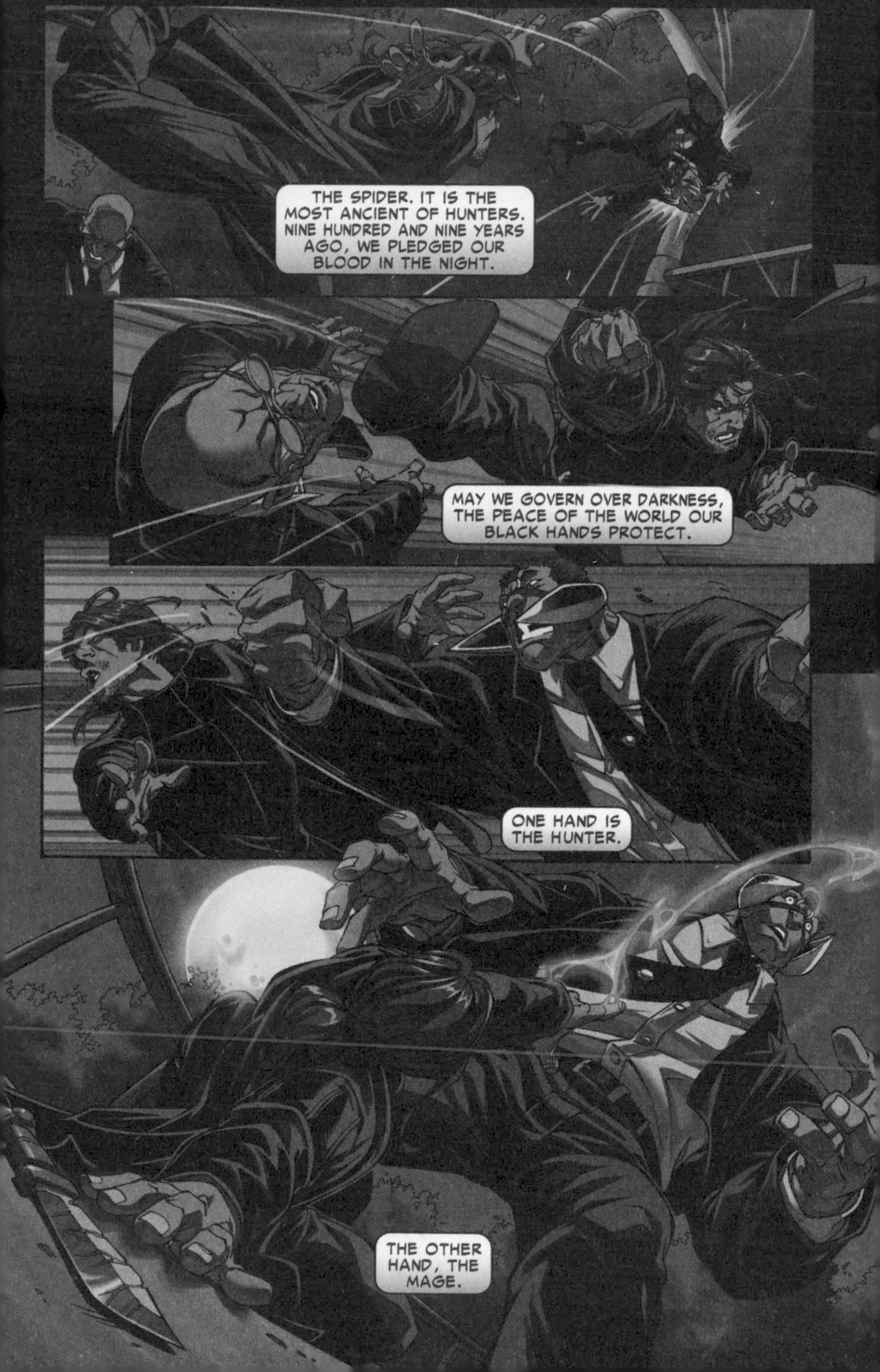
THE SPIDER. IT IS THE MOST ANCIENT OF HUNTERS. NINE HUNDRED AND NINE YEARS AGO, WE PLEDGED OUR BLOOD IN THE NIGHT.
MAY WE GOVERN OVER DARKNESS, THE PEACE OF THE WORLD OUR BLACK HANDS PROTECT.
ONE HAND IS THE HUNTER.
THE OTHER HAND, THE MAGE.

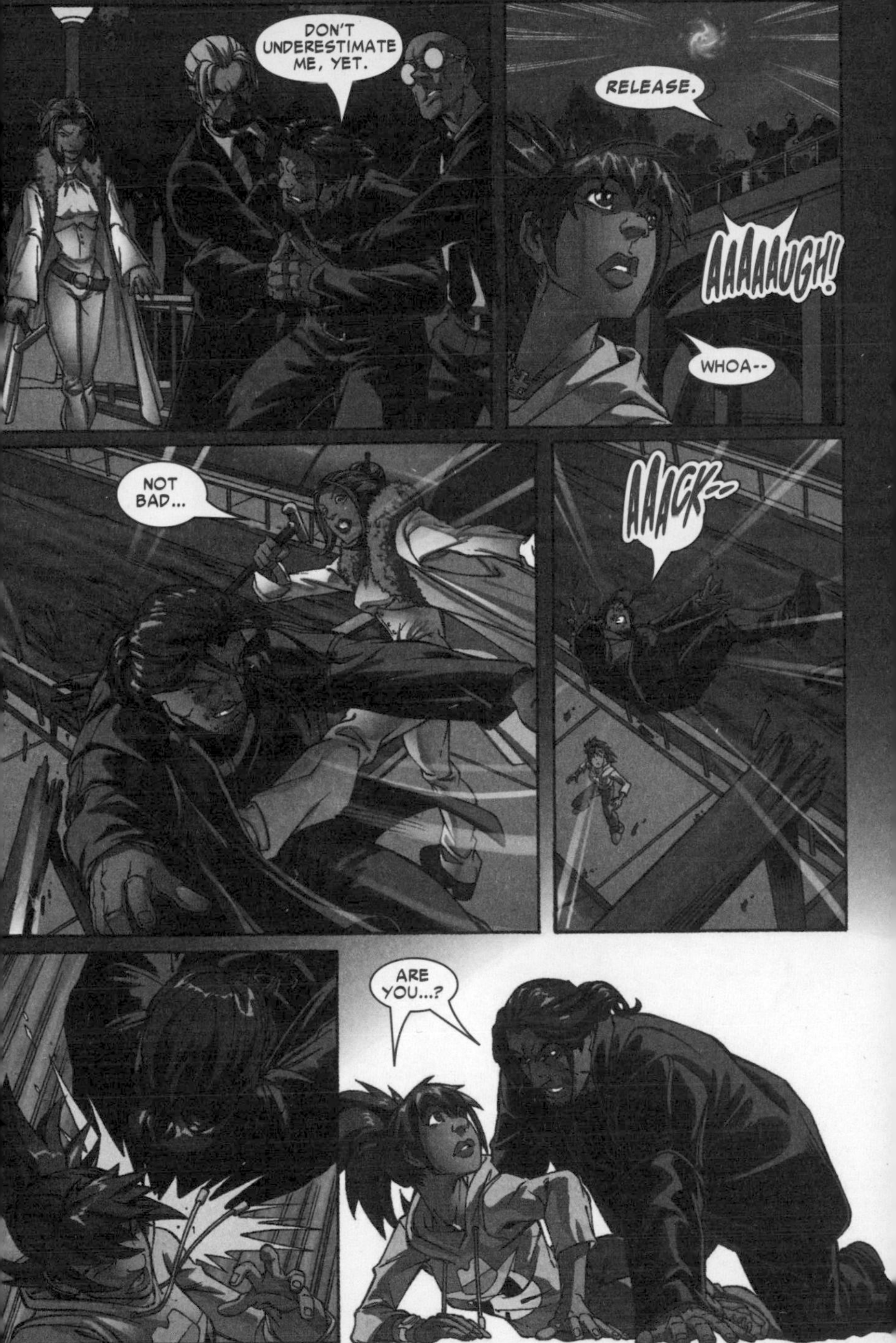
DON'T UNDERESTIMATE ME, YET.
RELEASE.
AAAAAUGH!
WHOA--
NOT BAD...
AAACK--
ARE YOU...?

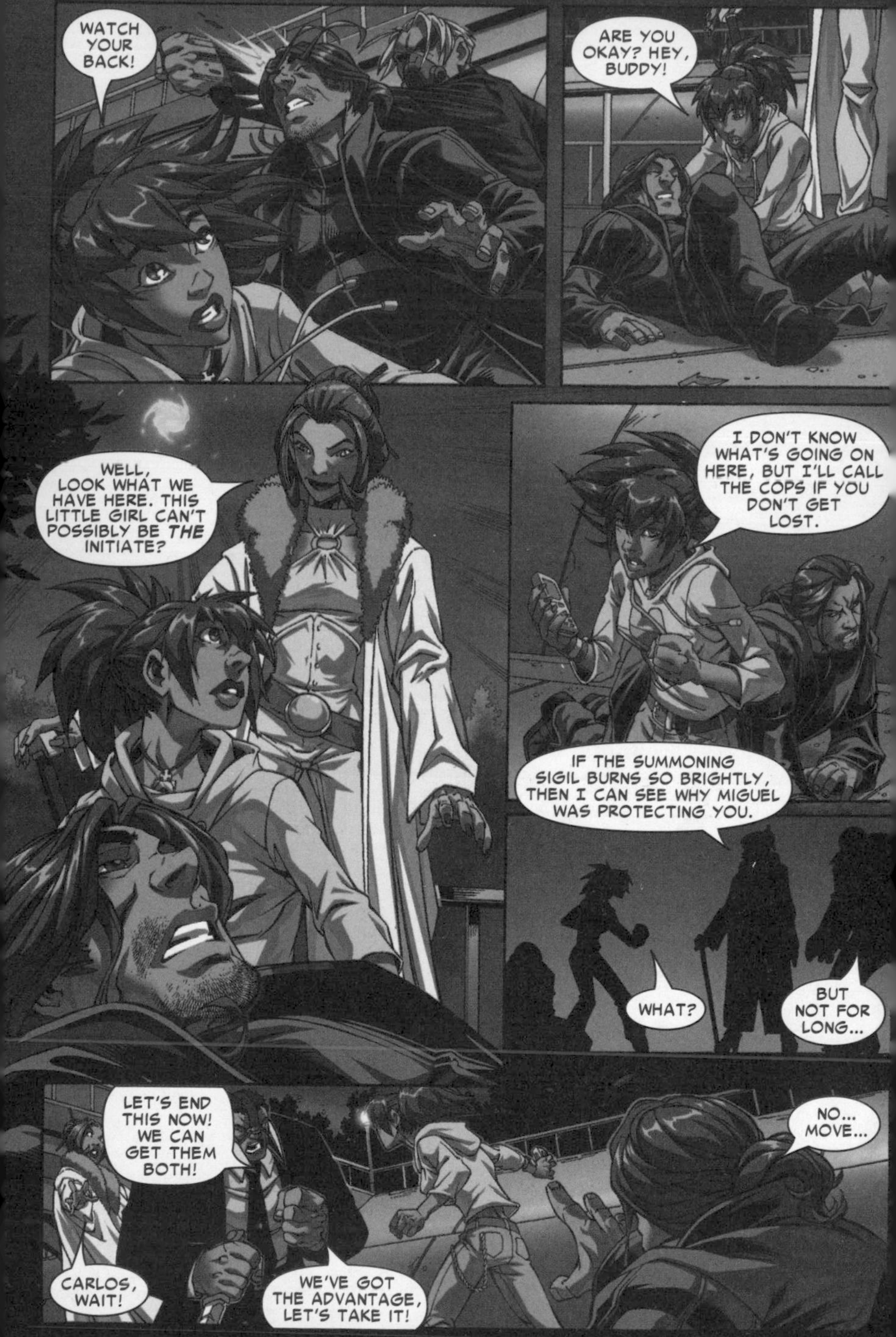
WATCH YOUR BACK!
ARE YOU OKAY? HEY, BUDDY!
WELL, LOOK WHAT WE HAVE HERE. THIS LITTLE GIRL CAN'T POSSIBLY BE *THE* INITIATE?
I DON'T KNOW WHAT'S GOING ON HERE, BUT I'LL CALL THE COPS IF YOU DON'T GET LOST.
IF THE SUMMONING SIGIL BURNS SO BRIGHTLY, THEN I CAN SEE WHY MIGUEL WAS PROTECTING YOU.
WHAT?
BUT NOT FOR LONG...
LET'S END THIS NOW! WE CAN GET THEM BOTH!
CARLOS, WAIT!
WE'VE GOT THE ADVANTAGE, LET'S TAKE IT!
NO... MOVE...

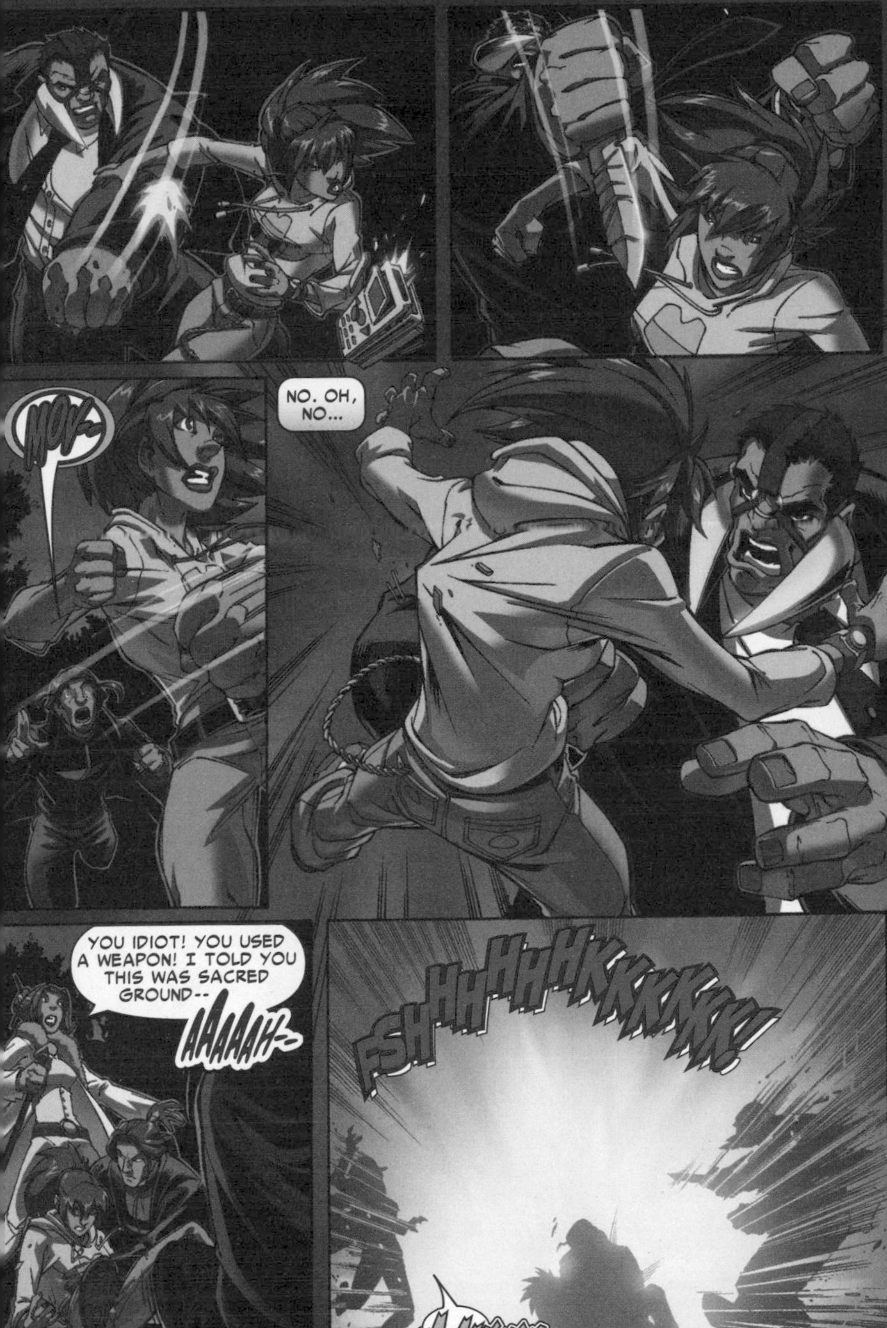
MOV-
NO. OH, NO...
YOU IDIOT! YOU USED A WEAPON! I TOLD YOU THIS WAS SACRED GROUND--
AAAAAH--
RUMMMMMMMBLE!
FSHHHHHHKKKKKK!
AAAAHHHH!

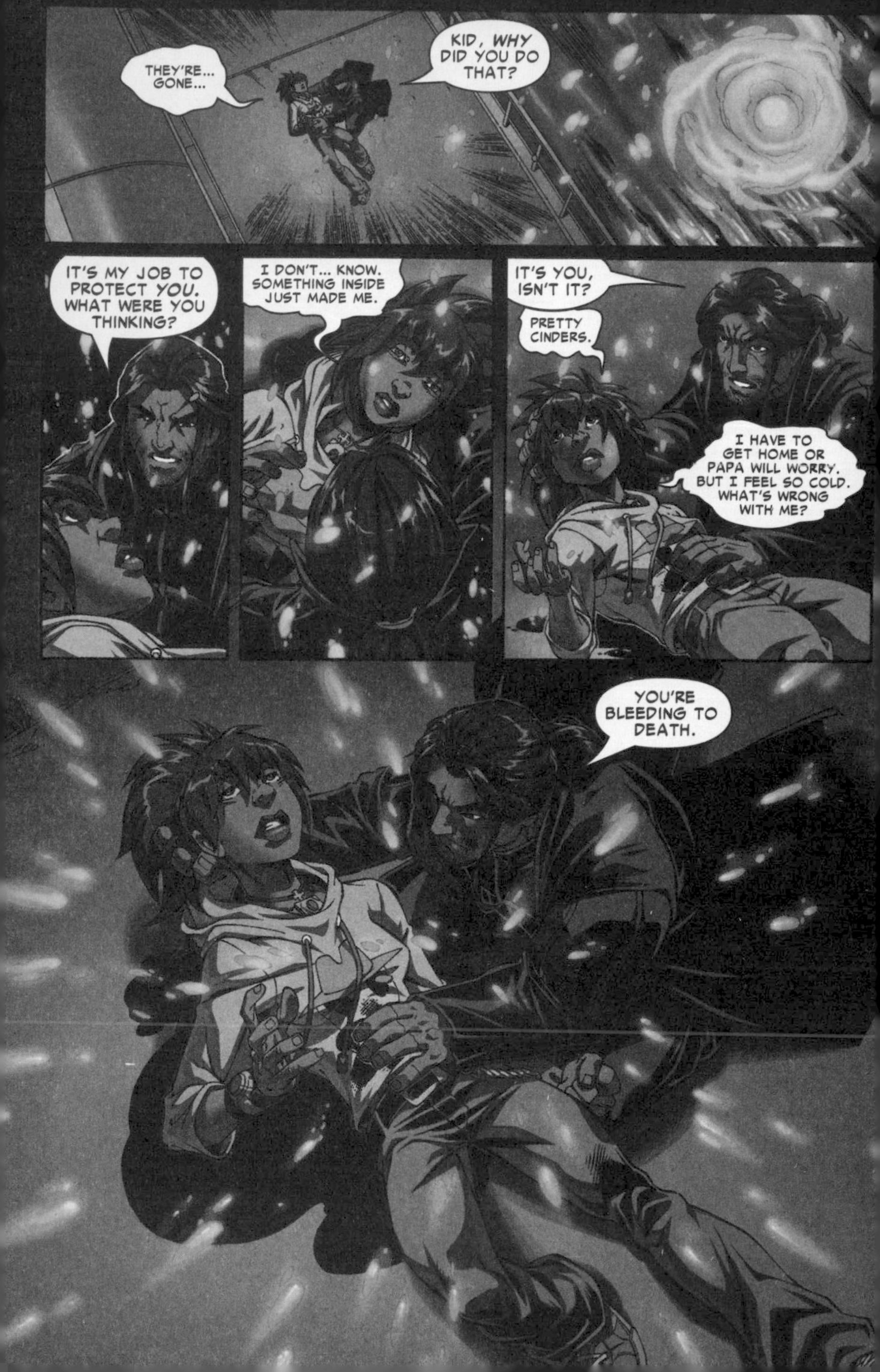
KID, WHY DID YOU DO THAT?
THEY'RE... GONE...
IT'S MY JOB TO PROTECT YOU. WHAT WERE YOU THINKING?
I DON'T... KNOW. SOMETHING INSIDE JUST MADE ME.
IT'S YOU, ISN'T IT?
PRETTY CINDERS.
I HAVE TO GET HOME OR PAPA WILL WORRY. BUT I FEEL SO COLD. WHAT'S WRONG WITH ME?
YOU'RE BLEEDING TO DEATH.

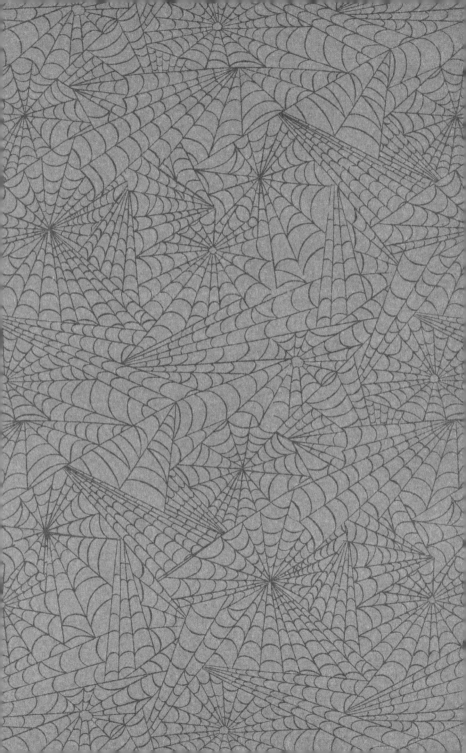

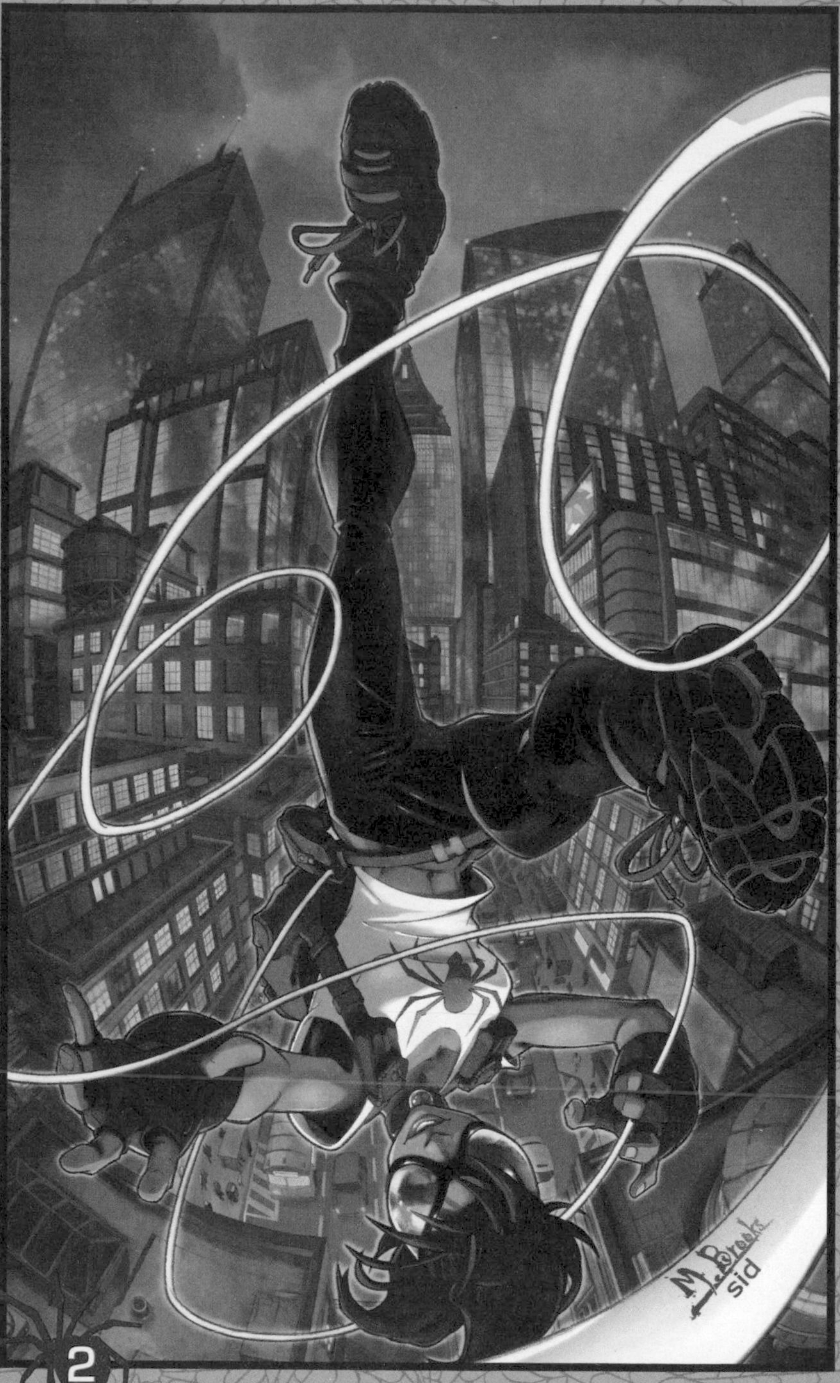
M. Brooks
sid

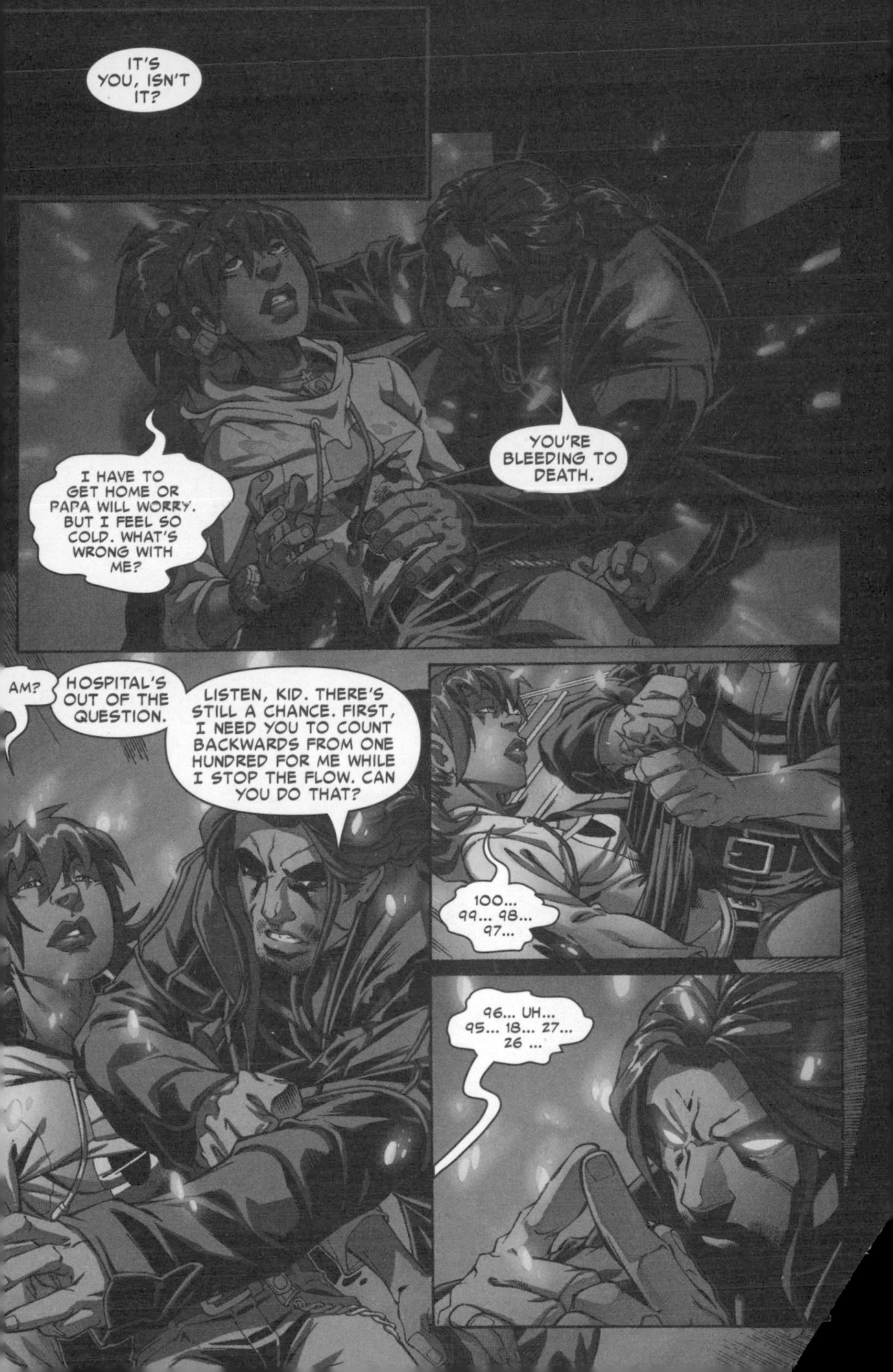
IT'S YOU, ISN'T IT?
YOU'RE BLEEDING TO DEATH.
I HAVE TO GET HOME OR PAPA WILL WORRY. BUT I FEEL SO COLD. WHAT'S WRONG WITH ME?
AM?
HOSPITAL'S OUT OF THE QUESTION.
LISTEN, KID. THERE'S STILL A CHANCE. FIRST, I NEED YOU TO COUNT BACKWARDS FROM ONE HUNDRED FOR ME WHILE I STOP THE FLOW. CAN YOU DO THAT?
100... 99... 98... 97...
96... UH... 95... 18... 27... 26 ...

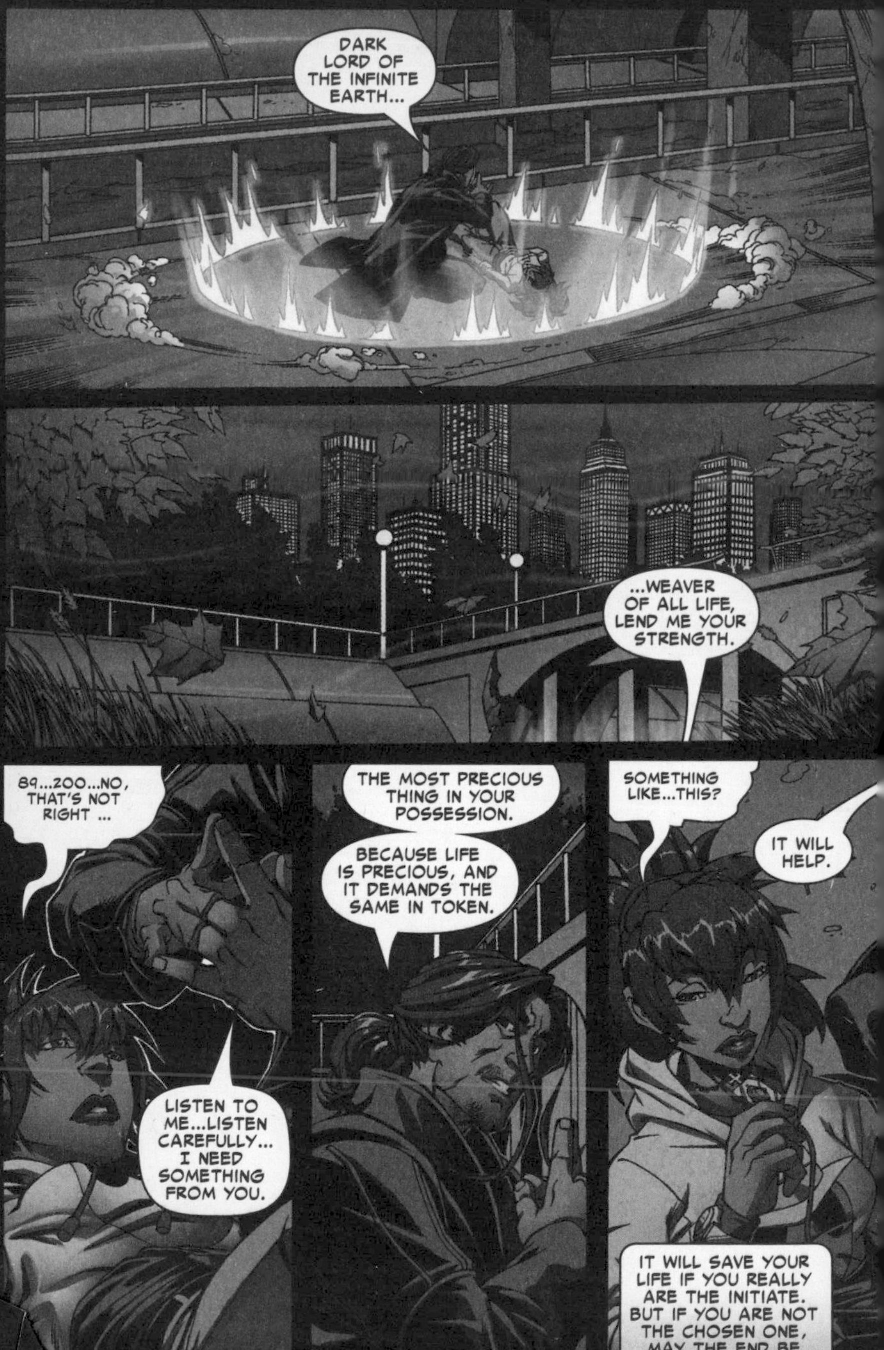
DARK LORD OF THE INFINITE EARTH...
...WEAVER OF ALL LIFE, LEND ME YOUR STRENGTH.
89...200...NO, THAT'S NOT RIGHT ...
LISTEN TO ME...LISTEN CAREFULLY... I NEED SOMETHING FROM YOU.
THE MOST PRECIOUS THING IN YOUR POSSESSION.
BECAUSE LIFE IS PRECIOUS, AND IT DEMANDS THE SAME IN TOKEN.
SOMETHING LIKE...THIS?
IT WILL HELP.
IT WILL SAVE YOUR LIFE IF YOU REALLY ARE THE INITIATE. BUT IF YOU ARE NOT THE CHOSEN ONE, MAY THE END BE SWIFT AND PAINLESS.

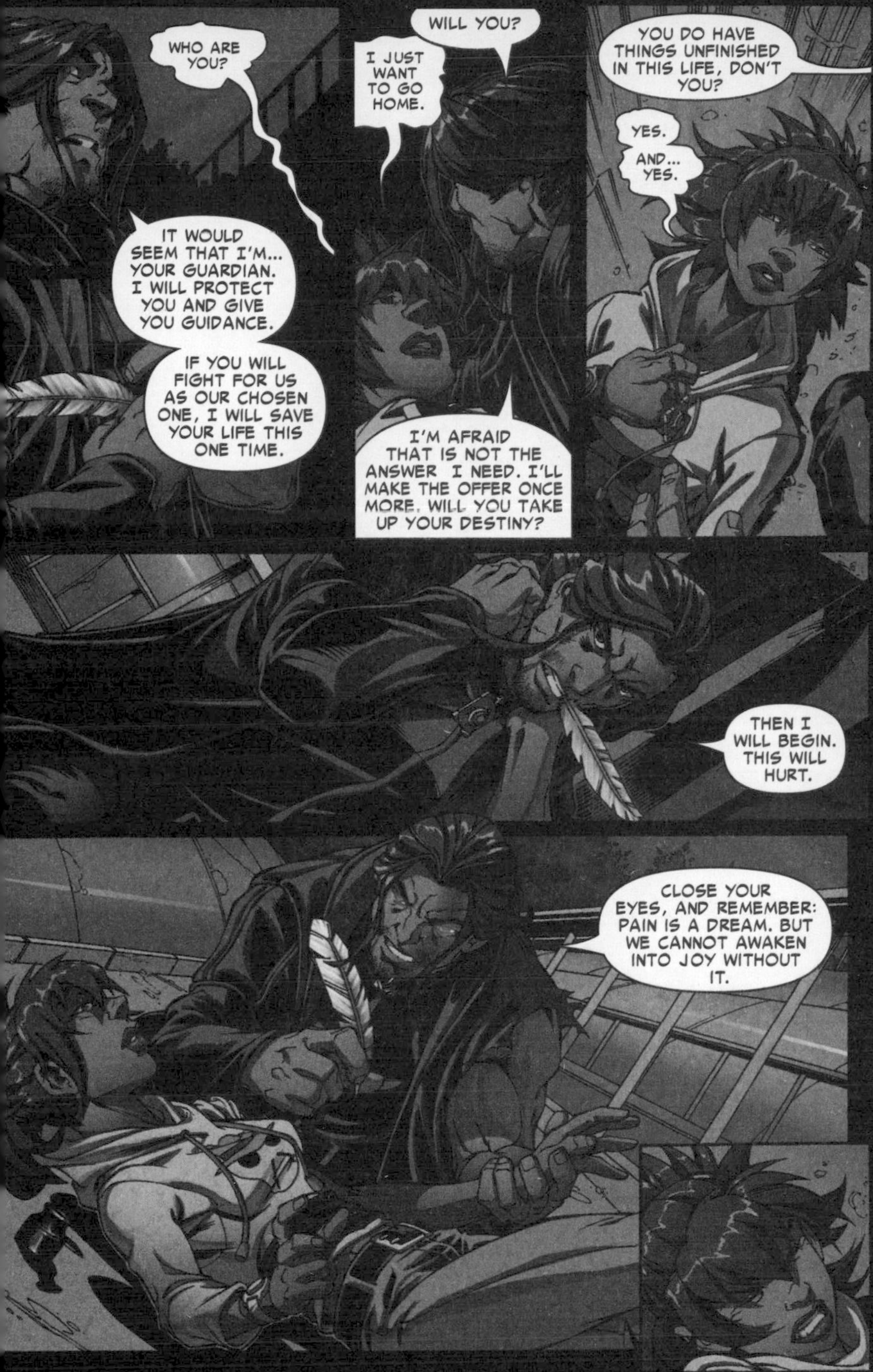
WHO ARE YOU?
IT WOULD SEEM THAT I'M... YOUR GUARDIAN. I WILL PROTECT YOU AND GIVE YOU GUIDANCE.
IF YOU WILL FIGHT FOR US AS OUR CHOSEN ONE, I WILL SAVE YOUR LIFE THIS ONE TIME.
I JUST WANT TO GO HOME.
WILL YOU?
I'M AFRAID THAT IS NOT THE ANSWER I NEED. I'LL MAKE THE OFFER ONCE MORE. WILL YOU TAKE UP YOUR DESTINY?
YOU DO HAVE THINGS UNFINISHED IN THIS LIFE, DON'T YOU?
YES.
AND... YES.
THEN I WILL BEGIN. THIS WILL HURT.
CLOSE YOUR EYES, AND REMEMBER: PAIN IS A DREAM. BUT WE CANNOT AWAKEN INTO JOY WITHOUT IT.

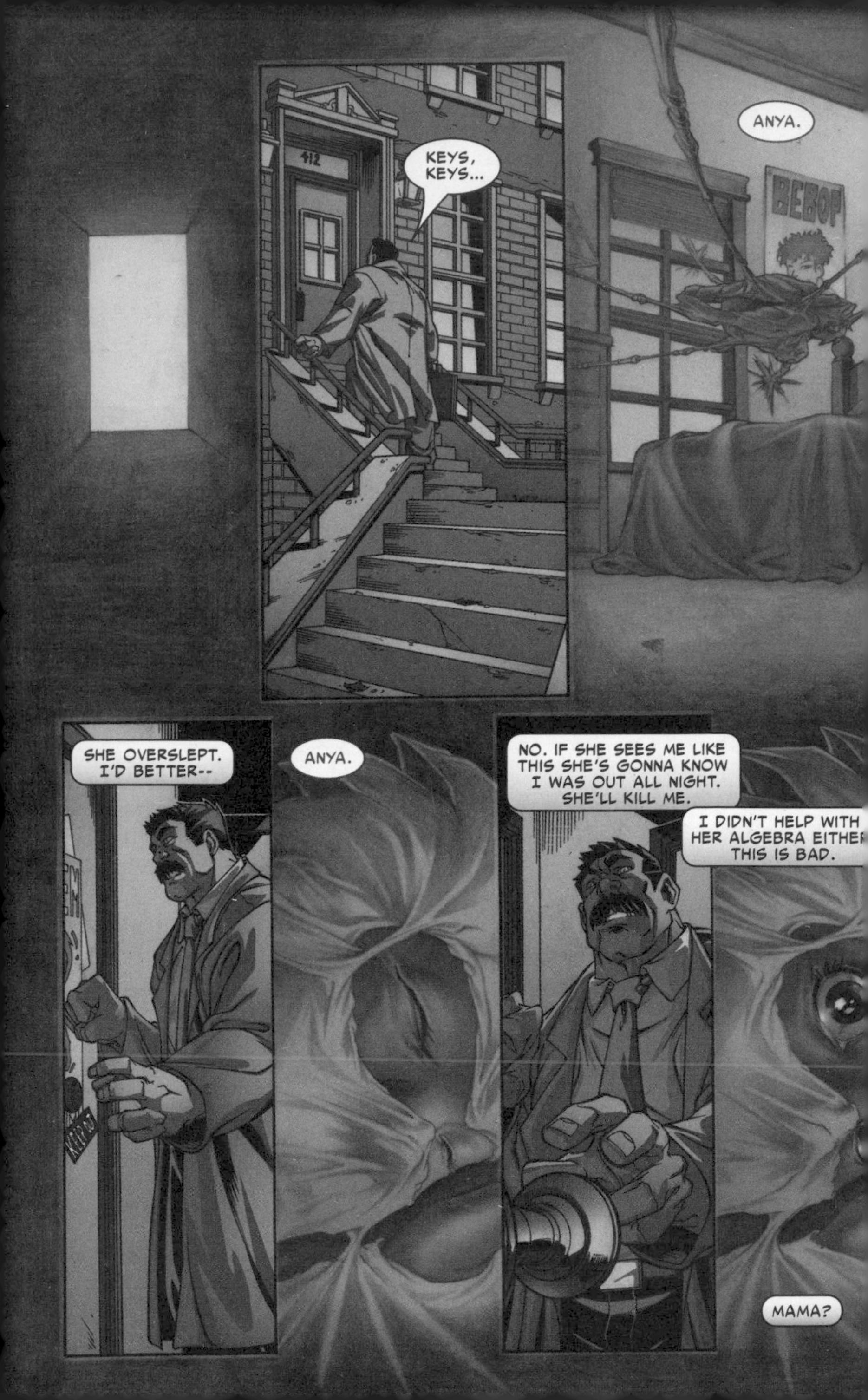
KEYS, KEYS...
ANYA.
SHE OVERSLEPT. I'D BETTER--
ANYA.
NO. IF SHE SEES ME LIKE THIS SHE'S GONNA KNOW I WAS OUT ALL NIGHT. SHE'LL KILL ME.
I DIDN'T HELP WITH HER ALGEBRA EITHER THIS IS BAD.
MAMA?

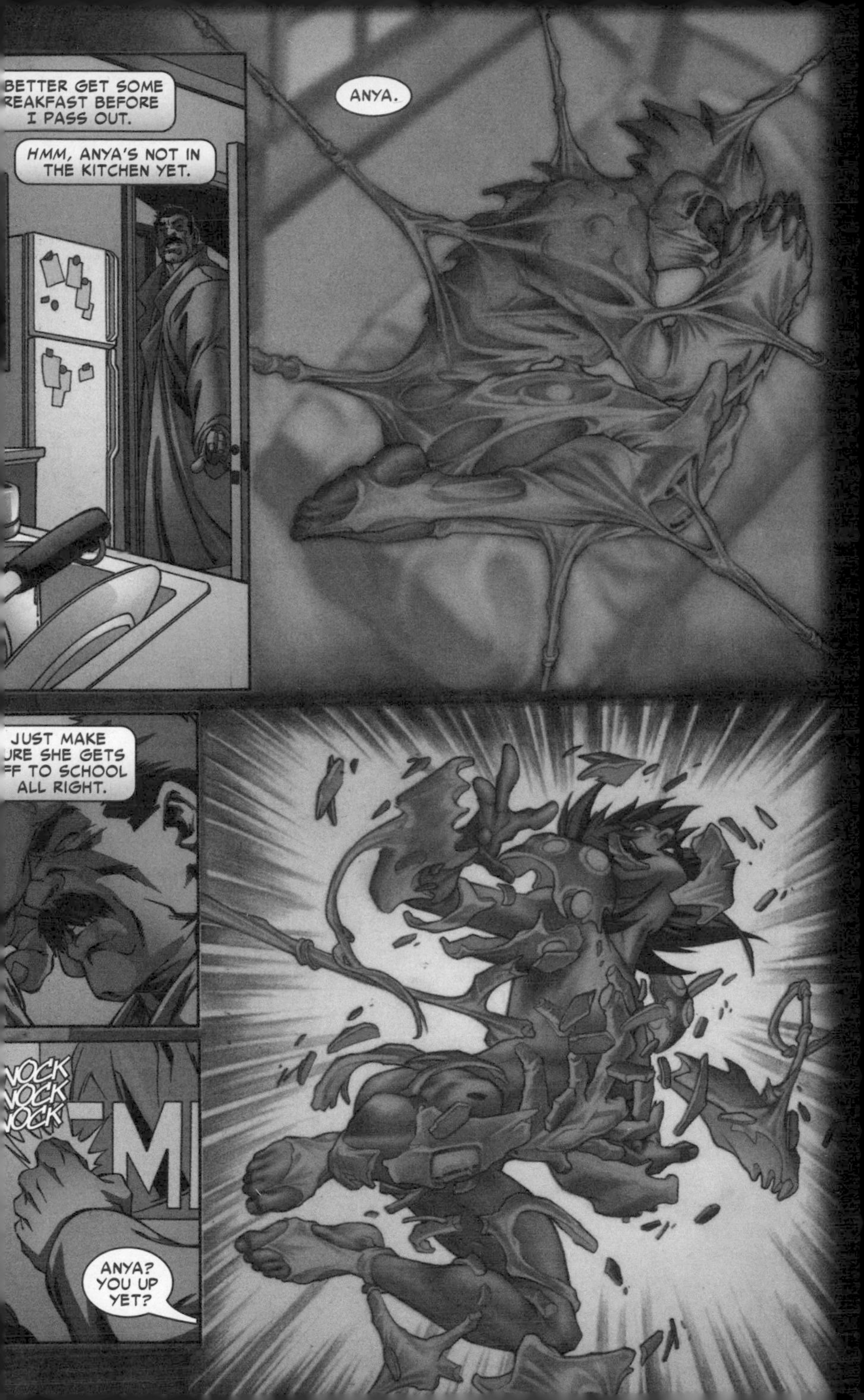
BETTER GET SOME
REAKFAST BEFORE
I PASS OUT.
HMM, ANYA'S NOT IN THE KITCHEN YET.
ANYA.
JUST MAKE
URE SHE GETS
FF TO SCHOOL
ALL RIGHT.
NOCK NOCK NOCK
ANYA? YOU UP YET?

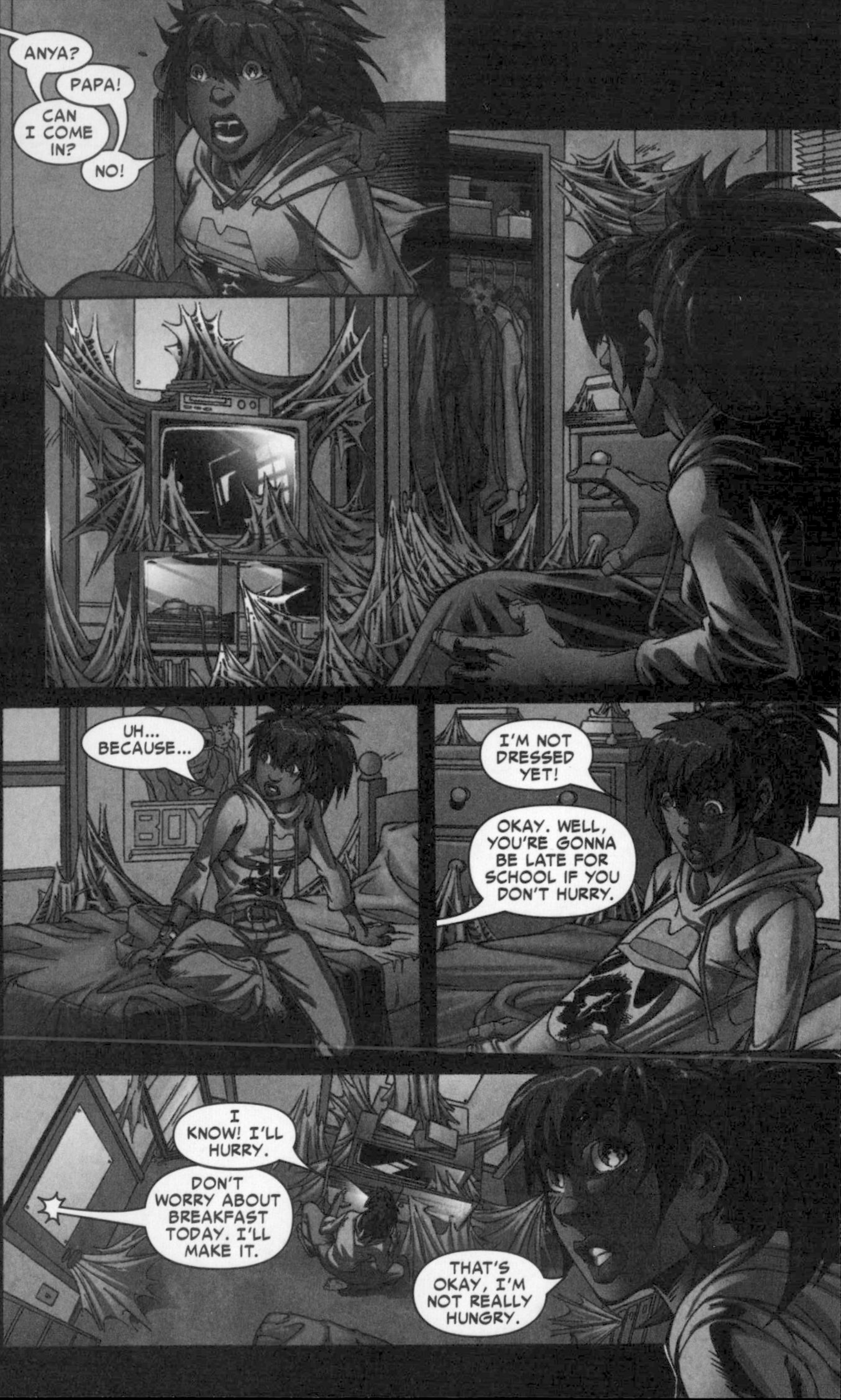
ANYA?
PAPA!
CAN I COME IN?
NO!
UH... BECAUSE...
I'M NOT DRESSED YET!
OKAY. WELL, YOU'RE GONNA BE LATE FOR SCHOOL IF YOU DON'T HURRY.
I KNOW! I'LL HURRY.
DON'T WORRY ABOUT BREAKFAST TODAY. I'LL MAKE IT.
THAT'S OKAY, I'M NOT REALLY HUNGRY.
BOY

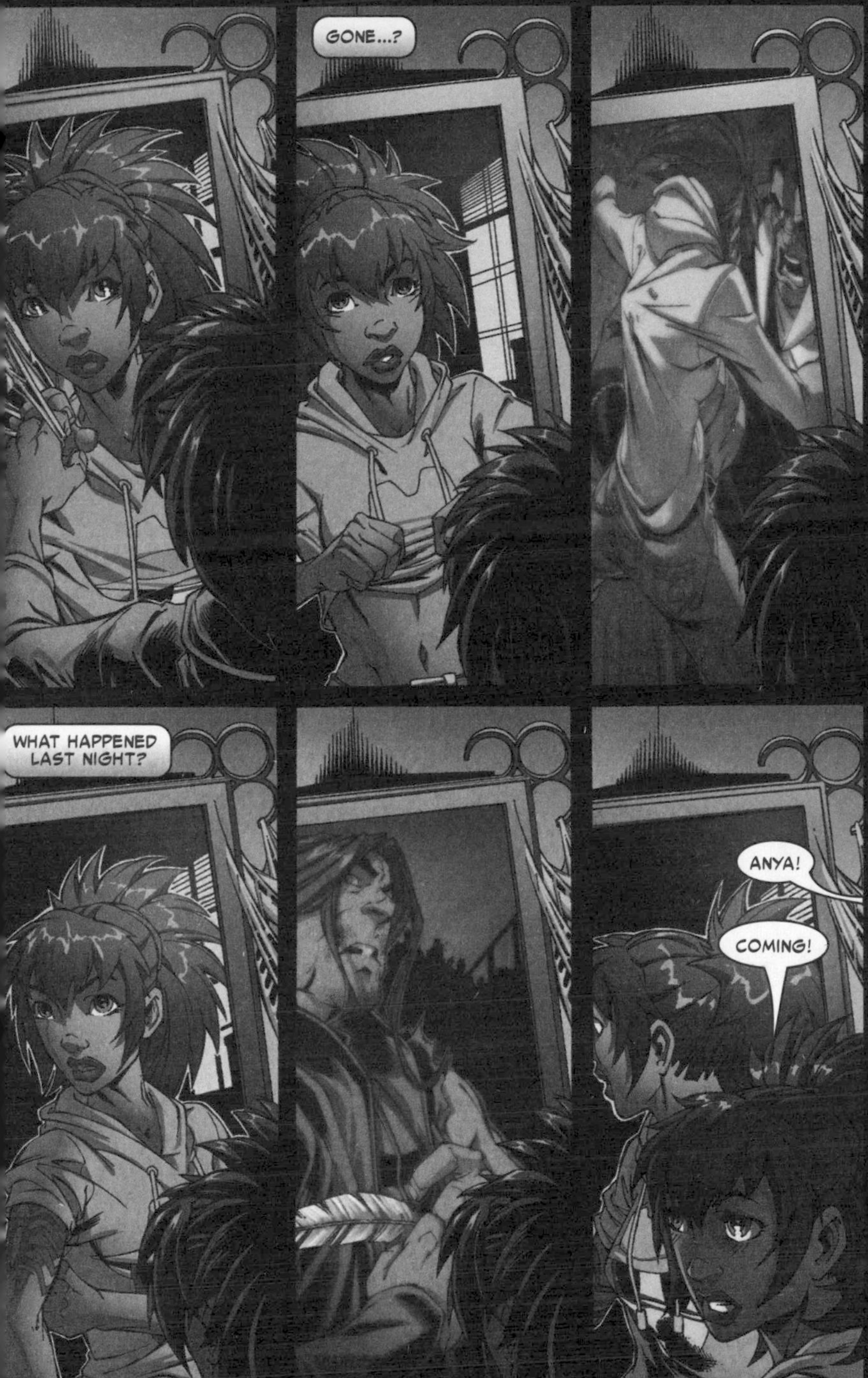
GONE...?
WHAT HAPPENED LAST NIGHT?
ANYA!
COMING!

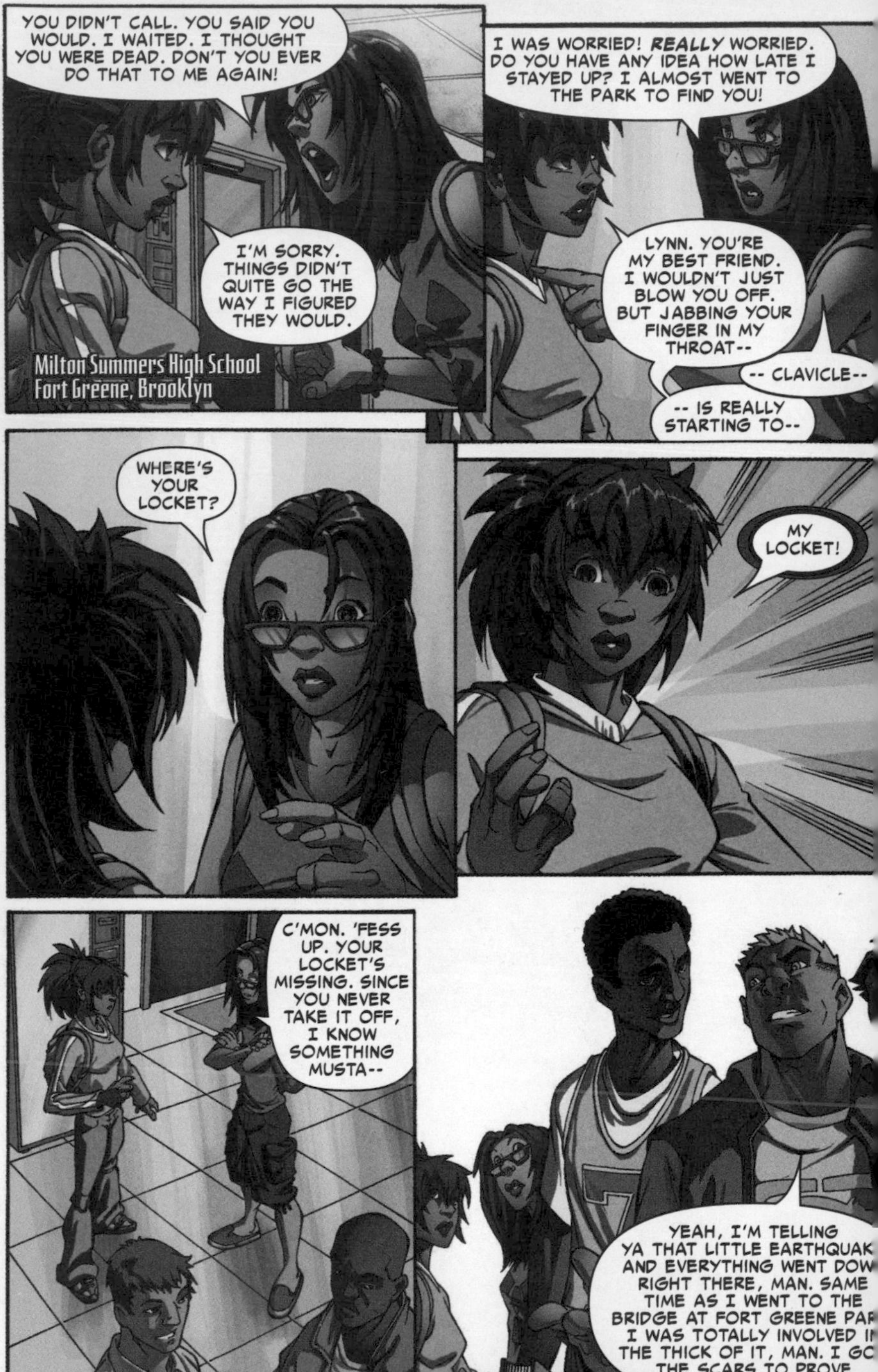
YOU DIDN'T CALL. YOU SAID YOU WOULD. I WAITED. I THOUGHT YOU WERE DEAD. DON'T YOU EVER DO THAT TO ME AGAIN!
I'M SORRY. THINGS DIDN'T QUITE GO THE WAY I FIGURED THEY WOULD.
Milton Summers High School Fort Greene, Brooklyn
I WAS WORRIED! REALLY WORRIED. DO YOU HAVE ANY IDEA HOW LATE I STAYED UP? I ALMOST WENT TO THE PARK TO FIND YOU!
LYNN. YOU'RE MY BEST FRIEND. I WOULDN'T JUST BLOW YOU OFF. BUT JABBING YOUR FINGER IN MY THROAT--
-- CLAVICLE--
-- IS REALLY STARTING TO--
WHERE'S YOUR LOCKET?
MY LOCKET!
C'MON. 'FESS UP. YOUR LOCKET'S MISSING. SINCE YOU NEVER TAKE IT OFF, I KNOW SOMETHING MUSTA--
YEAH, I'M TELLING YA THAT LITTLE EARTHQUAK AND EVERYTHING WENT DOW RIGHT THERE, MAN. SAME TIME AS I WENT TO THE BRIDGE AT FORT GREENE PA I WAS TOTALLY INVOLVED I THE THICK OF IT, MAN. I GO THE SCARS TO PROVE IT, TOO.

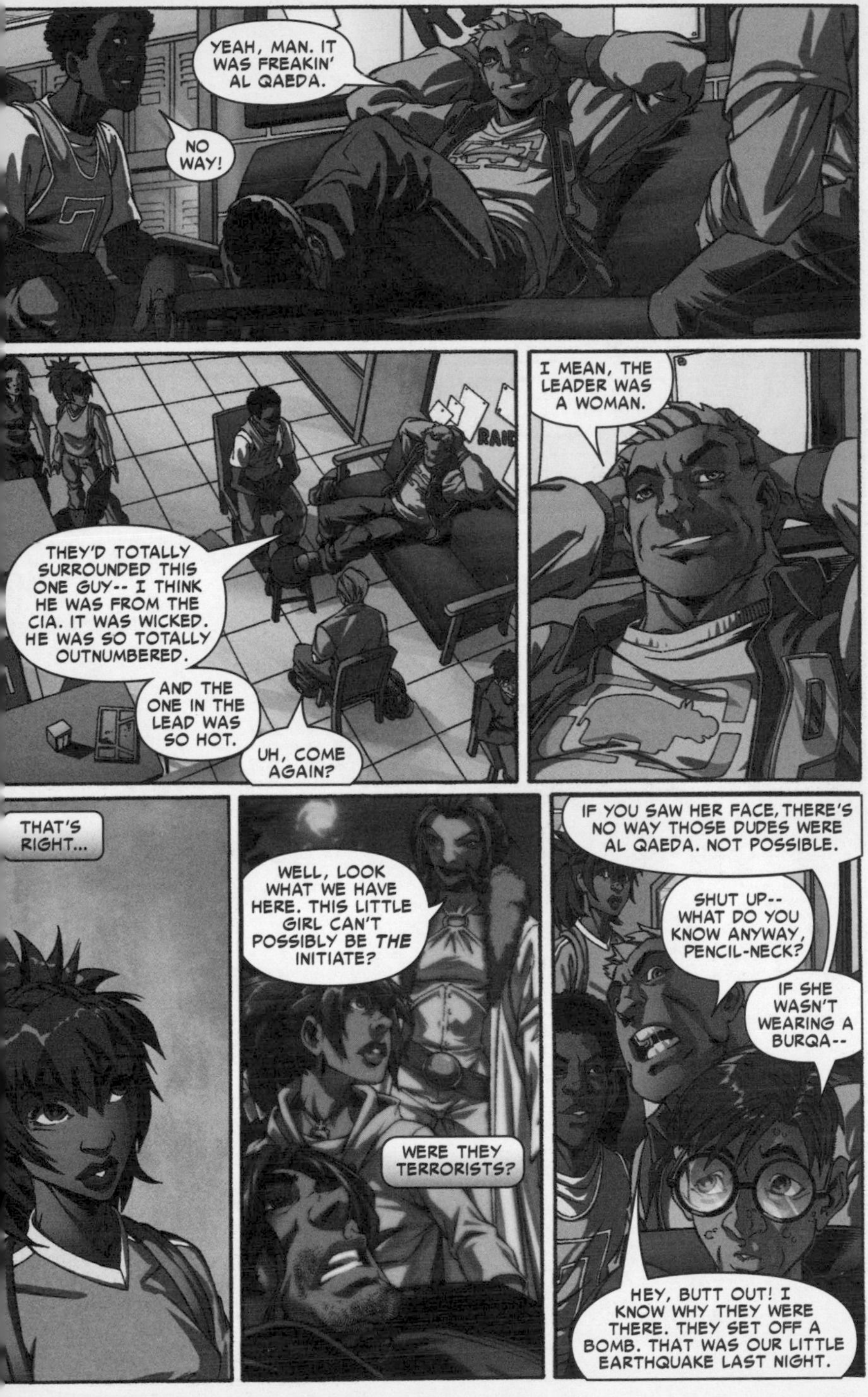
YEAH, MAN. IT WAS FREAKIN' AL QAEDA.
NO WAY!
THEY'D TOTALLY SURROUNDED THIS ONE GUY-- I THINK HE WAS FROM THE CIA. IT WAS WICKED. HE WAS SO TOTALLY OUTNUMBERED.
AND THE ONE IN THE LEAD WAS SO HOT.
UH, COME AGAIN?
RAID
I MEAN, THE LEADER WAS A WOMAN.
THAT'S RIGHT...
WELL, LOOK WHAT WE HAVE HERE. THIS LITTLE GIRL CAN'T POSSIBLY BE *THE* INITIATE?
WERE THEY TERRORISTS?
IF YOU SAW HER FACE, THERE'S NO WAY THOSE DUDES WERE AL QAEDA. NOT POSSIBLE.
SHUT UP-- WHAT DO YOU KNOW ANYWAY, PENCIL-NECK?
IF SHE WASN'T WEARING A BURQA--
HEY, BUTT OUT! I KNOW WHY THEY WERE THERE. THEY SET OFF A BOMB. THAT WAS OUR LITTLE EARTHQUAKE LAST NIGHT.

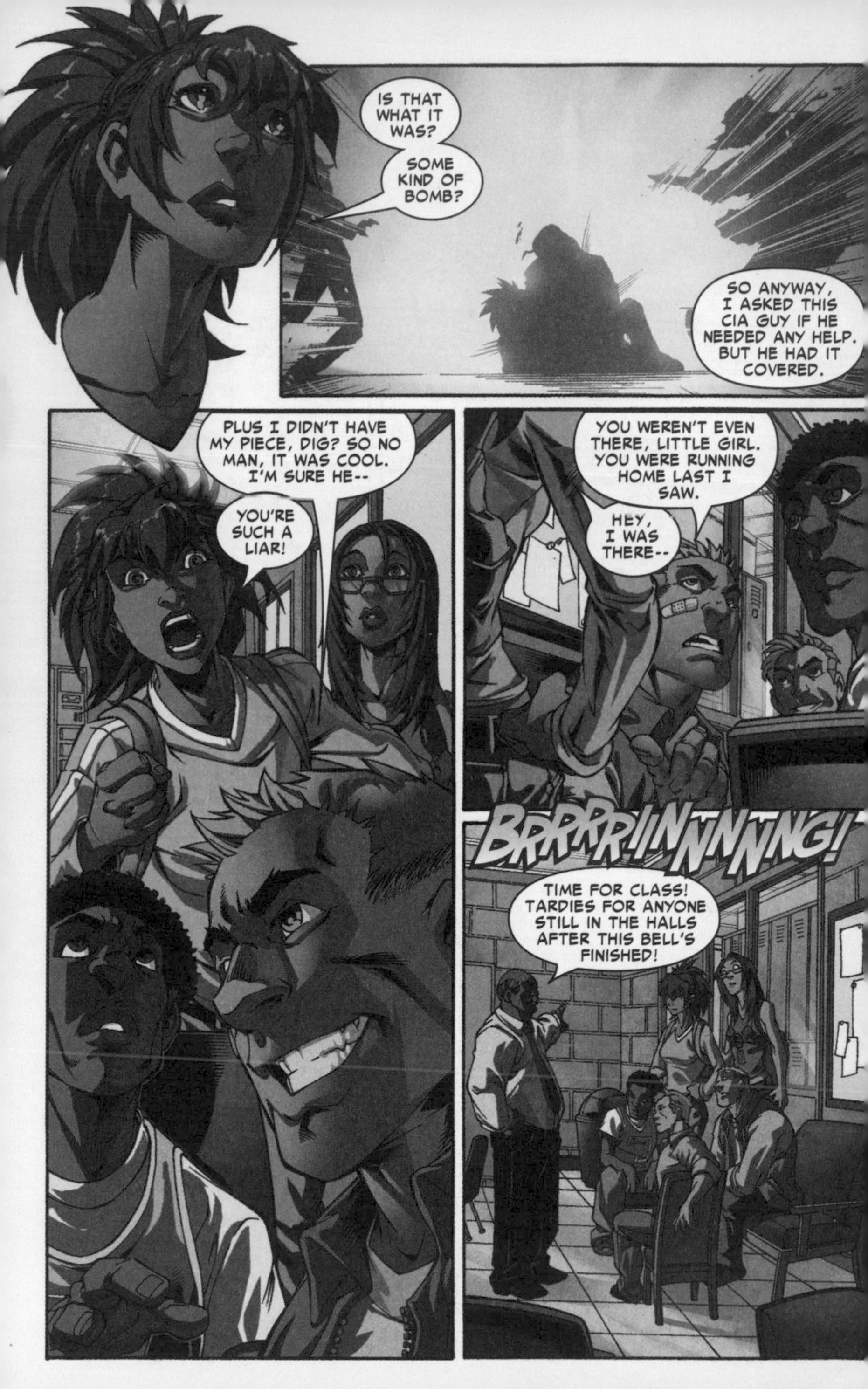
IS THAT WHAT IT WAS?
SOME KIND OF BOMB?
SO ANYWAY, I ASKED THIS CIA GUY IF HE NEEDED ANY HELP. BUT HE HAD IT COVERED.
PLUS I DIDN'T HAVE MY PIECE, DIG? SO NO MAN, IT WAS COOL. I'M SURE HE--
YOU'RE SUCH A LIAR!
YOU WEREN'T EVEN THERE, LITTLE GIRL. YOU WERE RUNNING HOME LAST I SAW.
HEY, I WAS THERE--
BRRRRIINNNNNG!
TIME FOR CLASS! TARDIES FOR ANYONE STILL IN THE HALLS AFTER THIS BELL'S FINISHED!

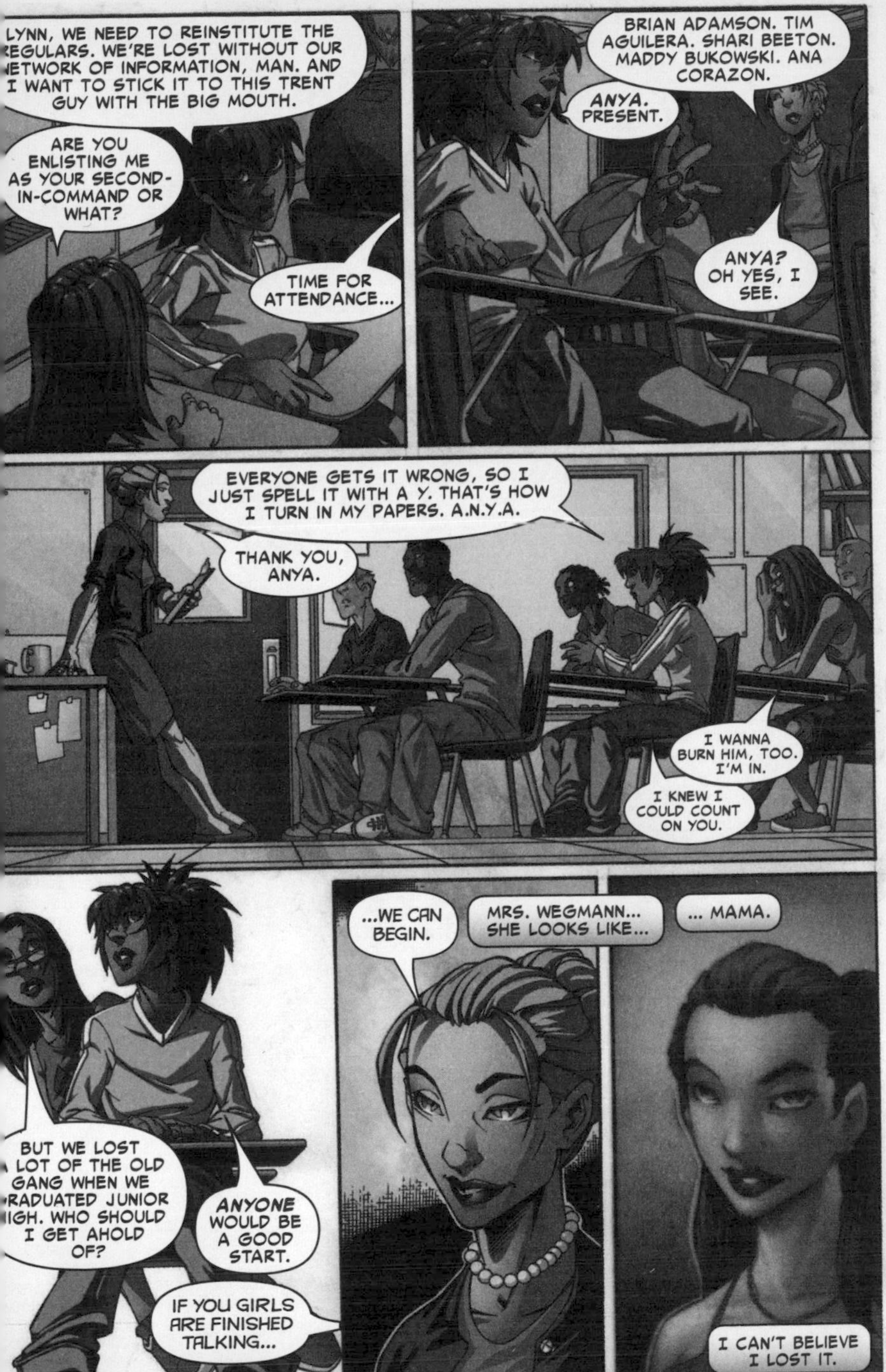
LYNN, WE NEED TO REINSTITUTE THE REGULARS. WE'RE LOST WITHOUT OUR NETWORK OF INFORMATION, MAN. AND I WANT TO STICK IT TO THIS TRENT GUY WITH THE BIG MOUTH.
ARE YOU ENLISTING ME AS YOUR SECOND-IN-COMMAND OR WHAT?
TIME FOR ATTENDANCE...
BRIAN ADAMSON. TIM AGUILERA. SHARI BEETON. MADDY BUKOWSKI. ANA CORAZON.
ANYA. PRESENT.
ANYA? OH YES, I SEE.
EVERYONE GETS IT WRONG, SO I JUST SPELL IT WITH A Y. THAT'S HOW I TURN IN MY PAPERS. A.N.Y.A.
THANK YOU, ANYA.
I WANNA BURN HIM, TOO. I'M IN.
I KNEW I COULD COUNT ON YOU.
BUT WE LOST LOT OF THE OLD GANG WHEN WE RADUATED JUNIOR IGH. WHO SHOULD I GET AHOLD OF?
ANYONE WOULD BE A GOOD START.
IF YOU GIRLS ARE FINISHED TALKING...
...WE CAN BEGIN.
MRS. WEGMANN... SHE LOOKS LIKE...
... MAMA.
I CAN'T BELIEVE I LOST IT.

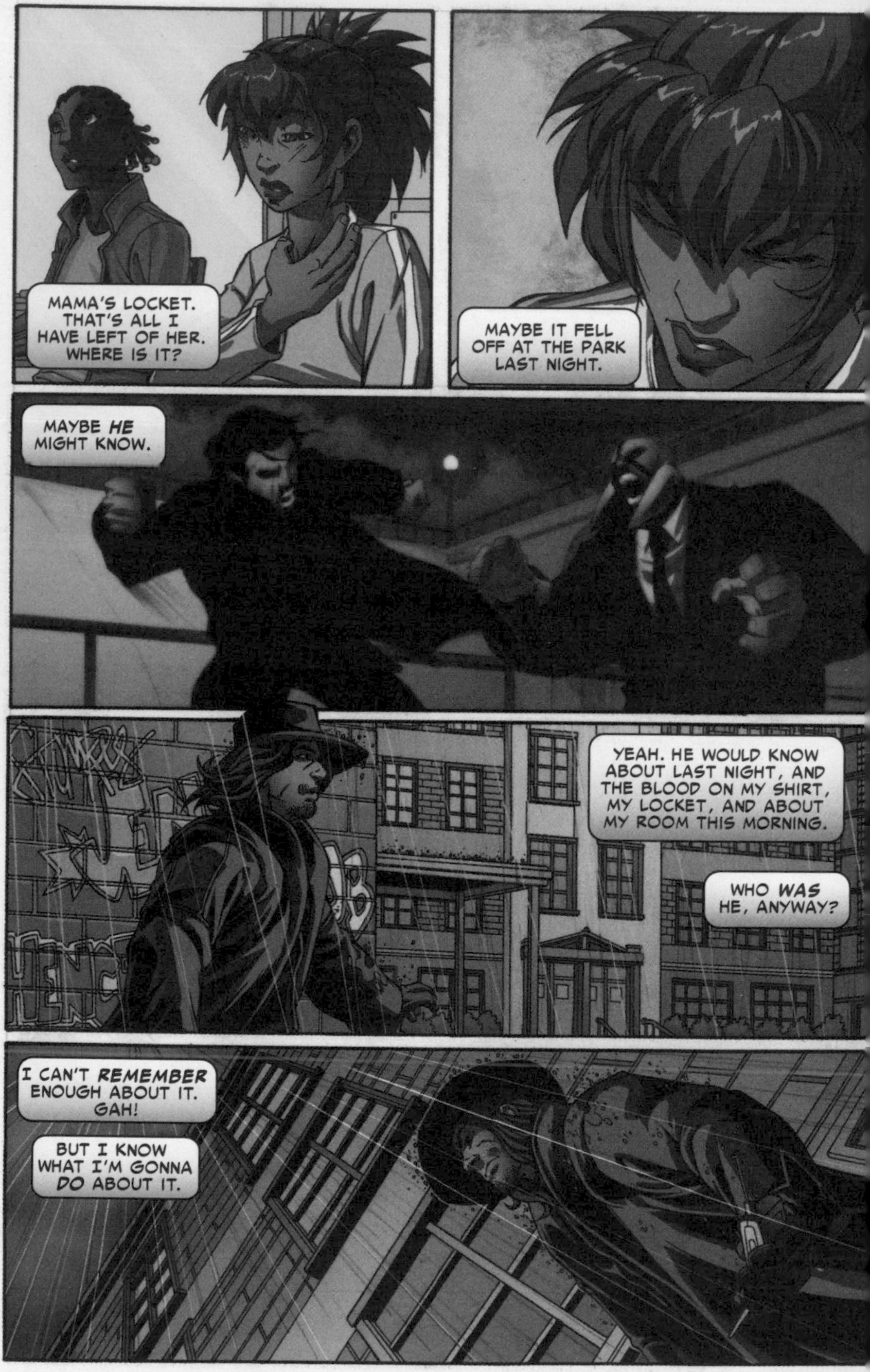
MAMA'S LOCKET. THAT'S ALL I HAVE LEFT OF HER. WHERE IS IT?
MAYBE IT FELL OFF AT THE PARK LAST NIGHT.
MAYBE *HE* MIGHT KNOW.
YEAH. HE WOULD KNOW ABOUT LAST NIGHT, AND THE BLOOD ON MY SHIRT, MY LOCKET, AND ABOUT MY ROOM THIS MORNING.
WHO *WAS* HE, ANYWAY?
I CAN'T *REMEMBER* ENOUGH ABOUT IT. GAH!
BUT I KNOW WHAT I'M GONNA *DO* ABOUT IT.

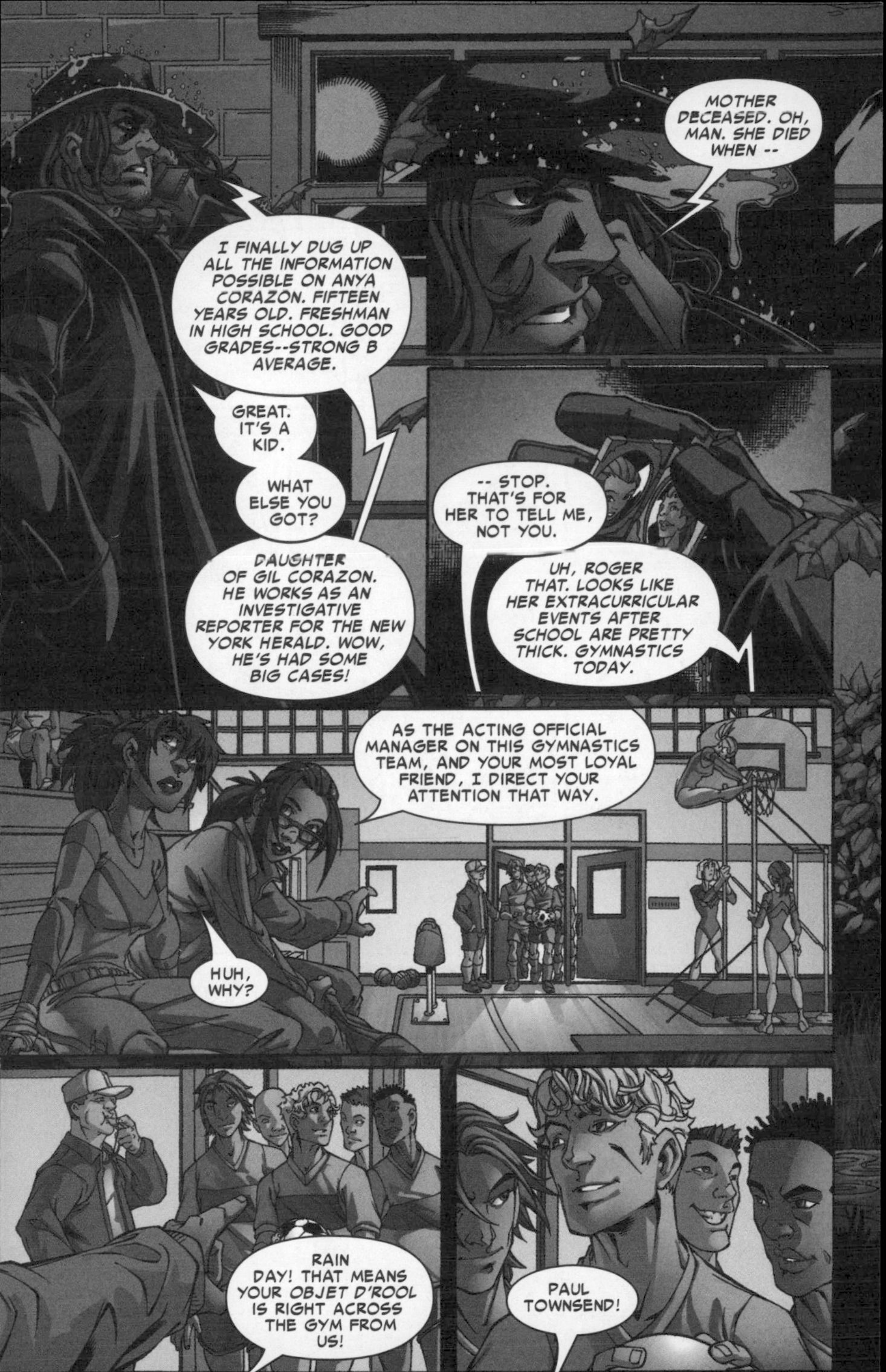

I FINALLY DUG UP ALL THE INFORMATION POSSIBLE ON ANYA CORAZON. FIFTEEN YEARS OLD. FRESHMAN IN HIGH SCHOOL. GOOD GRADES--STRONG B AVERAGE.
GREAT. IT'S A KID.
WHAT ELSE YOU GOT?
DAUGHTER OF GIL CORAZON. HE WORKS AS AN INVESTIGATIVE REPORTER FOR THE NEW YORK HERALD. WOW, HE'S HAD SOME BIG CASES!
MOTHER DECEASED. OH, MAN. SHE DIED WHEN --
-- STOP. THAT'S FOR HER TO TELL ME, NOT YOU.
UH, ROGER THAT. LOOKS LIKE HER EXTRACURRICULAR EVENTS AFTER SCHOOL ARE PRETTY THICK. GYMNASTICS TODAY.
AS THE ACTING OFFICIAL MANAGER ON THIS GYMNASTICS TEAM, AND YOUR MOST LOYAL FRIEND, I DIRECT YOUR ATTENTION THAT WAY.
HUH, WHY?
RAIN DAY! THAT MEANS YOUR OBJET D'ROOL IS RIGHT ACROSS THE GYM FROM US!
PAUL TOWNSEND!

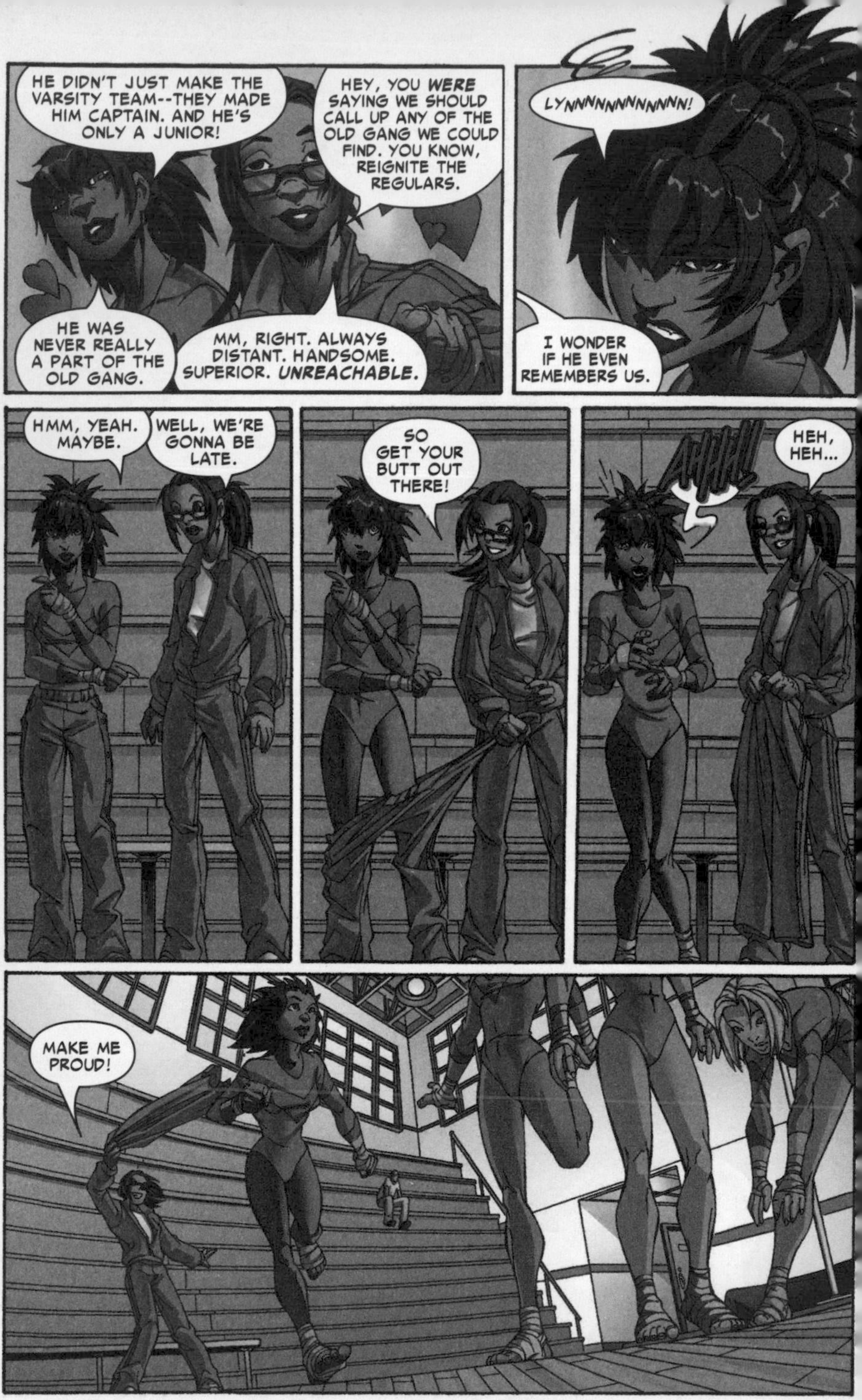
HE DIDN'T JUST MAKE THE VARSITY TEAM--THEY MADE HIM CAPTAIN. AND HE'S ONLY A JUNIOR!
HEY, YOU WERE SAYING WE SHOULD CALL UP ANY OF THE OLD GANG WE COULD FIND. YOU KNOW, REIGNITE THE REGULARS.
HE WAS NEVER REALLY A PART OF THE OLD GANG.
MM, RIGHT. ALWAYS DISTANT. HANDSOME. SUPERIOR. UNREACHABLE.
LYNNNNNNNNNNNN!
I WONDER IF HE EVEN REMEMBERS US.
HMM, YEAH. MAYBE.
WELL, WE'RE GONNA BE LATE.
SO GET YOUR BUTT OUT THERE!
AHHH!
HEH, HEH...
MAKE ME PROUD!

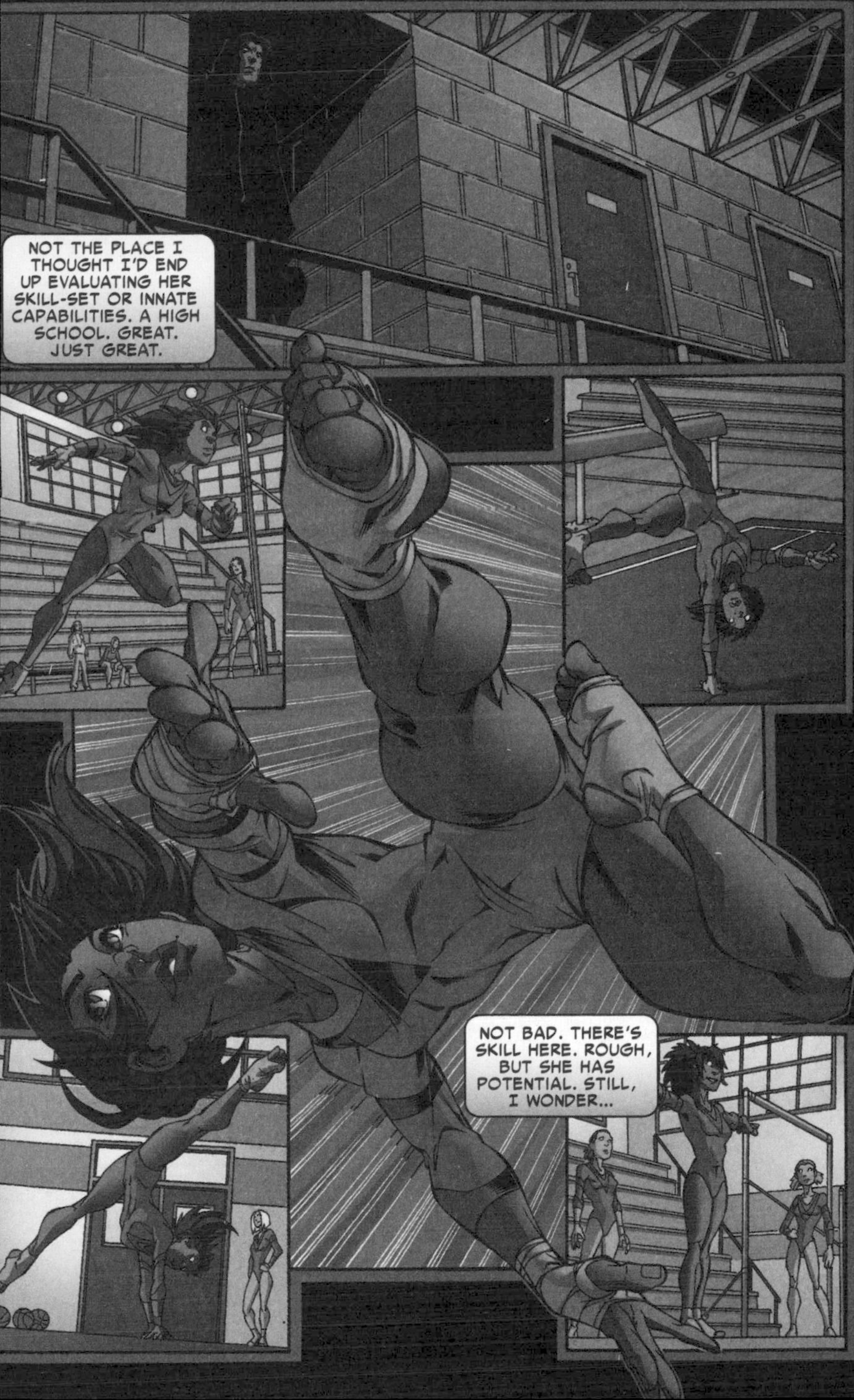
NOT THE PLACE I THOUGHT I'D END UP EVALUATING HER SKILL-SET OR INNATE CAPABILITIES. A HIGH SCHOOL. GREAT. JUST GREAT.
NOT BAD. THERE'S SKILL HERE. ROUGH, BUT SHE HAS POTENTIAL. STILL, I WONDER...

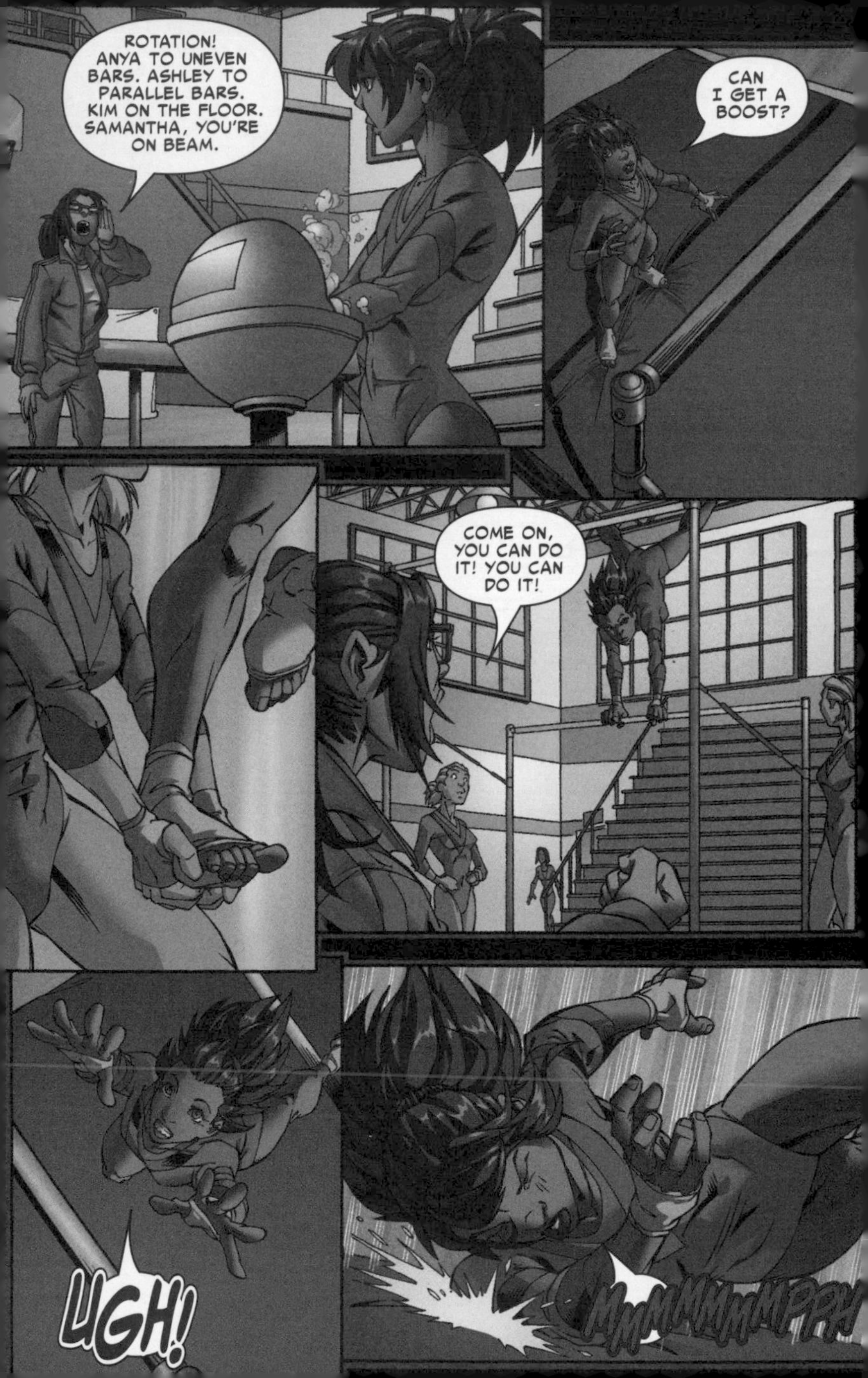
ROTATION! ANYA TO UNEVEN BARS. ASHLEY TO PARALLEL BARS. KIM ON THE FLOOR. SAMANTHA, YOU'RE ON BEAM.
CAN I GET A BOOST?
COME ON, YOU CAN DO IT! YOU CAN DO IT!
UGH!
MMMMMMMPPH

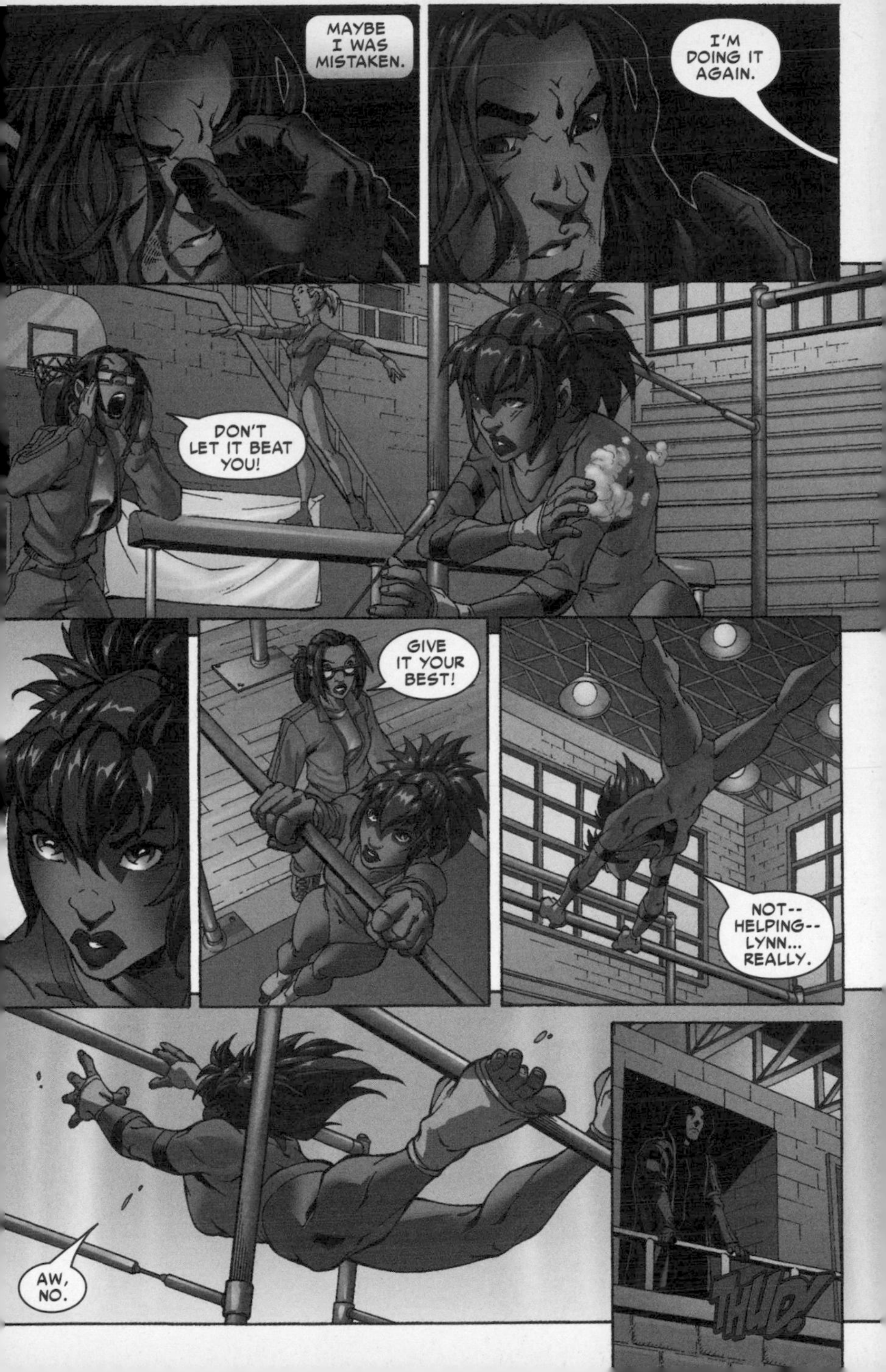
MAYBE I WAS MISTAKEN.
I'M DOING IT AGAIN.
DON'T LET IT BEAT YOU!
GIVE IT YOUR BEST!
NOT-- HELPING-- LYNN... REALLY.
AW, NO.
THUD!

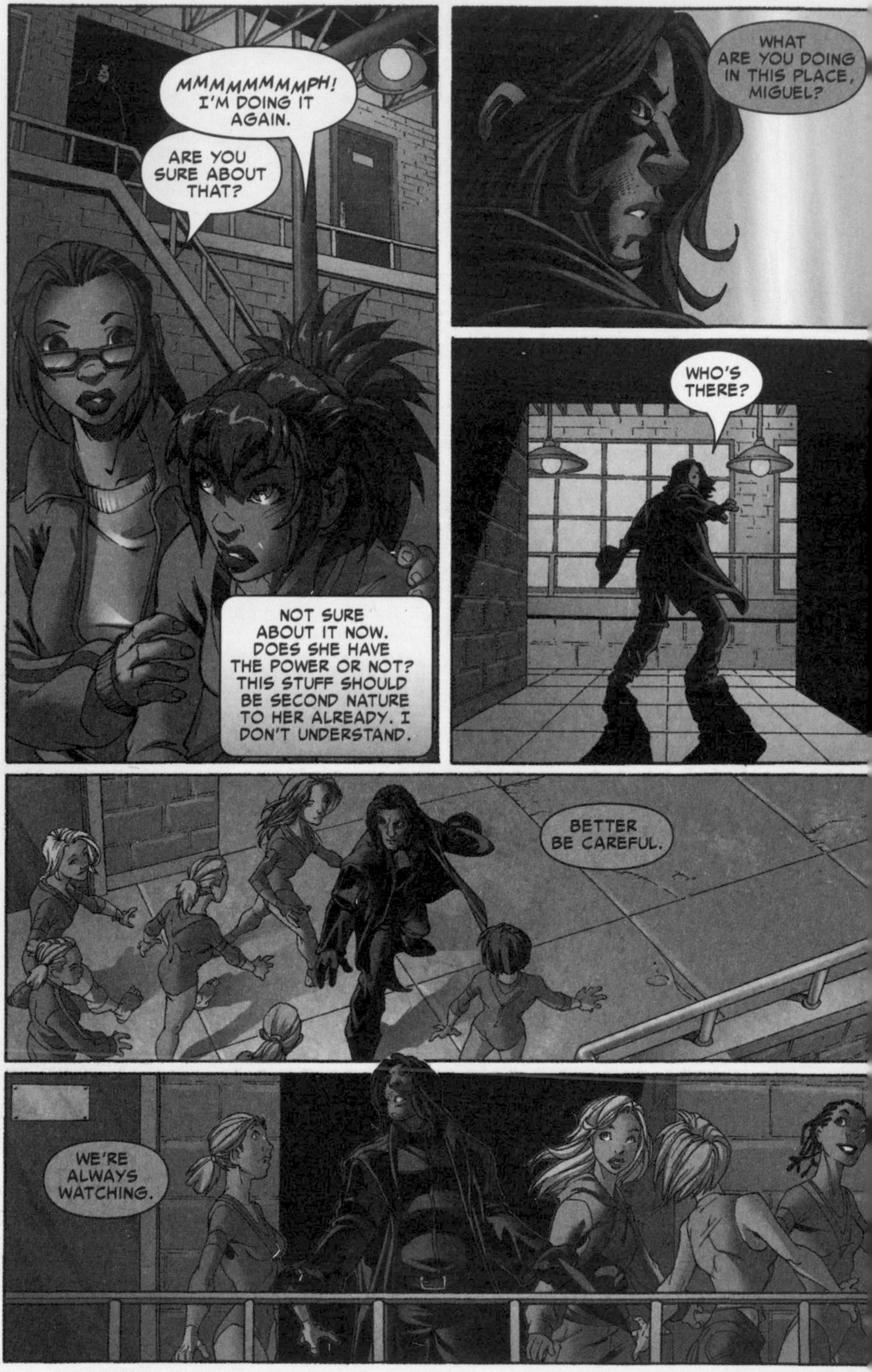

MMMMMMMMPH! I'M DOING IT AGAIN.
ARE YOU SURE ABOUT THAT?
NOT SURE ABOUT IT NOW. DOES SHE HAVE THE POWER OR NOT? THIS STUFF SHOULD BE SECOND NATURE TO HER ALREADY. I DON'T UNDERSTAND.
WHAT ARE YOU DOING IN THIS PLACE, MIGUEL?
WHO'S THERE?
BETTER BE CAREFUL.
WE'RE ALWAYS WATCHING.

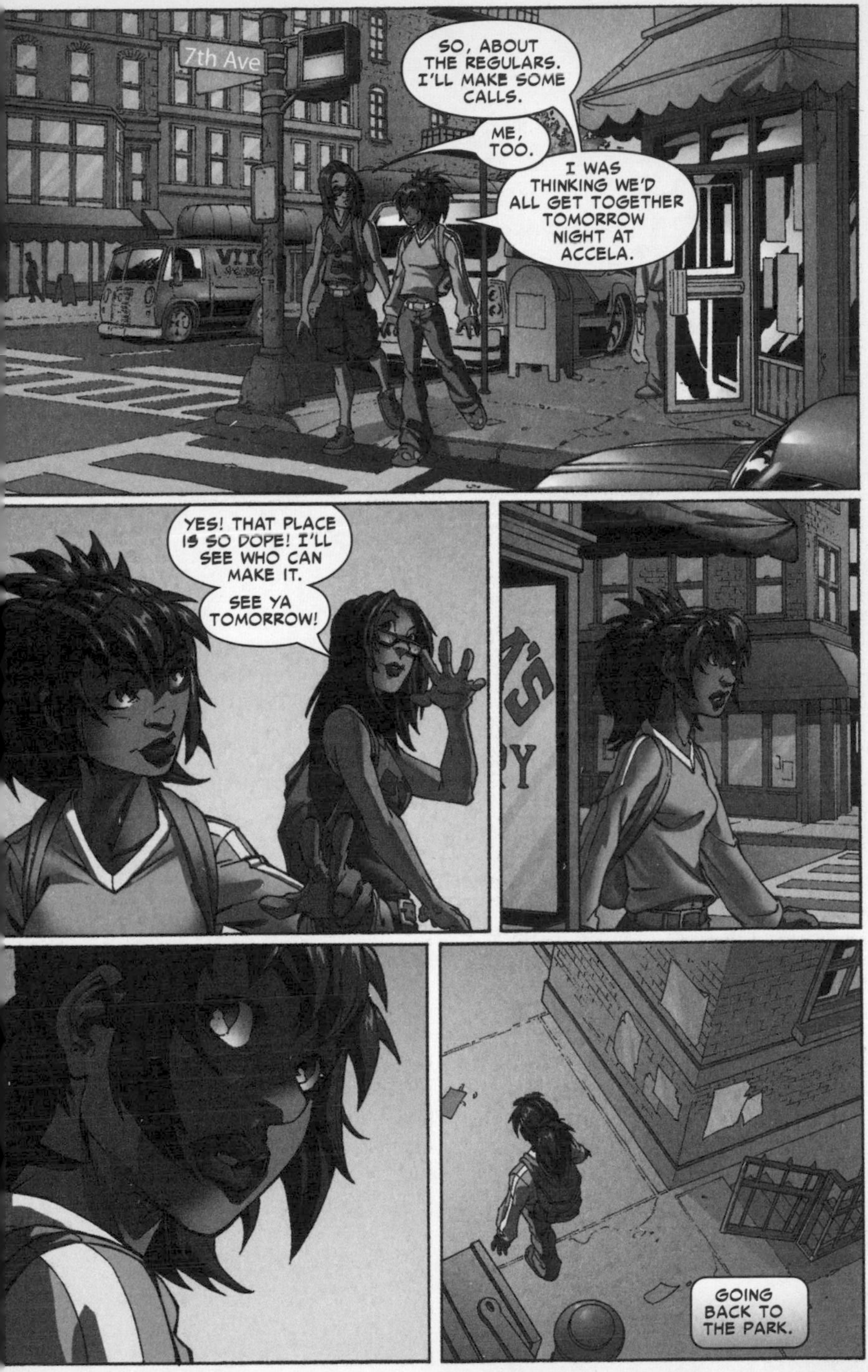

7th Ave
SO, ABOUT THE REGULARS. I'LL MAKE SOME CALLS.
ME, TOO.
I WAS THINKING WE'D ALL GET TOGETHER TOMORROW NIGHT AT ACCELA.
YES! THAT PLACE IS SO DOPE! I'LL SEE WHO CAN MAKE IT.
SEE YA TOMORROW!
GOING BACK TO THE PARK.

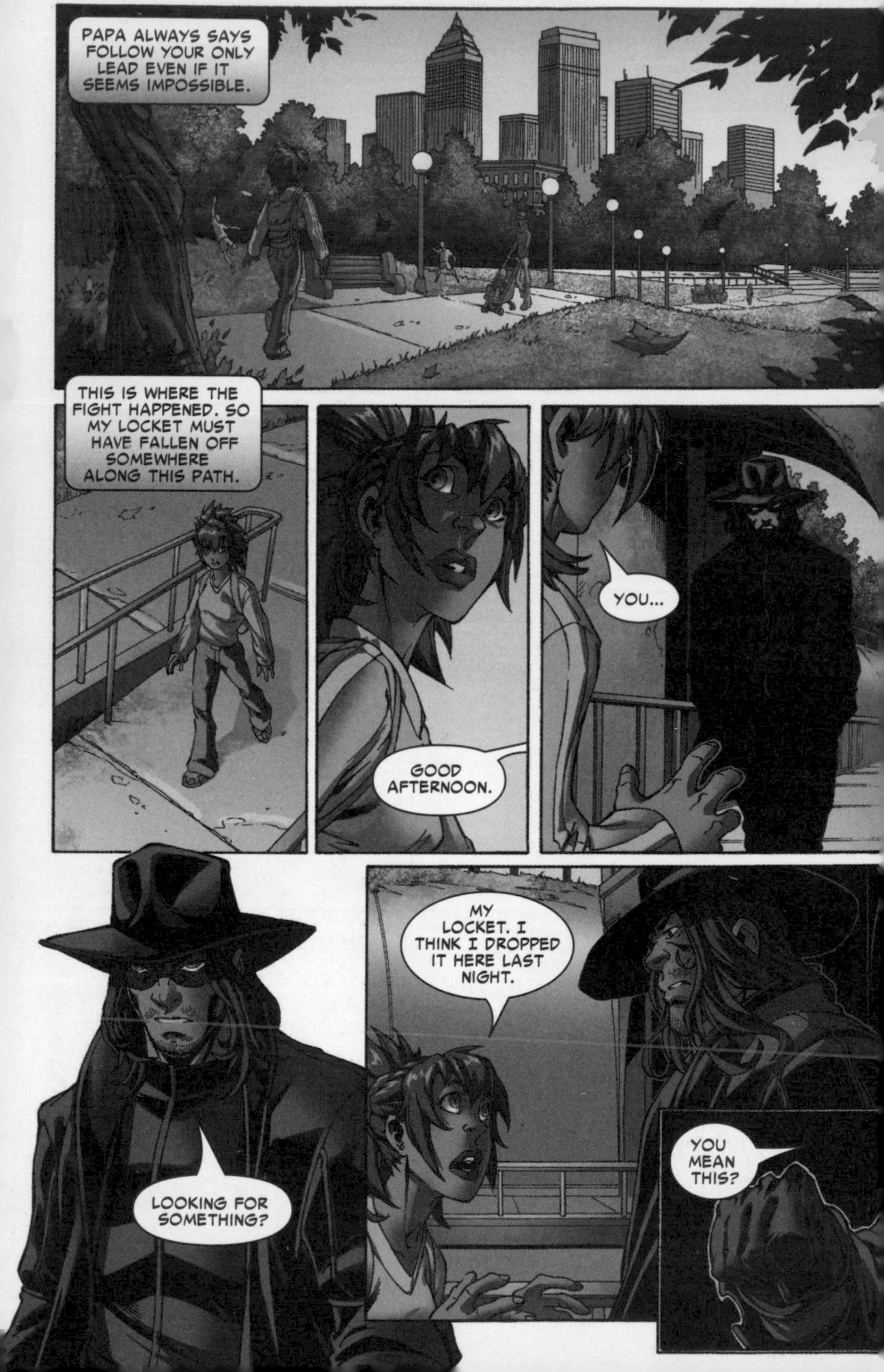
PAPA ALWAYS SAYS FOLLOW YOUR ONLY LEAD EVEN IF IT SEEMS IMPOSSIBLE.
THIS IS WHERE THE FIGHT HAPPENED. SO MY LOCKET MUST HAVE FALLEN OFF SOMEWHERE ALONG THIS PATH.
GOOD AFTERNOON.
YOU...
LOOKING FOR SOMETHING?
MY LOCKET. I THINK I DROPPED IT HERE LAST NIGHT.
YOU MEAN THIS?

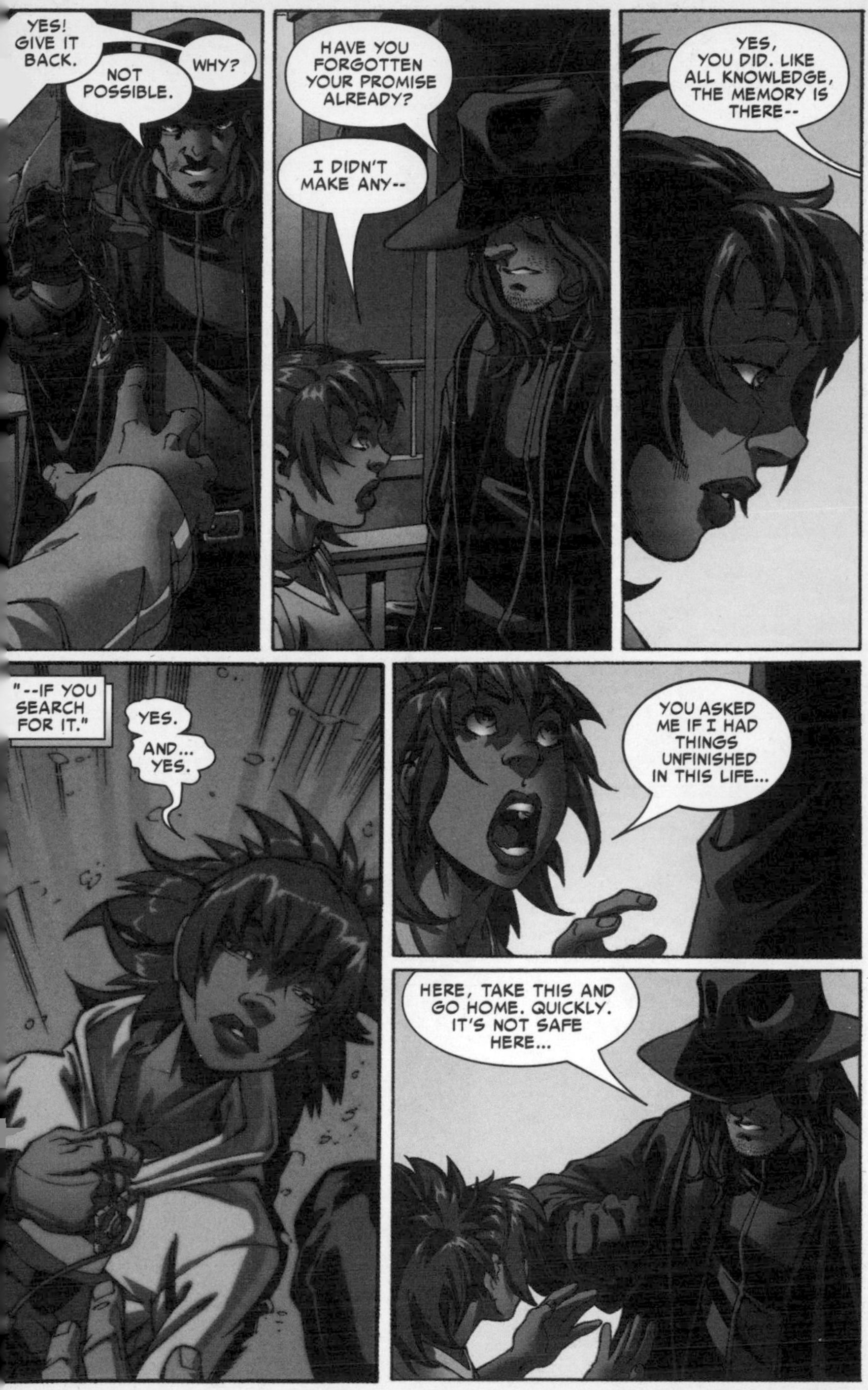
YES! GIVE IT BACK.
WHY?
NOT POSSIBLE.
HAVE YOU FORGOTTEN YOUR PROMISE ALREADY?
I DIDN'T MAKE ANY--
YES, YOU DID. LIKE ALL KNOWLEDGE, THE MEMORY IS THERE--
"--IF YOU SEARCH FOR IT."
YES.
AND... YES.
YOU ASKED ME IF I HAD THINGS UNFINISHED IN THIS LIFE...
HERE, TAKE THIS AND GO HOME. QUICKLY. IT'S NOT SAFE HERE...

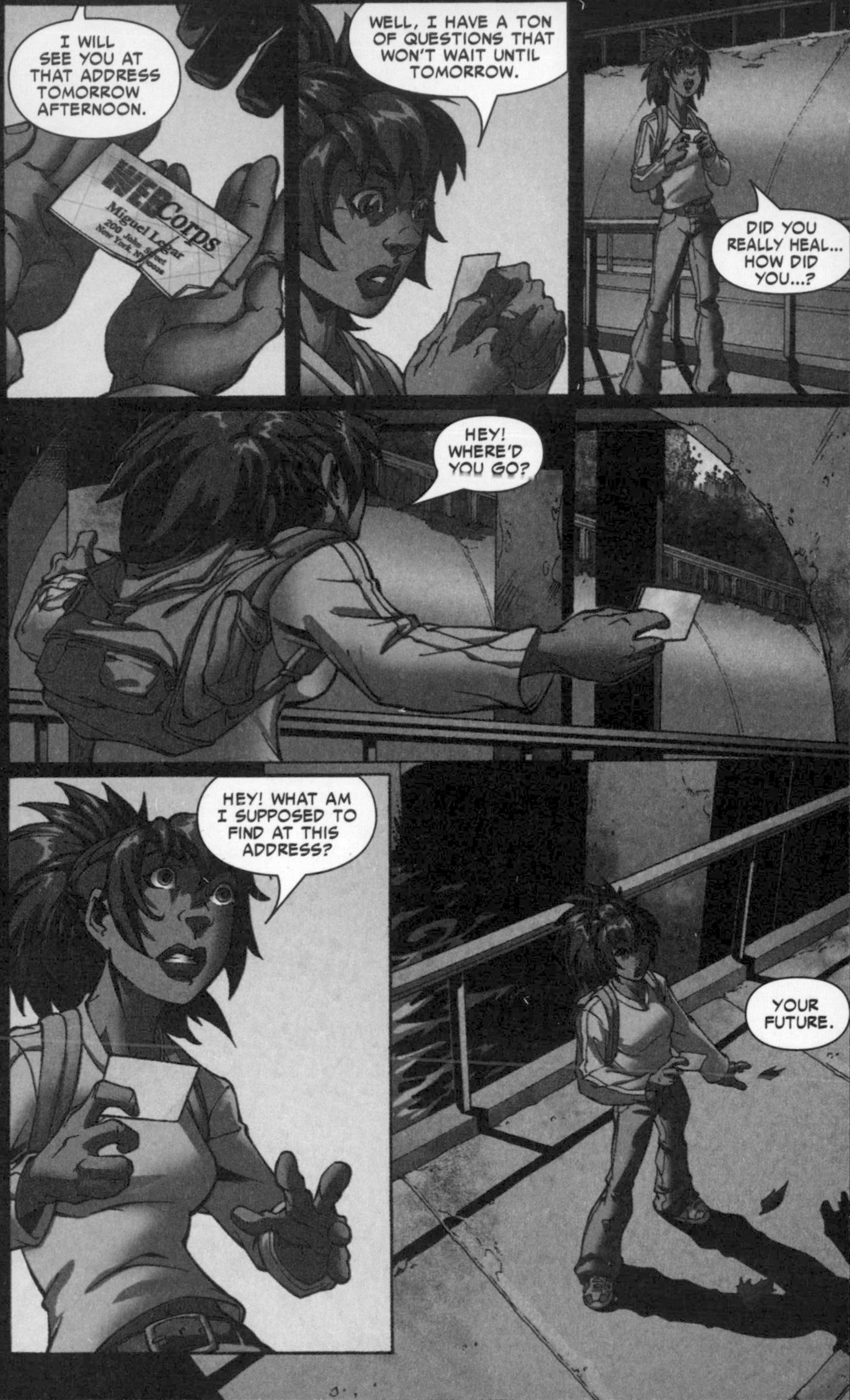
I WILL SEE YOU AT THAT ADDRESS TOMORROW AFTERNOON.
WEBCorps
Miguel Legar
WELL, I HAVE A TON OF QUESTIONS THAT WON'T WAIT UNTIL TOMORROW.
DID YOU REALLY HEAL... HOW DID YOU...?
HEY! WHERE'D YOU GO?
HEY! WHAT AM I SUPPOSED TO FIND AT THIS ADDRESS?
YOUR FUTURE.

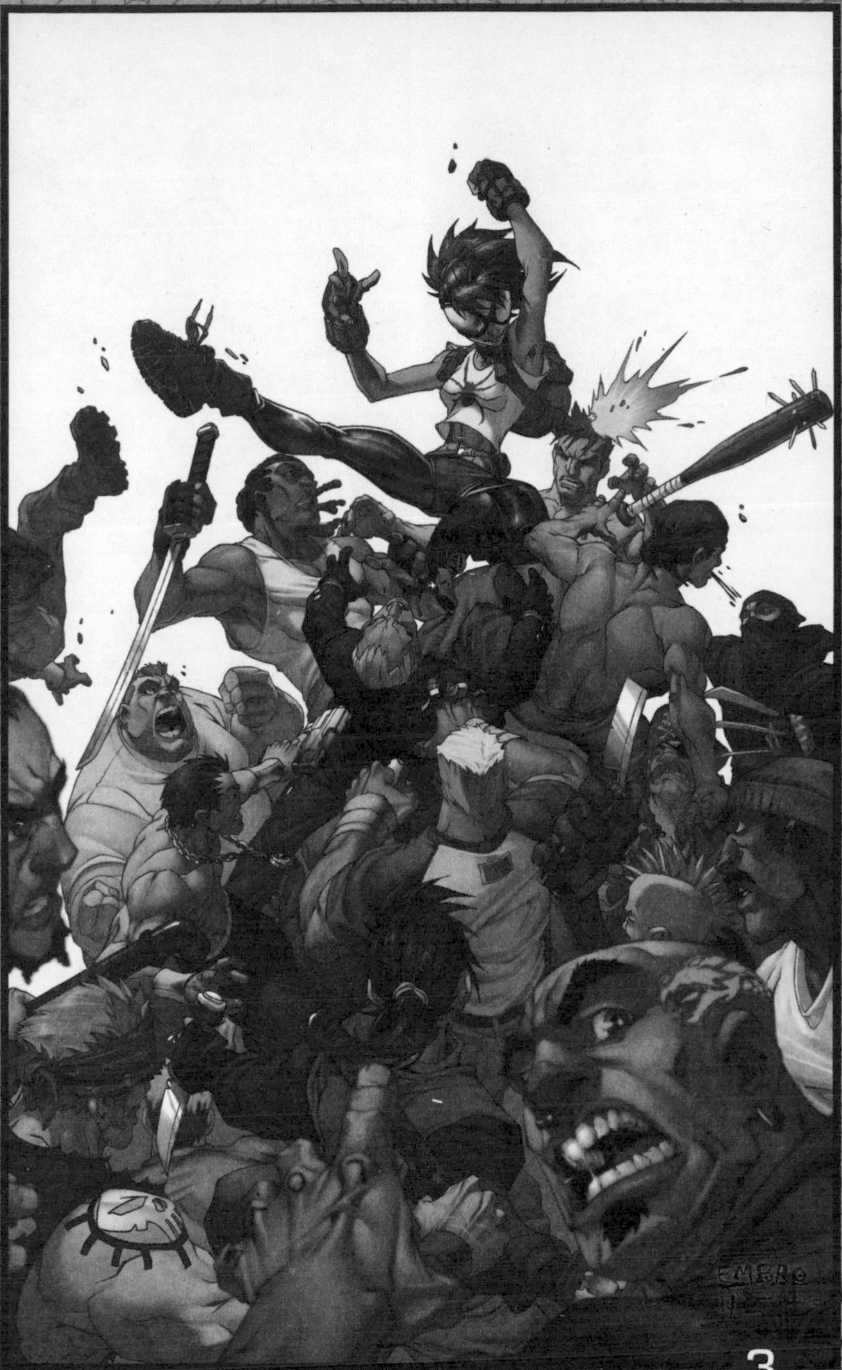

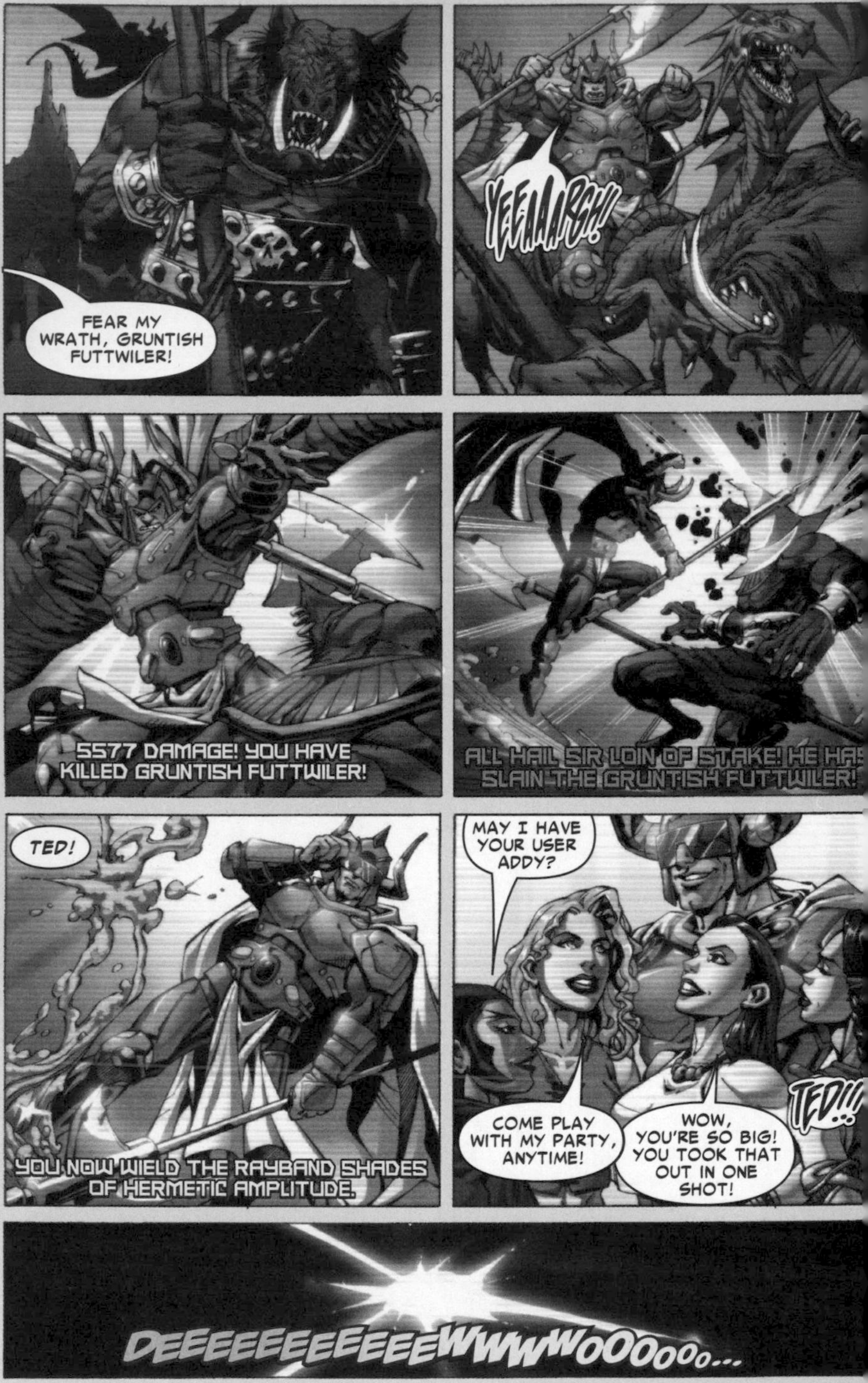
FEAR MY WRATH, GRUNTISH FUTTWILER!
YEEAAARGH!
5577 DAMAGE! YOU HAVE KILLED GRUNTISH FUTTWILER!
ALL HAIL SIR LOIN OF STAKE! HE HAS SLAIN THE GRUNTISH FUTTWILER!
TED!
YOU NOW WIELD THE RAYBAND SHADES OF HERMETIC AMPLITUDE.
MAY I HAVE YOUR USER ADDY?
COME PLAY WITH MY PARTY, ANYTIME!
WOW, YOU'RE SO BIG! YOU TOOK THAT OUT IN ONE SHOT!
TED!!!
DEEEEEEEEEEEEWWWWWOOOOOoo...

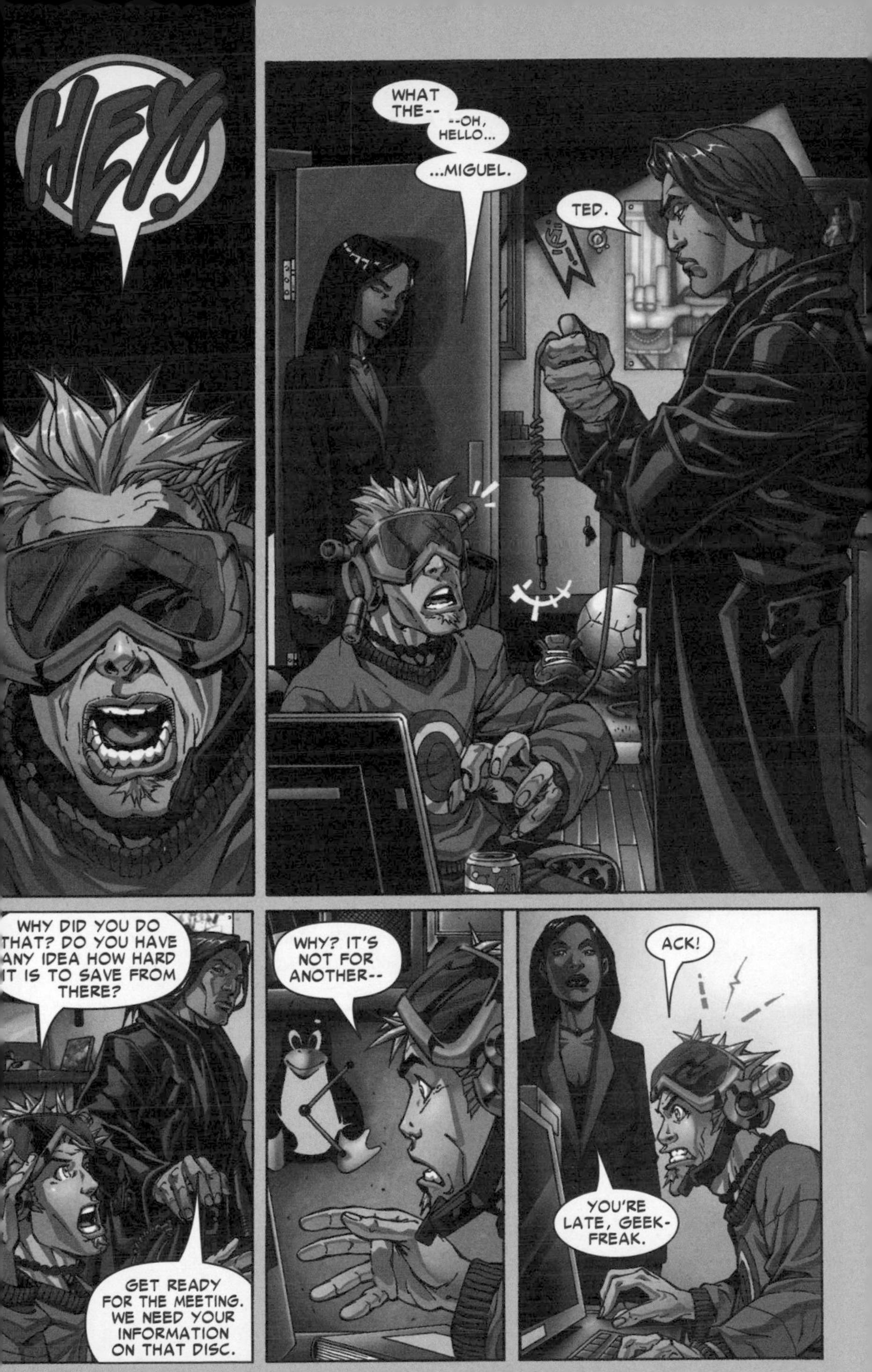
HEY!!
WHAT THE--
--OH, HELLO...
...MIGUEL.
TED.
WHY DID YOU DO THAT? DO YOU HAVE ANY IDEA HOW HARD IT IS TO SAVE FROM THERE?
GET READY FOR THE MEETING. WE NEED YOUR INFORMATION ON THAT DISC.
WHY? IT'S NOT FOR ANOTHER--
ACK!
YOU'RE LATE, GEEK-FREAK.

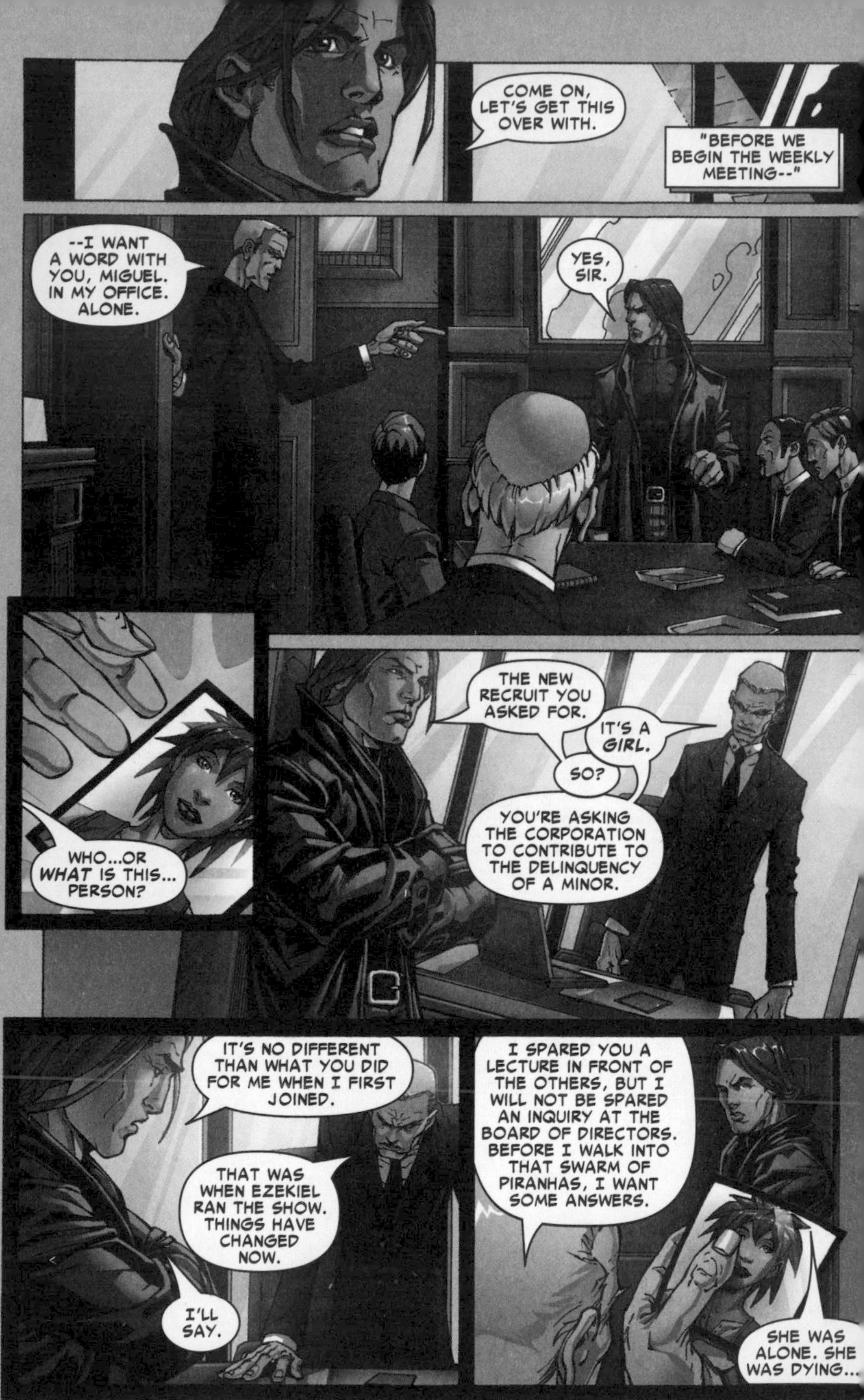
COME ON, LET'S GET THIS OVER WITH.
"BEFORE WE BEGIN THE WEEKLY MEETING--"
--I WANT A WORD WITH YOU, MIGUEL. IN MY OFFICE. ALONE.
YES, SIR.
WHO...OR *WHAT* IS THIS... PERSON?
THE NEW RECRUIT YOU ASKED FOR.
IT'S A *GIRL*.
SO?
YOU'RE ASKING THE CORPORATION TO CONTRIBUTE TO THE DELINQUENCY OF A MINOR.
IT'S NO DIFFERENT THAN WHAT YOU DID FOR ME WHEN I FIRST JOINED.
THAT WAS WHEN EZEKIEL RAN THE SHOW. THINGS HAVE CHANGED NOW.
I'LL SAY.
I SPARED YOU A LECTURE IN FRONT OF THE OTHERS, BUT I WILL NOT BE SPARED AN INQUIRY AT THE BOARD OF DIRECTORS. BEFORE I WALK INTO THAT SWARM OF PIRANHAS, I WANT SOME ANSWERS.
SHE WAS ALONE. SHE WAS DYING...

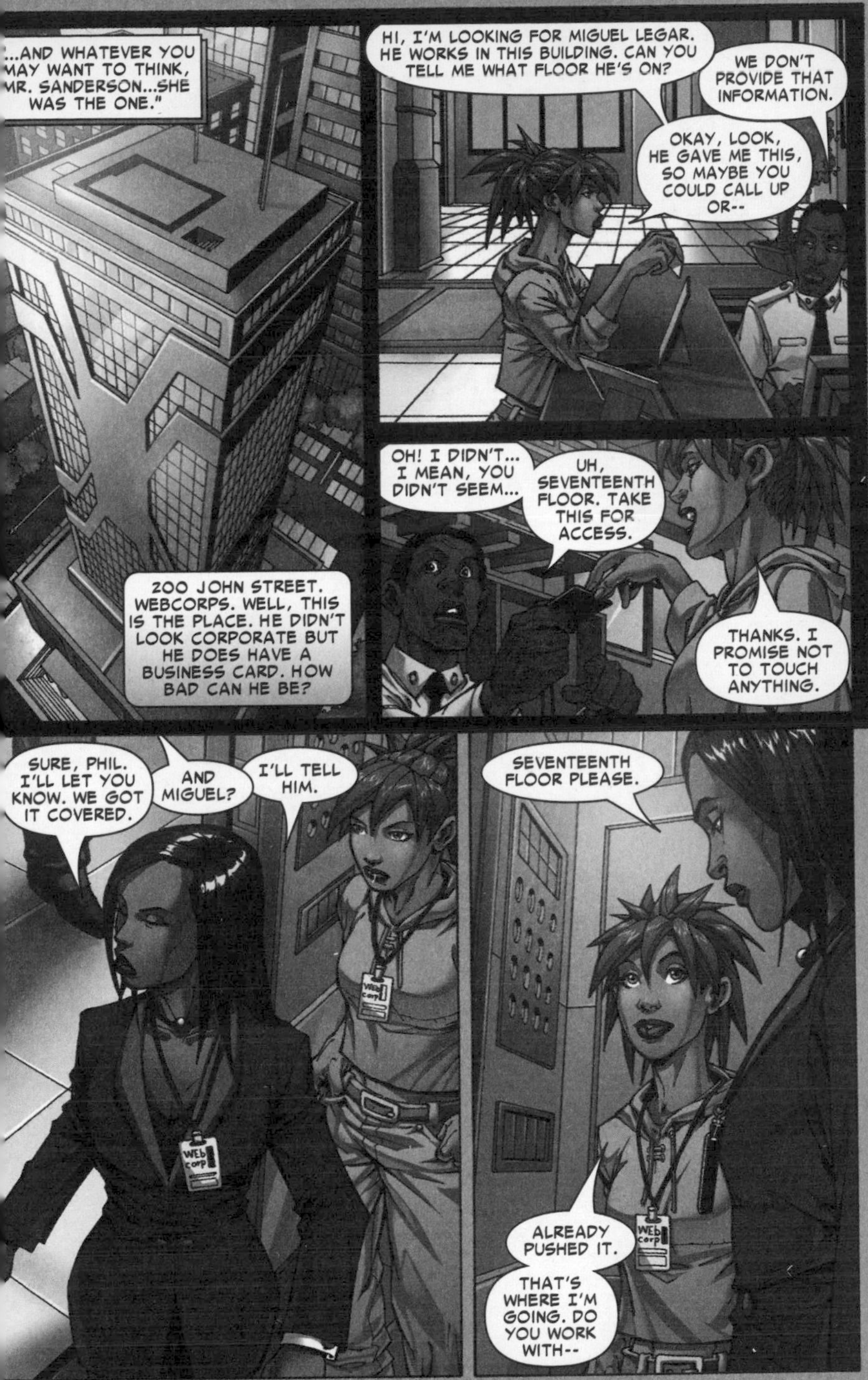

...AND WHATEVER YOU MAY WANT TO THINK, MR. SANDERSON...SHE WAS THE ONE."
200 JOHN STREET. WEBCORPS. WELL, THIS IS THE PLACE. HE DIDN'T LOOK CORPORATE BUT HE DOES HAVE A BUSINESS CARD. HOW BAD CAN HE BE?
HI, I'M LOOKING FOR MIGUEL LEGAR. HE WORKS IN THIS BUILDING. CAN YOU TELL ME WHAT FLOOR HE'S ON?
WE DON'T PROVIDE THAT INFORMATION.
OKAY, LOOK, HE GAVE ME THIS, SO MAYBE YOU COULD CALL UP OR--
OH! I DIDN'T... I MEAN, YOU DIDN'T SEEM...
UH, SEVENTEENTH FLOOR. TAKE THIS FOR ACCESS.
THANKS. I PROMISE NOT TO TOUCH ANYTHING.
SURE, PHIL. I'LL LET YOU KNOW. WE GOT IT COVERED.
AND MIGUEL?
I'LL TELL HIM.
SEVENTEENTH FLOOR PLEASE.
ALREADY PUSHED IT.
THAT'S WHERE I'M GOING. DO YOU WORK WITH--

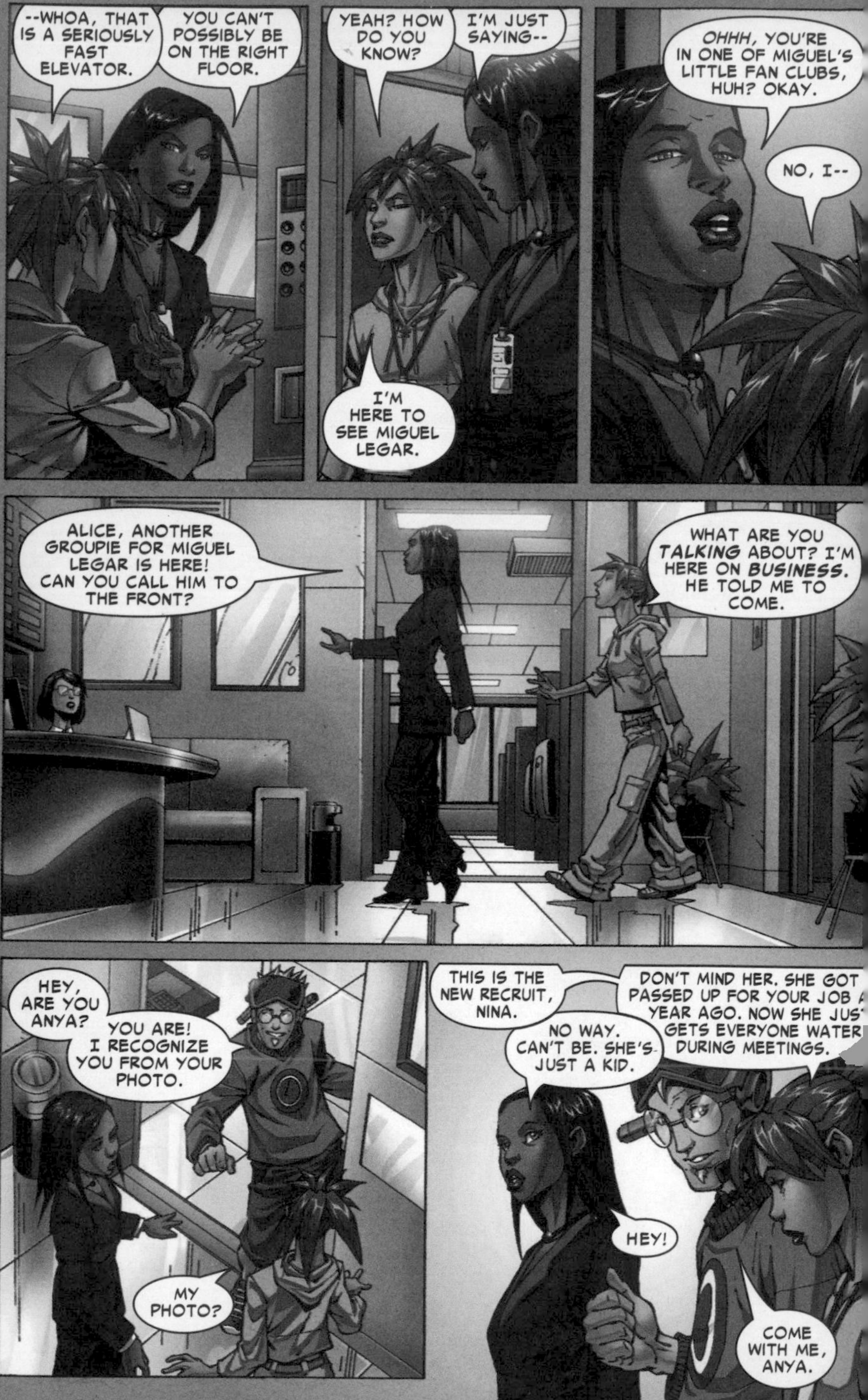
--WHOA, THAT IS A SERIOUSLY FAST ELEVATOR.
YOU CAN'T POSSIBLY BE ON THE RIGHT FLOOR.
YEAH? HOW DO YOU KNOW?
I'M JUST SAYING--
I'M HERE TO SEE MIGUEL LEGAR.
OHHH, YOU'RE IN ONE OF MIGUEL'S LITTLE FAN CLUBS, HUH? OKAY.
NO, I--
ALICE, ANOTHER GROUPIE FOR MIGUEL LEGAR IS HERE! CAN YOU CALL HIM TO THE FRONT?
WHAT ARE YOU *TALKING* ABOUT? I'M HERE ON *BUSINESS.* HE TOLD ME TO COME.
HEY, ARE YOU ANYA?
YOU ARE! I RECOGNIZE YOU FROM YOUR PHOTO.
MY PHOTO?
THIS IS THE NEW RECRUIT, NINA.
NO WAY. CAN'T BE. SHE'S JUST A KID.
DON'T MIND HER. SHE GOT PASSED UP FOR YOUR JOB A YEAR AGO. NOW SHE JUST GETS EVERYONE WATER DURING MEETINGS.
HEY!
COME WITH ME, ANYA.

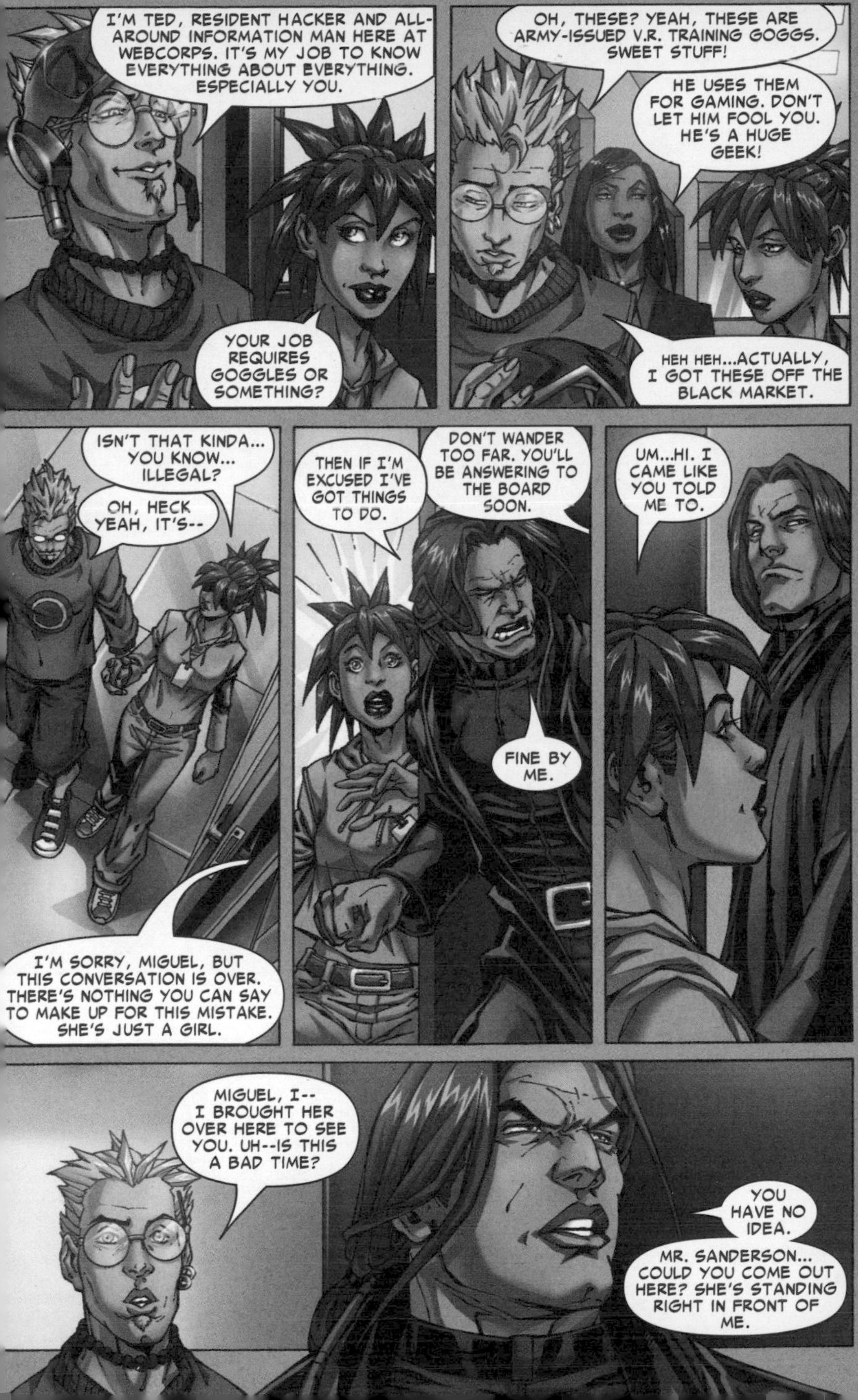

I'M TED, RESIDENT HACKER AND ALL-AROUND INFORMATION MAN HERE AT WEBCORPS. IT'S MY JOB TO KNOW EVERYTHING ABOUT EVERYTHING. ESPECIALLY YOU.
YOUR JOB REQUIRES GOGGLES OR SOMETHING?
OH, THESE? YEAH, THESE ARE ARMY-ISSUED V.R. TRAINING GOGGS. SWEET STUFF!
HE USES THEM FOR GAMING. DON'T LET HIM FOOL YOU. HE'S A HUGE GEEK!
HEH HEH...ACTUALLY, I GOT THESE OFF THE BLACK MARKET.
ISN'T THAT KINDA... YOU KNOW... ILLEGAL?
OH, HECK YEAH, IT'S--
I'M SORRY, MIGUEL, BUT THIS CONVERSATION IS OVER. THERE'S NOTHING YOU CAN SAY TO MAKE UP FOR THIS MISTAKE. SHE'S JUST A GIRL.
THEN IF I'M EXCUSED I'VE GOT THINGS TO DO.
DON'T WANDER TOO FAR. YOU'LL BE ANSWERING TO THE BOARD SOON.
FINE BY ME.
UM...HI. I CAME LIKE YOU TOLD ME TO.
MIGUEL, I-- I BROUGHT HER OVER HERE TO SEE YOU. UH--IS THIS A BAD TIME?
YOU HAVE NO IDEA.
MR. SANDERSON... COULD YOU COME OUT HERE? SHE'S STANDING RIGHT IN FRONT OF ME.

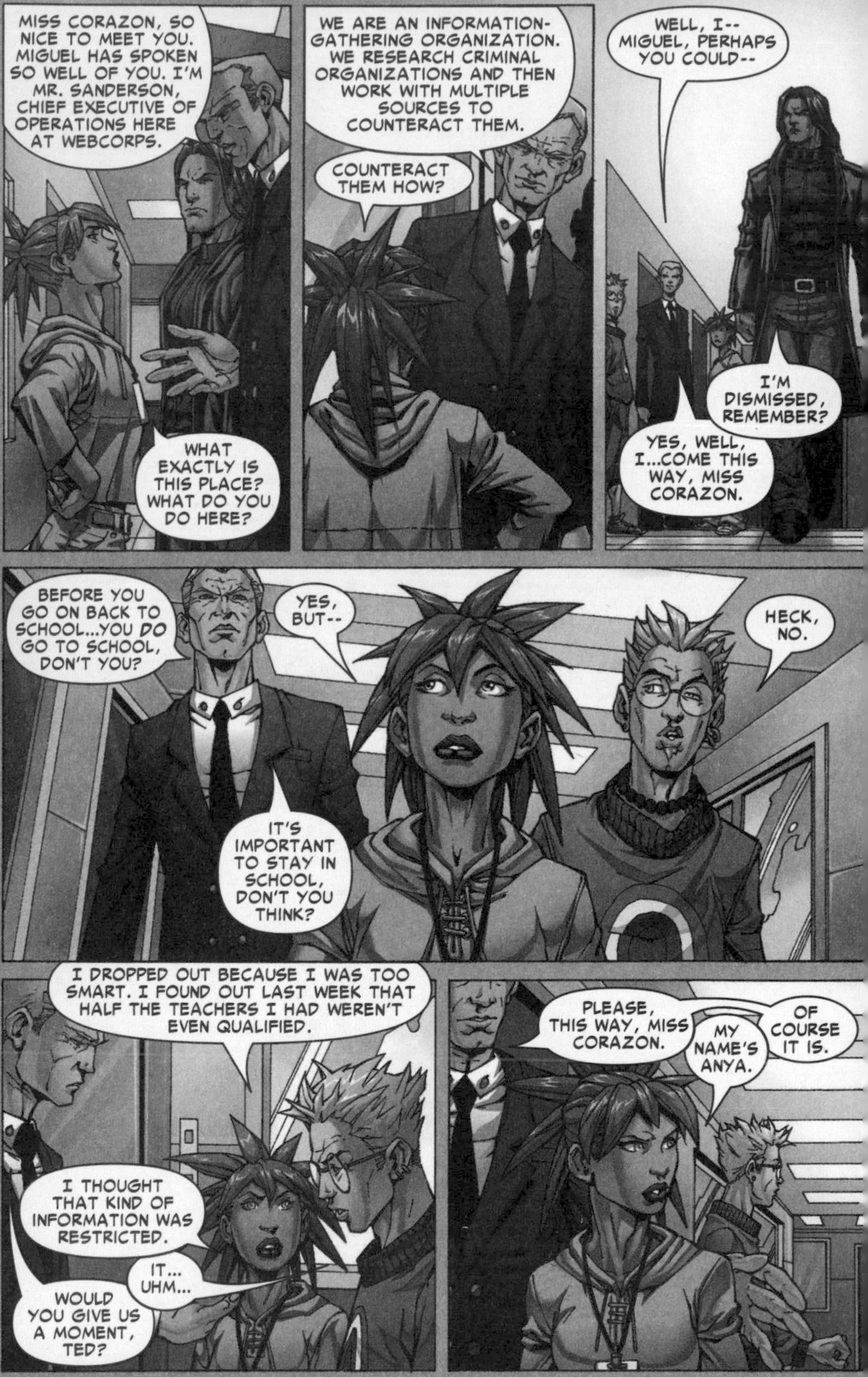

MISS CORAZON, SO NICE TO MEET YOU. MIGUEL HAS SPOKEN SO WELL OF YOU. I'M MR. SANDERSON, CHIEF EXECUTIVE OF OPERATIONS HERE AT WEBCORPS.
WHAT EXACTLY IS THIS PLACE? WHAT DO YOU DO HERE?
WE ARE AN INFORMATION-GATHERING ORGANIZATION. WE RESEARCH CRIMINAL ORGANIZATIONS AND THEN WORK WITH MULTIPLE SOURCES TO COUNTERACT THEM.
COUNTERACT THEM HOW?
WELL, I-- MIGUEL, PERHAPS YOU COULD--
I'M DISMISSED, REMEMBER?
YES, WELL, I...COME THIS WAY, MISS CORAZON.
BEFORE YOU GO ON BACK TO SCHOOL...YOU *DO* GO TO SCHOOL, DON'T YOU?
YES, BUT--
HECK, NO.
IT'S IMPORTANT TO STAY IN SCHOOL, DON'T YOU THINK?
I DROPPED OUT BECAUSE I WAS TOO SMART. I FOUND OUT LAST WEEK THAT HALF THE TEACHERS I HAD WEREN'T EVEN QUALIFIED.
I THOUGHT THAT KIND OF INFORMATION WAS RESTRICTED.
IT... UHM...
WOULD YOU GIVE US A MOMENT, TED?
PLEASE, THIS WAY, MISS CORAZON.
MY NAME'S ANYA.
OF COURSE IT IS.

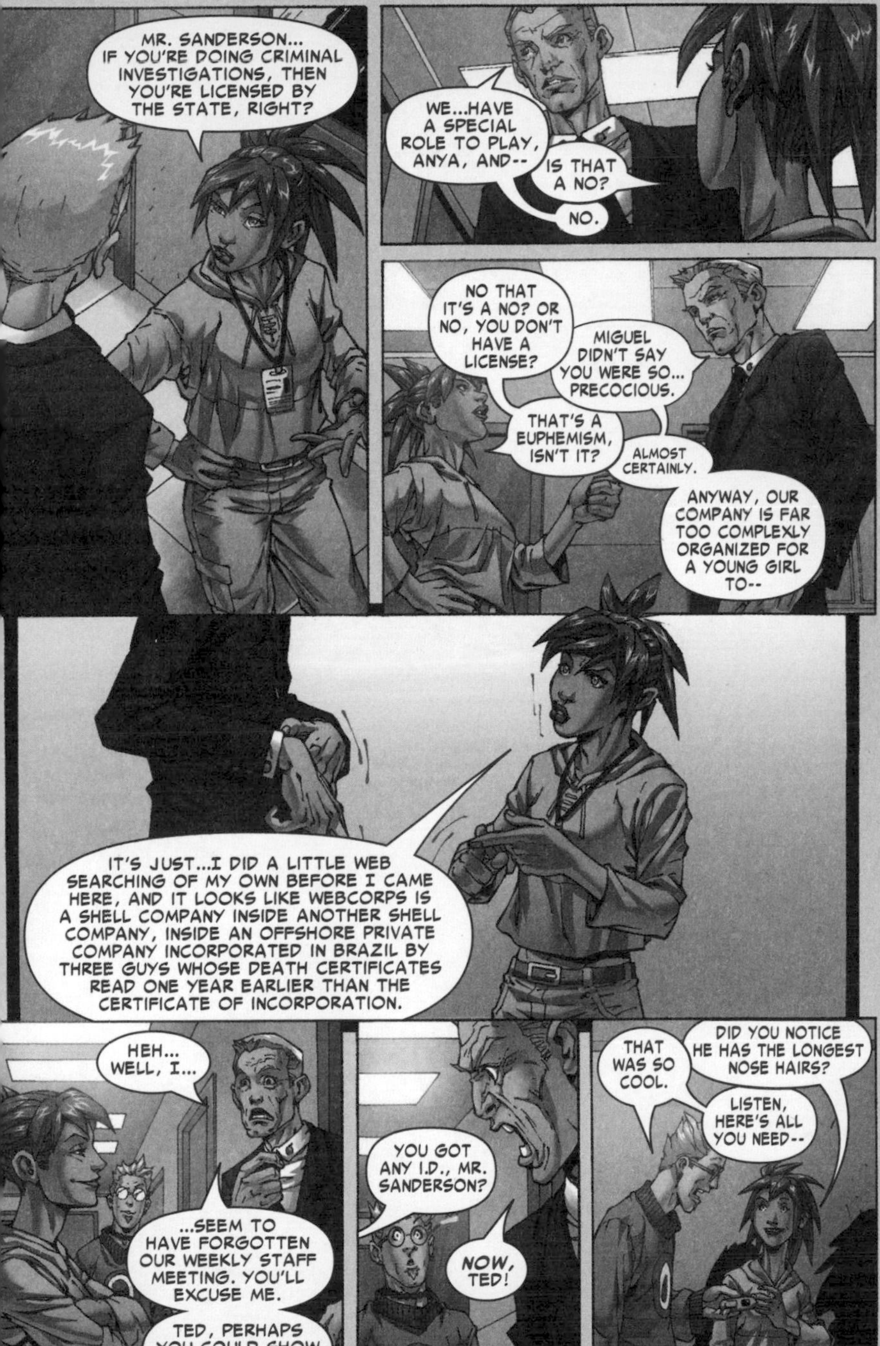
MR. SANDERSON... IF YOU'RE DOING CRIMINAL INVESTIGATIONS, THEN YOU'RE LICENSED BY THE STATE, RIGHT?
WE...HAVE A SPECIAL ROLE TO PLAY, ANYA, AND--
IS THAT A NO?
NO.
NO THAT IT'S A NO? OR NO, YOU DON'T HAVE A LICENSE?
MIGUEL DIDN'T SAY YOU WERE SO... PRECOCIOUS.
THAT'S A EUPHEMISM, ISN'T IT?
ALMOST CERTAINLY.
ANYWAY, OUR COMPANY IS FAR TOO COMPLEXLY ORGANIZED FOR A YOUNG GIRL TO--
IT'S JUST...I DID A LITTLE WEB SEARCHING OF MY OWN BEFORE I CAME HERE, AND IT LOOKS LIKE WEBCORPS IS A SHELL COMPANY INSIDE ANOTHER SHELL COMPANY, INSIDE AN OFFSHORE PRIVATE COMPANY INCORPORATED IN BRAZIL BY THREE GUYS WHOSE DEATH CERTIFICATES READ ONE YEAR EARLIER THAN THE CERTIFICATE OF INCORPORATION.
HEH... WELL, I...
...SEEM TO HAVE FORGOTTEN OUR WEEKLY STAFF MEETING. YOU'LL EXCUSE ME.
TED, PERHAPS YOU COULD SHOW THE YOUNG LADY OUT.
YOU GOT ANY I.D., MR. SANDERSON?
NOW, TED!
THAT WAS SO COOL.
DID YOU NOTICE HE HAS THE LONGEST NOSE HAIRS?
LISTEN, HERE'S ALL YOU NEED--

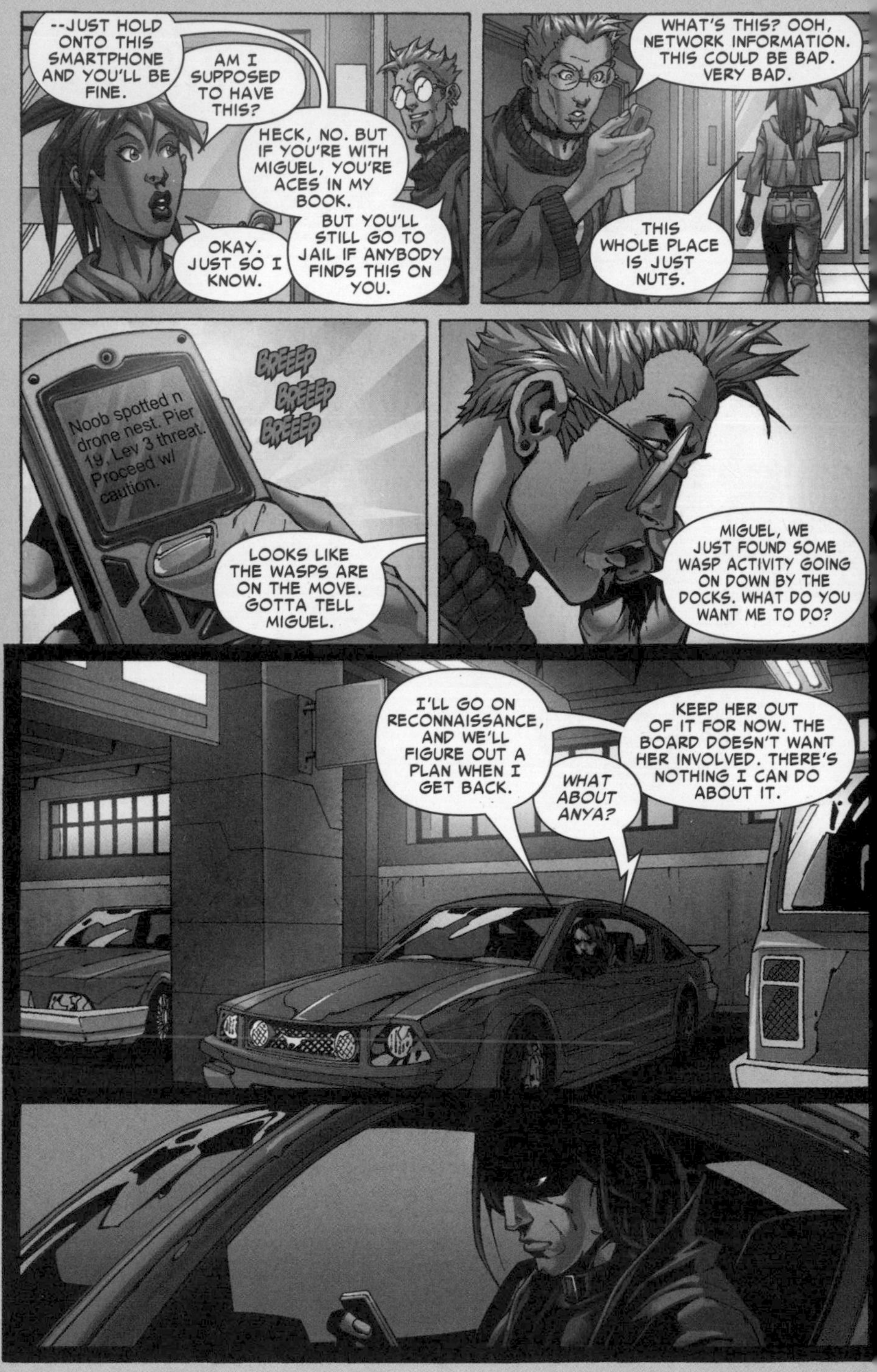
--JUST HOLD ONTO THIS SMARTPHONE AND YOU'LL BE FINE.
AM I SUPPOSED TO HAVE THIS?
HECK, NO. BUT IF YOU'RE WITH MIGUEL, YOU'RE ACES IN MY BOOK.
BUT YOU'LL STILL GO TO JAIL IF ANYBODY FINDS THIS ON YOU.
OKAY. JUST SO I KNOW.
WHAT'S THIS? OOH, NETWORK INFORMATION. THIS COULD BE BAD. VERY BAD.
THIS WHOLE PLACE IS JUST NUTS.
Noob spotted n drone nest. Pier 19, Lev 3 threat. Proceed w/ caution.
BREEEP BREEEP BREEEP
LOOKS LIKE THE WASPS ARE ON THE MOVE. GOTTA TELL MIGUEL.
MIGUEL, WE JUST FOUND SOME WASP ACTIVITY GOING ON DOWN BY THE DOCKS. WHAT DO YOU WANT ME TO DO?
I'LL GO ON RECONNAISSANCE, AND WE'LL FIGURE OUT A PLAN WHEN I GET BACK.
WHAT ABOUT ANYA?
KEEP HER OUT OF IT FOR NOW. THE BOARD DOESN'T WANT HER INVOLVED. THERE'S NOTHING I CAN DO ABOUT IT.

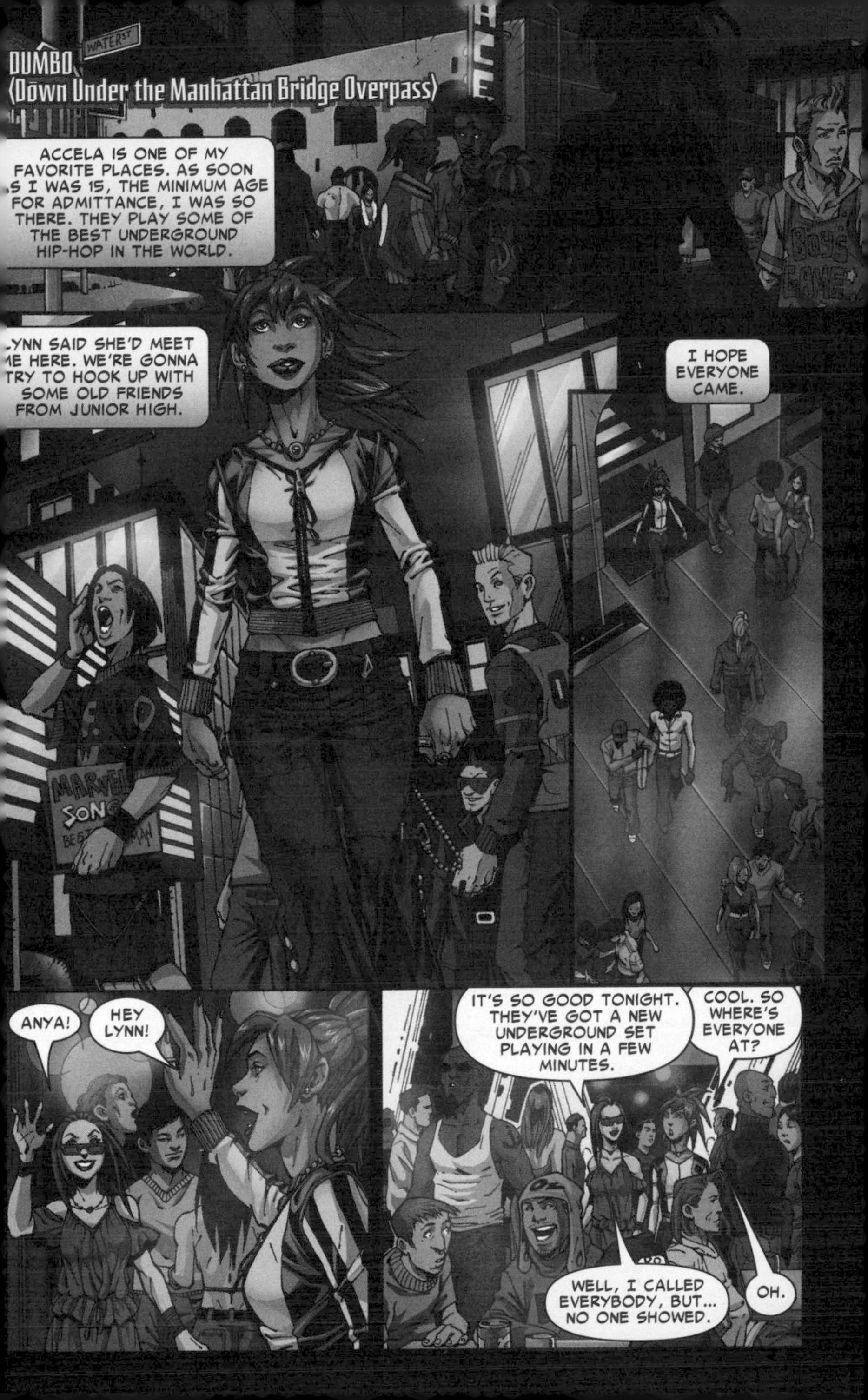
DUMBO
(Down Under the Manhattan Bridge Overpass)
WATER ST
ACCELA IS ONE OF MY FAVORITE PLACES. AS SOON AS I WAS 15, THE MINIMUM AGE FOR ADMITTANCE, I WAS SO THERE. THEY PLAY SOME OF THE BEST UNDERGROUND HIP-HOP IN THE WORLD.
LYNN SAID SHE'D MEET ME HERE. WE'RE GONNA TRY TO HOOK UP WITH SOME OLD FRIENDS FROM JUNIOR HIGH.
I HOPE EVERYONE CAME.
ANYA!
HEY LYNN!
IT'S SO GOOD TONIGHT. THEY'VE GOT A NEW UNDERGROUND SET PLAYING IN A FEW MINUTES.
COOL. SO WHERE'S EVERYONE AT?
WELL, I CALLED EVERYBODY, BUT... NO ONE SHOWED.
OH.

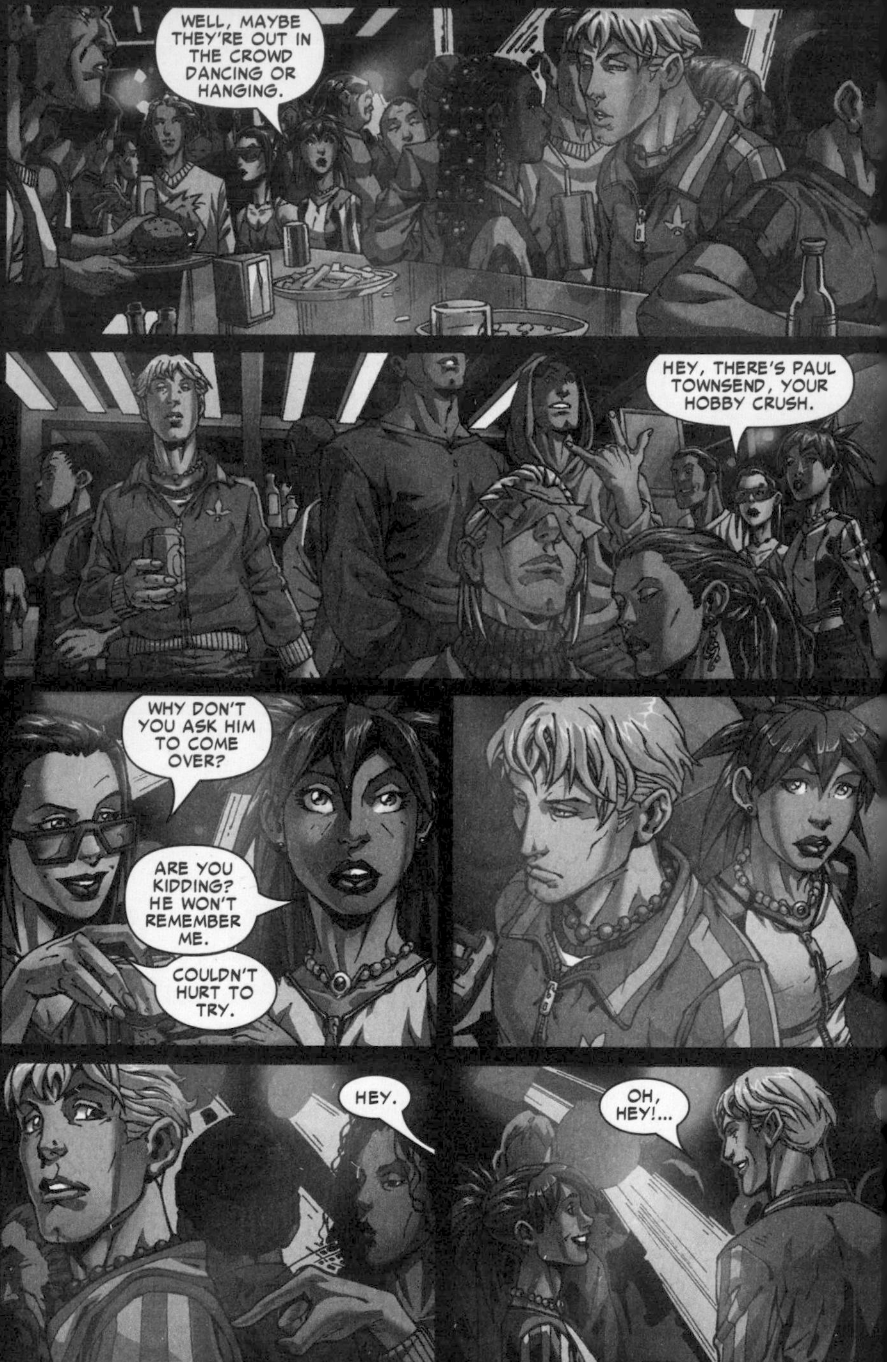
WELL, MAYBE THEY'RE OUT IN THE CROWD DANCING OR HANGING.
HEY, THERE'S PAUL TOWNSEND, YOUR HOBBY CRUSH.
WHY DON'T YOU ASK HIM TO COME OVER?
ARE YOU KIDDING? HE WON'T REMEMBER ME.
COULDN'T HURT TO TRY.
HEY.
OH, HEY!...

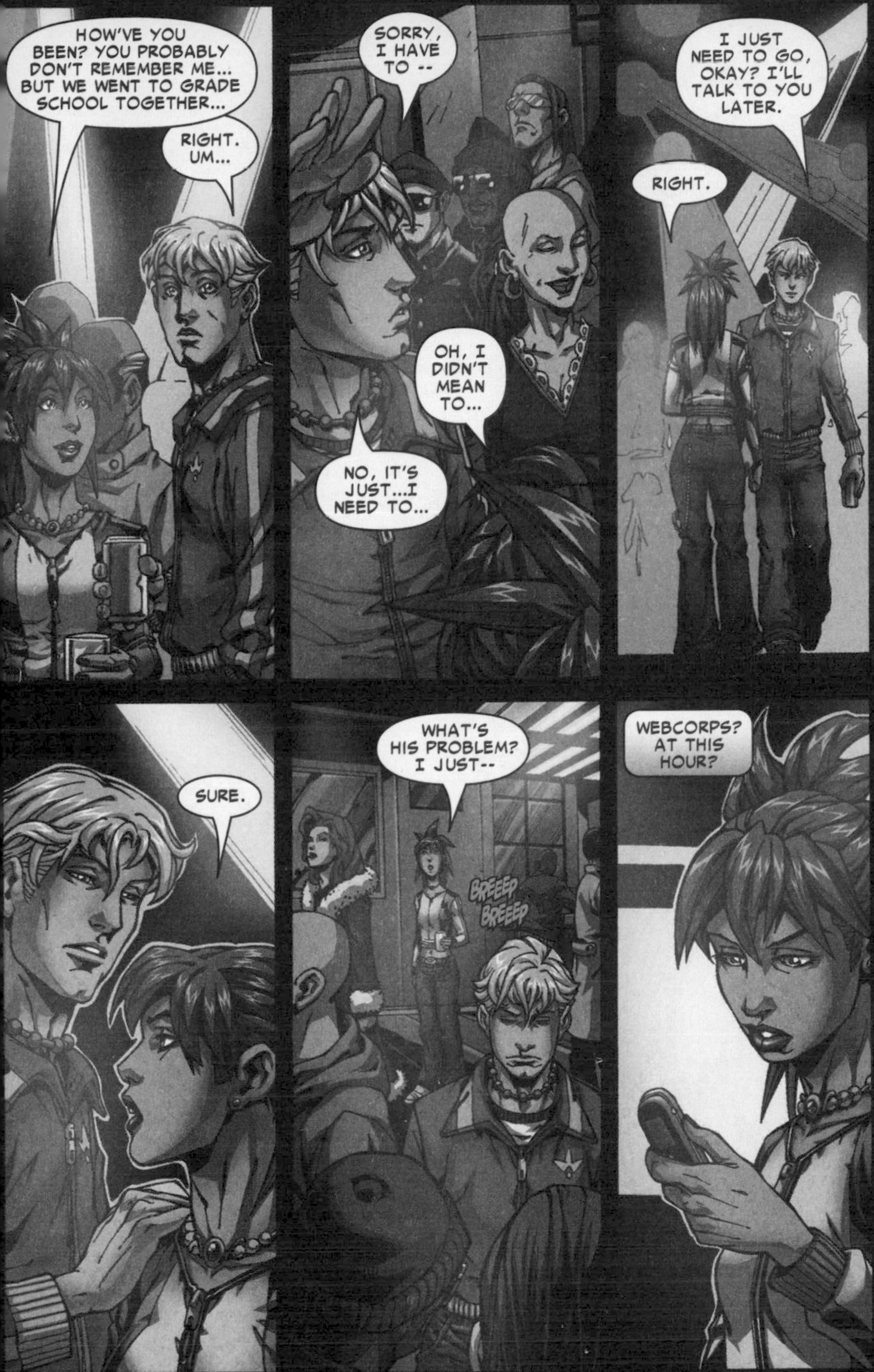
HOW'VE YOU BEEN? YOU PROBABLY DON'T REMEMBER ME... BUT WE WENT TO GRADE SCHOOL TOGETHER...
RIGHT. UM...
SORRY, I HAVE TO --
OH, I DIDN'T MEAN TO...
NO, IT'S JUST...I NEED TO...
I JUST NEED TO GO, OKAY? I'LL TALK TO YOU LATER.
RIGHT.
SURE.
WHAT'S HIS PROBLEM? I JUST--
BREEEP BREEEP
WEBCORPS? AT THIS HOUR?

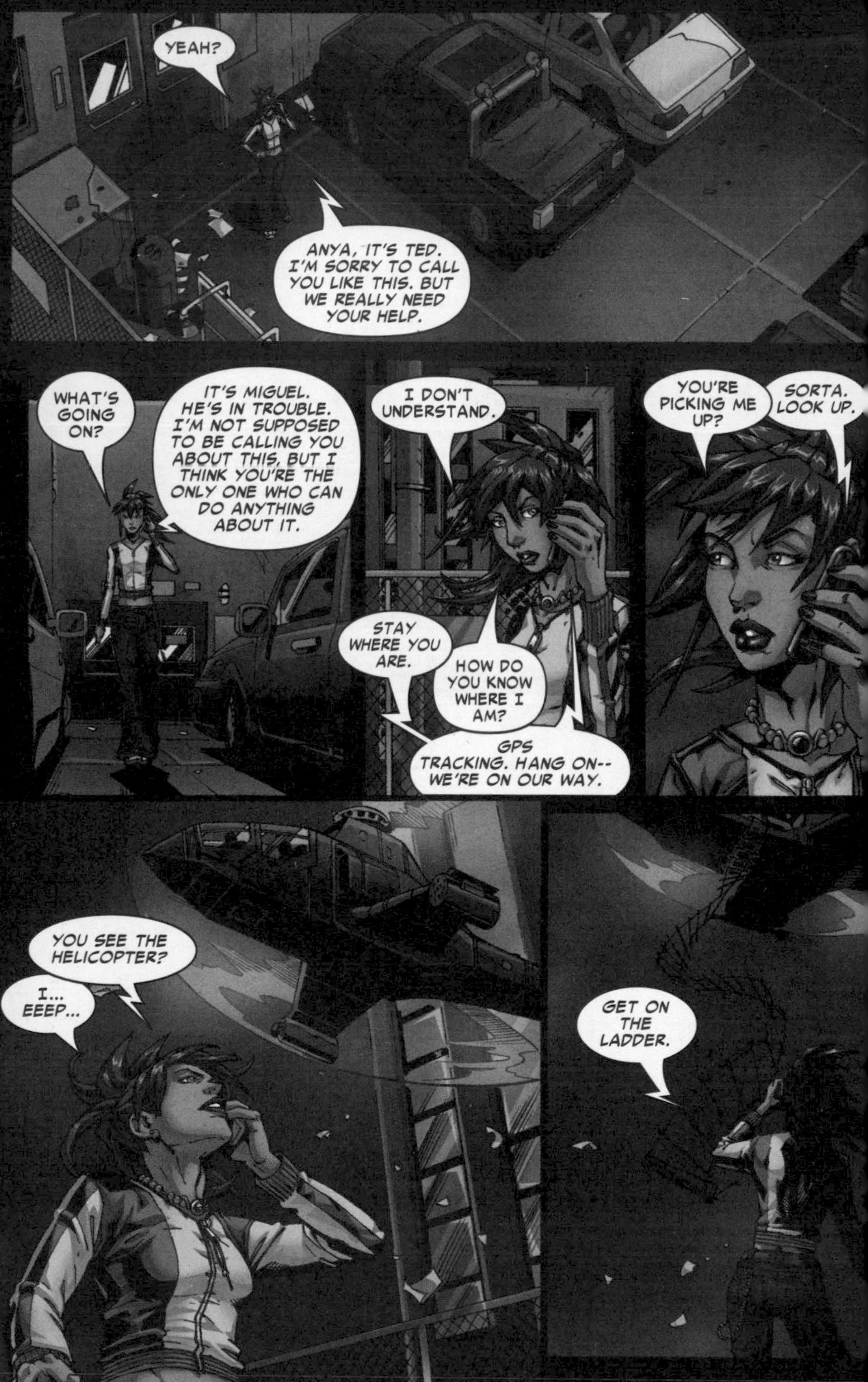
YEAH?
ANYA, IT'S TED. I'M SORRY TO CALL YOU LIKE THIS. BUT WE REALLY NEED YOUR HELP.
WHAT'S GOING ON?
IT'S MIGUEL. HE'S IN TROUBLE. I'M NOT SUPPOSED TO BE CALLING YOU ABOUT THIS, BUT I THINK YOU'RE THE ONLY ONE WHO CAN DO ANYTHING ABOUT IT.
I DON'T UNDERSTAND.
STAY WHERE YOU ARE.
HOW DO YOU KNOW WHERE I AM?
GPS TRACKING. HANG ON-- WE'RE ON OUR WAY.
YOU'RE PICKING ME UP?
SORTA. LOOK UP.
YOU SEE THE HELICOPTER?
I... EEEP...
GET ON THE LADDER.

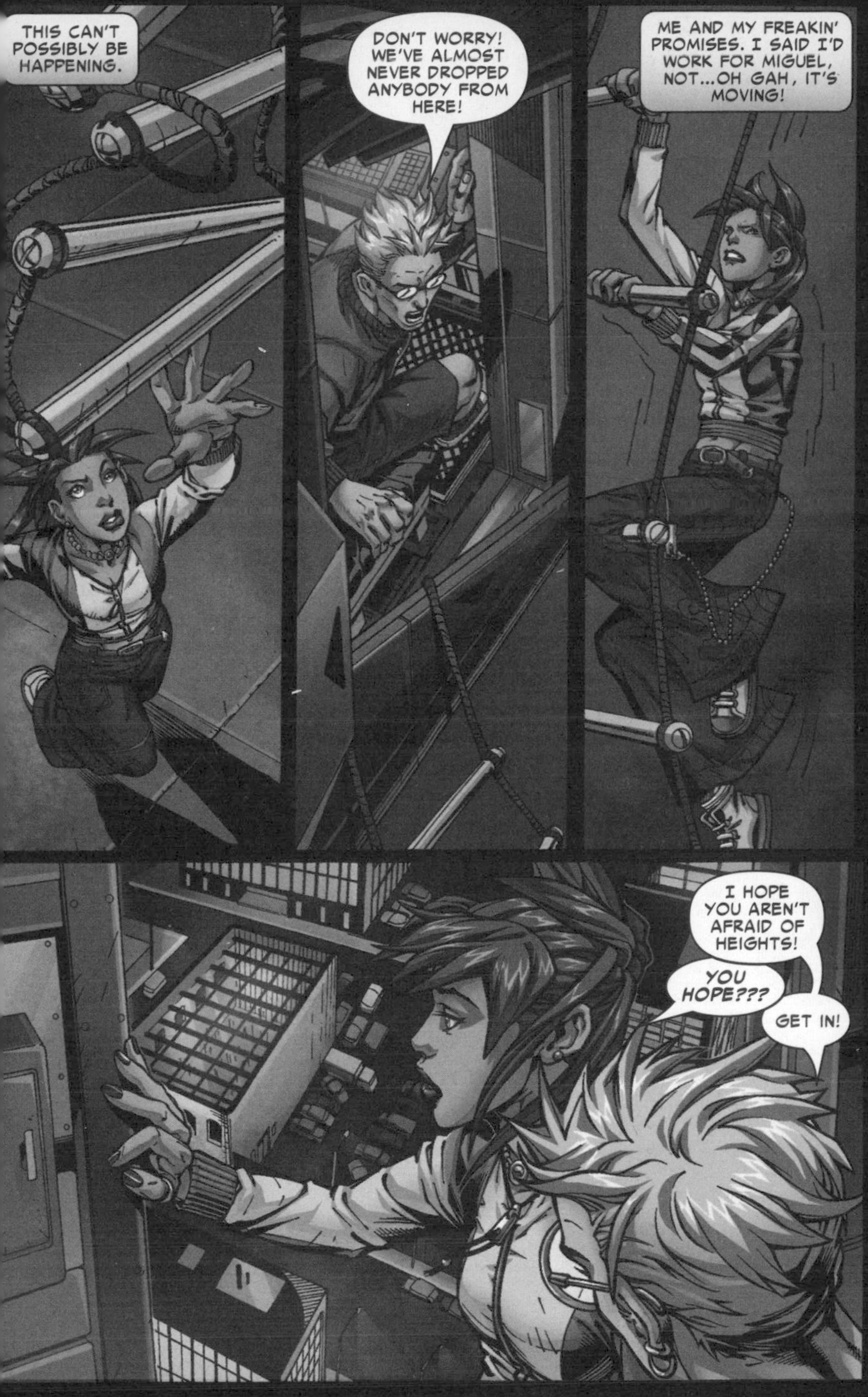
THIS CAN'T POSSIBLY BE HAPPENING.
DON'T WORRY! WE'VE ALMOST NEVER DROPPED ANYBODY FROM HERE!
ME AND MY FREAKIN' PROMISES. I SAID I'D WORK FOR MIGUEL, NOT...OH GAH, IT'S MOVING!
I HOPE YOU AREN'T AFRAID OF HEIGHTS!
YOU HOPE???
GET IN!

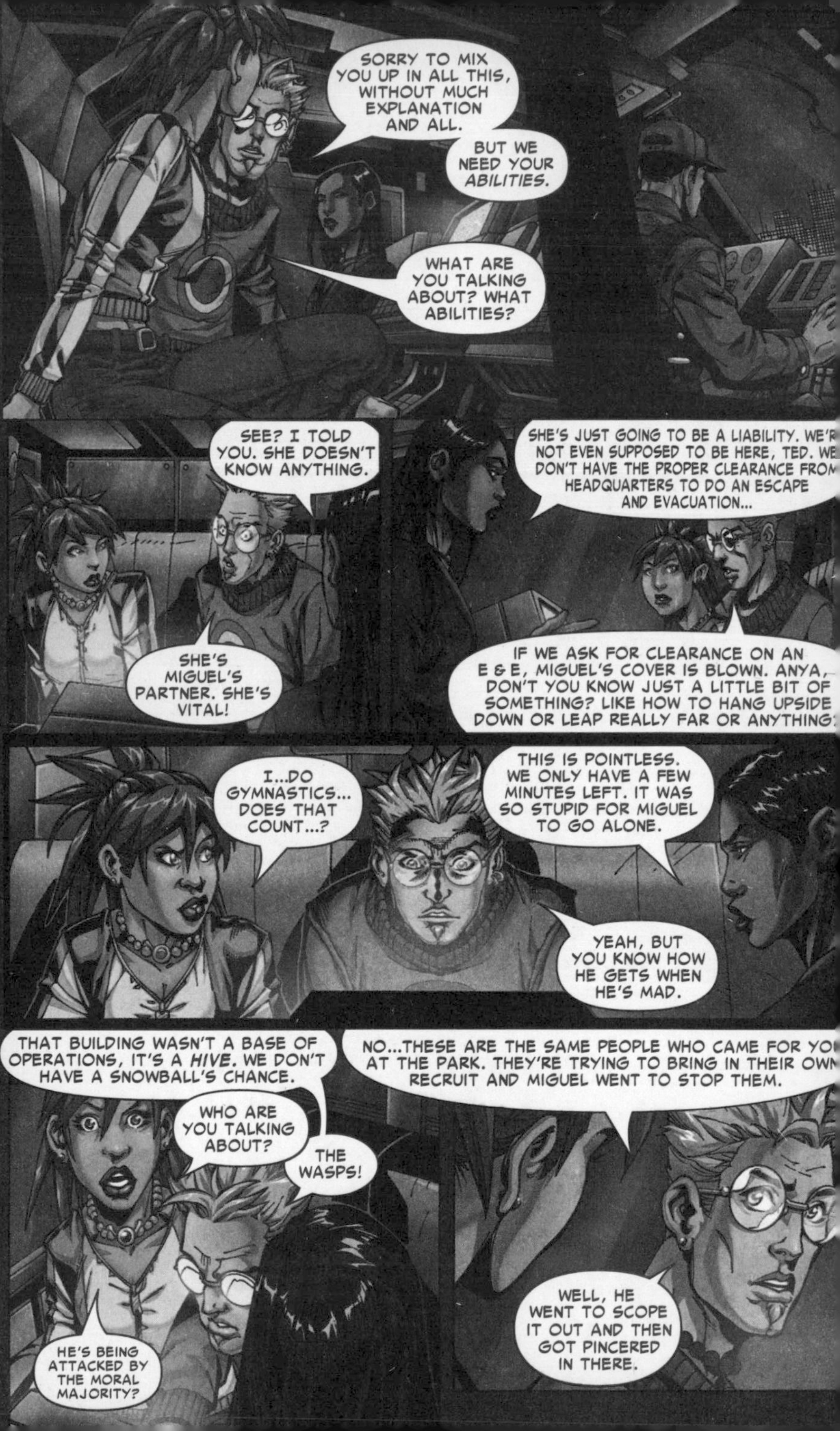
SORRY TO MIX YOU UP IN ALL THIS, WITHOUT MUCH EXPLANATION AND ALL.
BUT WE NEED YOUR *ABILITIES.*
WHAT ARE YOU TALKING ABOUT? WHAT ABILITIES?
SEE? I TOLD YOU. SHE DOESN'T KNOW ANYTHING.
SHE'S MIGUEL'S PARTNER. SHE'S VITAL!
SHE'S JUST GOING TO BE A LIABILITY. WE'R NOT EVEN SUPPOSED TO BE HERE, TED. WE DON'T HAVE THE PROPER CLEARANCE FROM HEADQUARTERS TO DO AN ESCAPE AND EVACUATION...
IF WE ASK FOR CLEARANCE ON AN E & E, MIGUEL'S COVER IS BLOWN. ANYA, DON'T YOU KNOW JUST A LITTLE BIT OF SOMETHING? LIKE HOW TO HANG UPSIDE DOWN OR LEAP REALLY FAR OR ANYTHING
I...DO GYMNASTICS... DOES THAT COUNT...?
THIS IS POINTLESS. WE ONLY HAVE A FEW MINUTES LEFT. IT WAS SO STUPID FOR MIGUEL TO GO ALONE.
YEAH, BUT YOU KNOW HOW HE GETS WHEN HE'S MAD.
THAT BUILDING WASN'T A BASE OF OPERATIONS, IT'S A *HIVE.* WE DON'T HAVE A SNOWBALL'S CHANCE.
WHO ARE YOU TALKING ABOUT?
THE WASPS!
HE'S BEING ATTACKED BY THE MORAL MAJORITY?
NO...THESE ARE THE SAME PEOPLE WHO CAME FOR YO AT THE PARK. THEY'RE TRYING TO BRING IN THEIR OWN RECRUIT AND MIGUEL WENT TO STOP THEM.
WELL, HE WENT TO SCOPE IT OUT AND THEN GOT PINCERED IN THERE.

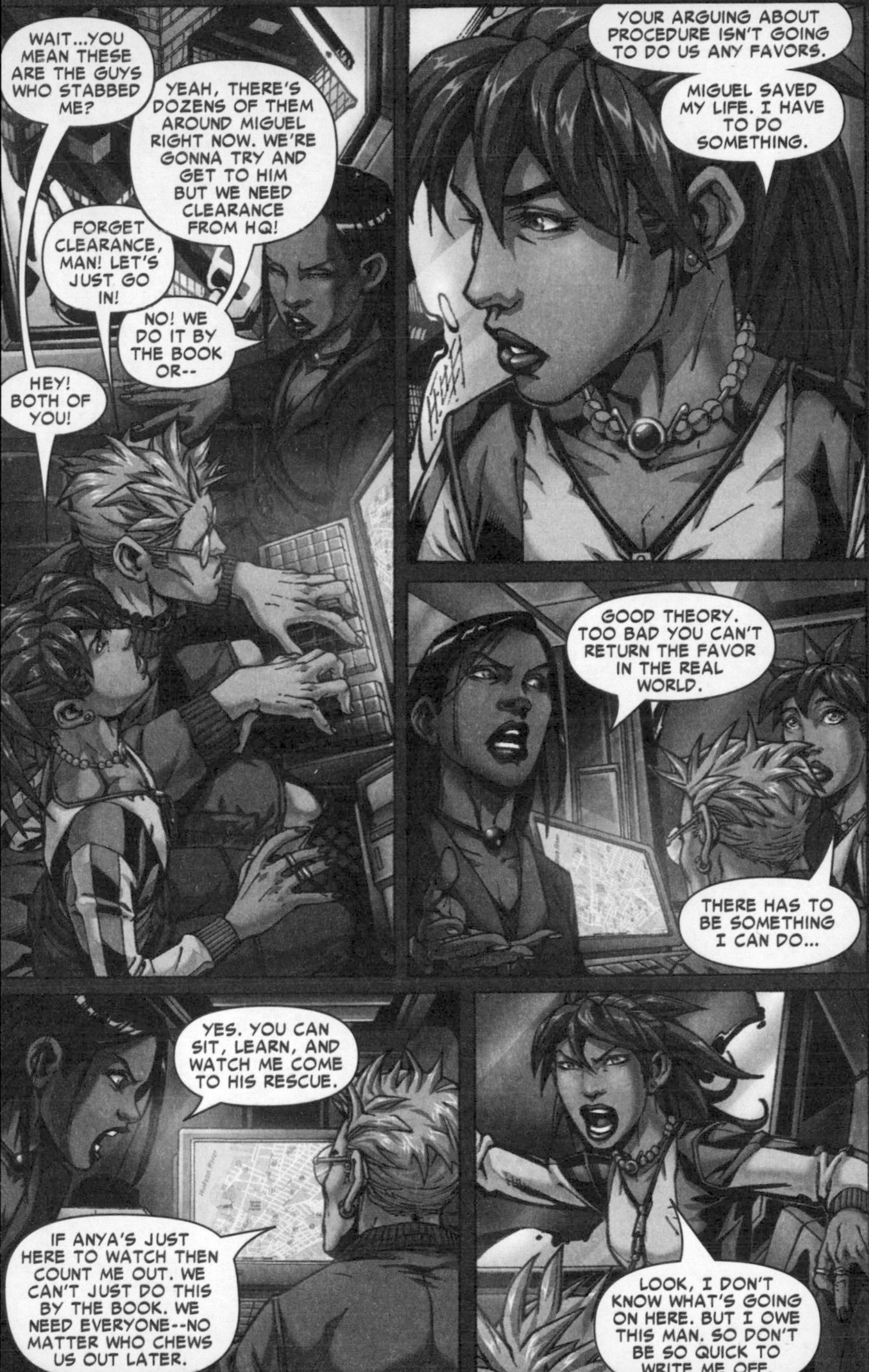
WAIT...YOU MEAN THESE ARE THE GUYS WHO STABBED ME?
YEAH, THERE'S DOZENS OF THEM AROUND MIGUEL RIGHT NOW. WE'RE GONNA TRY AND GET TO HIM BUT WE NEED CLEARANCE FROM HQ!
FORGET CLEARANCE, MAN! LET'S JUST GO IN!
NO! WE DO IT BY THE BOOK OR--
HEY! BOTH OF YOU!
YOUR ARGUING ABOUT PROCEDURE ISN'T GOING TO DO US ANY FAVORS.
MIGUEL SAVED MY LIFE. I HAVE TO DO SOMETHING.
GOOD THEORY. TOO BAD YOU CAN'T RETURN THE FAVOR IN THE REAL WORLD.
THERE HAS TO BE SOMETHING I CAN DO...
YES. YOU CAN SIT, LEARN, AND WATCH ME COME TO HIS RESCUE.
IF ANYA'S JUST HERE TO WATCH THEN COUNT ME OUT. WE CAN'T JUST DO THIS BY THE BOOK. WE NEED EVERYONE--NO MATTER WHO CHEWS US OUT LATER.
LOOK, I DON'T KNOW WHAT'S GOING ON HERE. BUT I OWE THIS MAN. SO DON'T BE SO QUICK TO WRITE ME OFF.

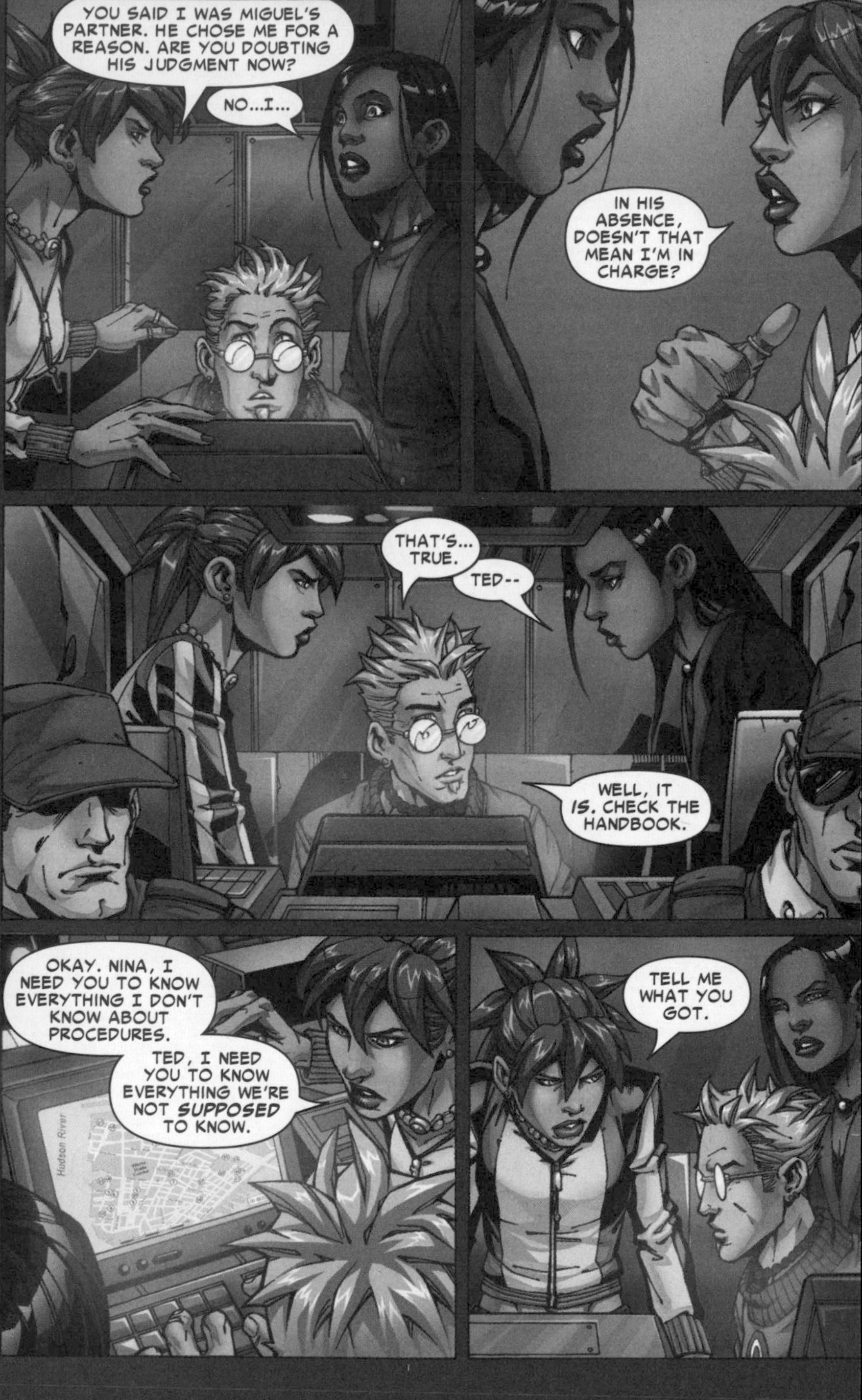
YOU SAID I WAS MIGUEL'S PARTNER. HE CHOSE ME FOR A REASON. ARE YOU DOUBTING HIS JUDGMENT NOW?
NO...I...
IN HIS ABSENCE, DOESN'T THAT MEAN I'M IN CHARGE?
THAT'S... TRUE.
TED--
WELL, IT *IS*. CHECK THE HANDBOOK.
OKAY. NINA, I NEED YOU TO KNOW EVERYTHING I DON'T KNOW ABOUT PROCEDURES.
TED, I NEED YOU TO KNOW EVERYTHING WE'RE NOT *SUPPOSED* TO KNOW.
Hudson River
TELL ME WHAT YOU GOT.

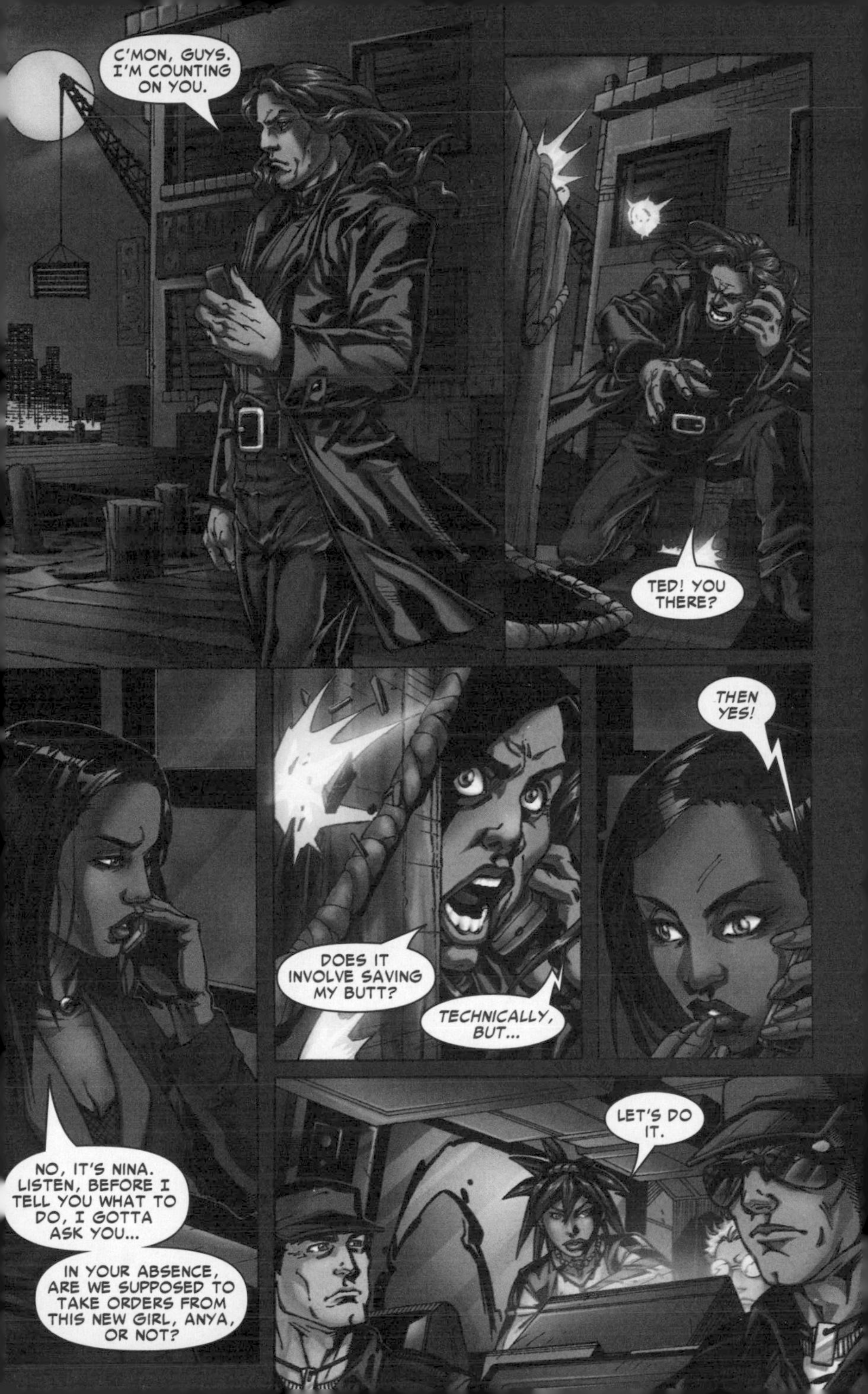
C'MON, GUYS. I'M COUNTING ON YOU.
TED! YOU THERE?
NO, IT'S NINA. LISTEN, BEFORE I TELL YOU WHAT TO DO, I GOTTA ASK YOU...
IN YOUR ABSENCE, ARE WE SUPPOSED TO TAKE ORDERS FROM THIS NEW GIRL, ANYA, OR NOT?
DOES IT INVOLVE SAVING MY BUTT?
TECHNICALLY, BUT...
THEN YES!
LET'S DO IT.

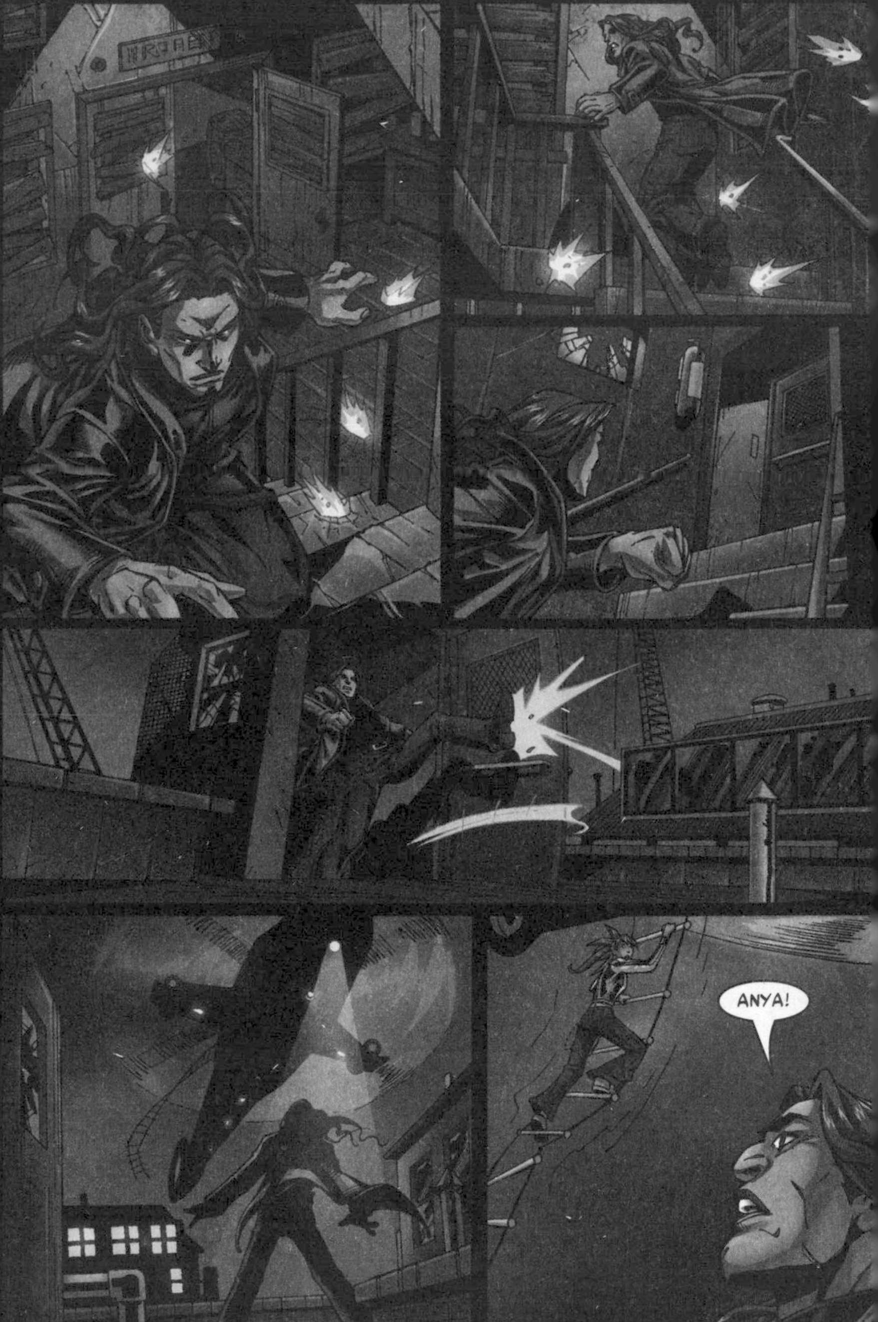
ANYA!

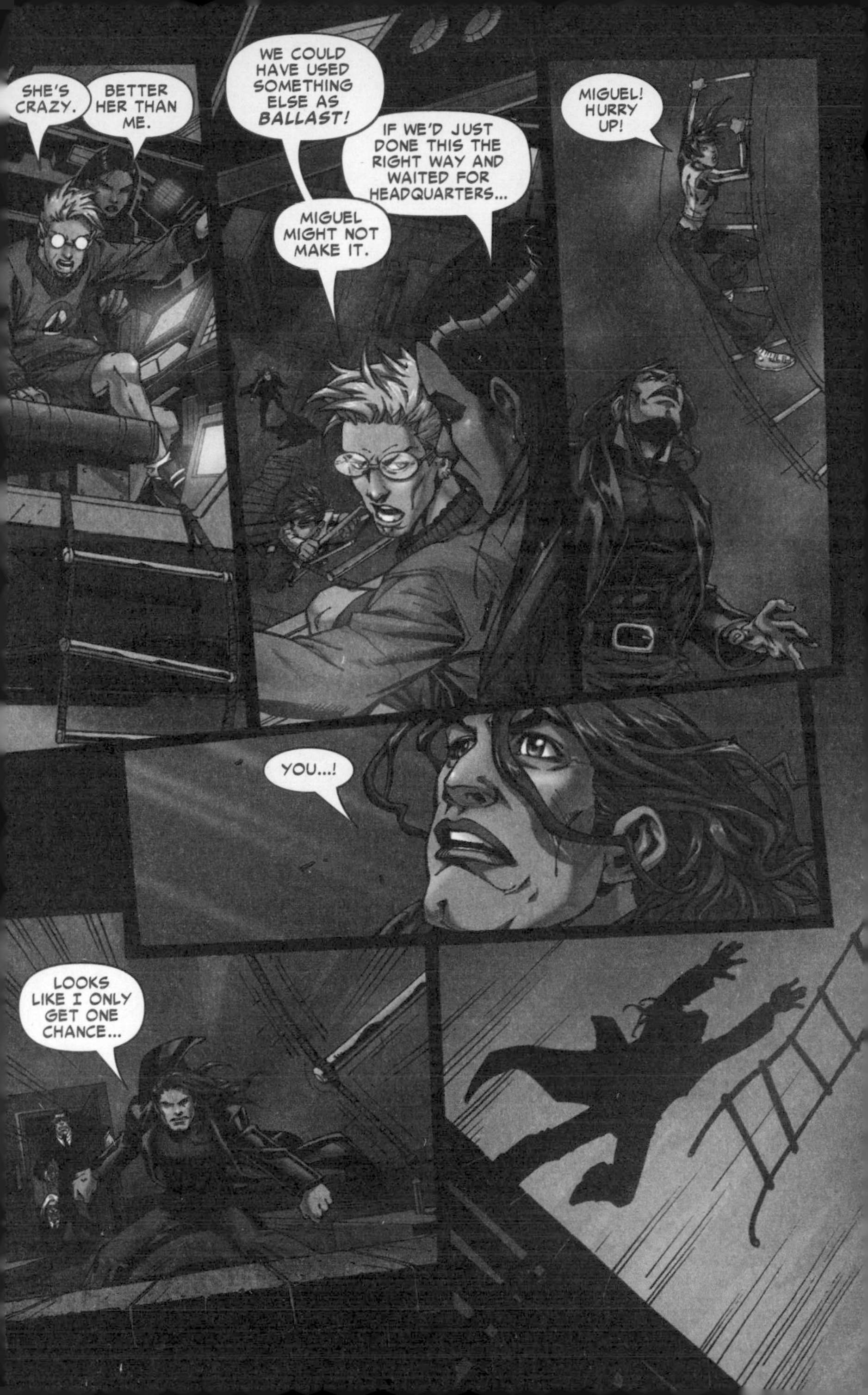
SHE'S CRAZY.
BETTER HER THAN ME.
WE COULD HAVE USED SOMETHING ELSE AS *BALLAST!*
IF WE'D JUST DONE THIS THE RIGHT WAY AND WAITED FOR HEADQUARTERS...
MIGUEL MIGHT NOT MAKE IT.
MIGUEL! HURRY UP!
YOU...!
LOOKS LIKE I ONLY GET ONE CHANCE...

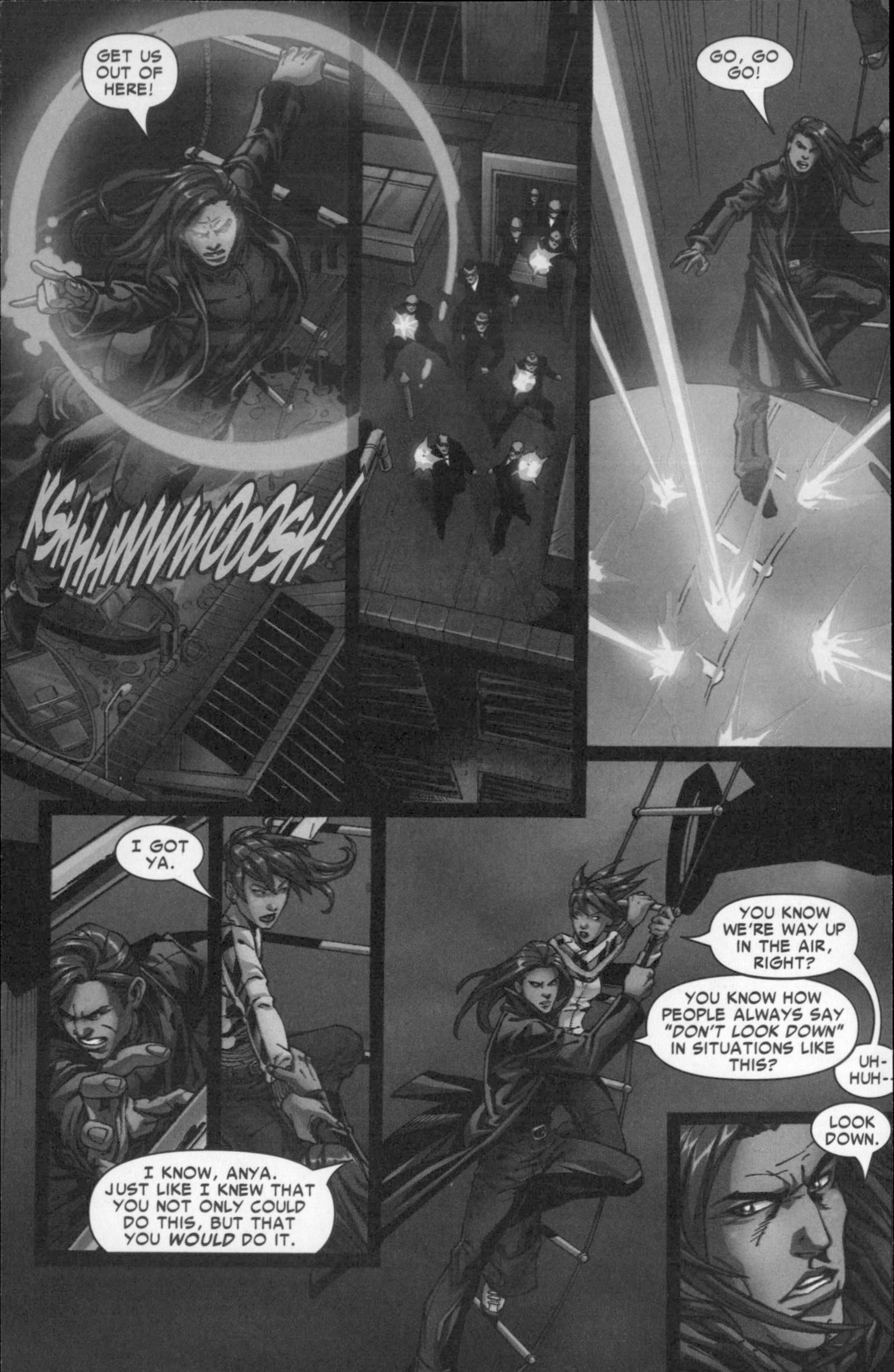
GET US OUT OF HERE!
KSHHHWWWWOOSH!
GO, GO GO!
I GOT YA.
I KNOW, ANYA. JUST LIKE I KNEW THAT YOU NOT ONLY COULD DO THIS, BUT THAT YOU *WOULD* DO IT.
YOU KNOW WE'RE WAY UP IN THE AIR, RIGHT?
YOU KNOW HOW PEOPLE ALWAYS SAY *"DON'T LOOK DOWN"* IN SITUATIONS LIKE THIS?
UH-HUH--
LOOK DOWN.

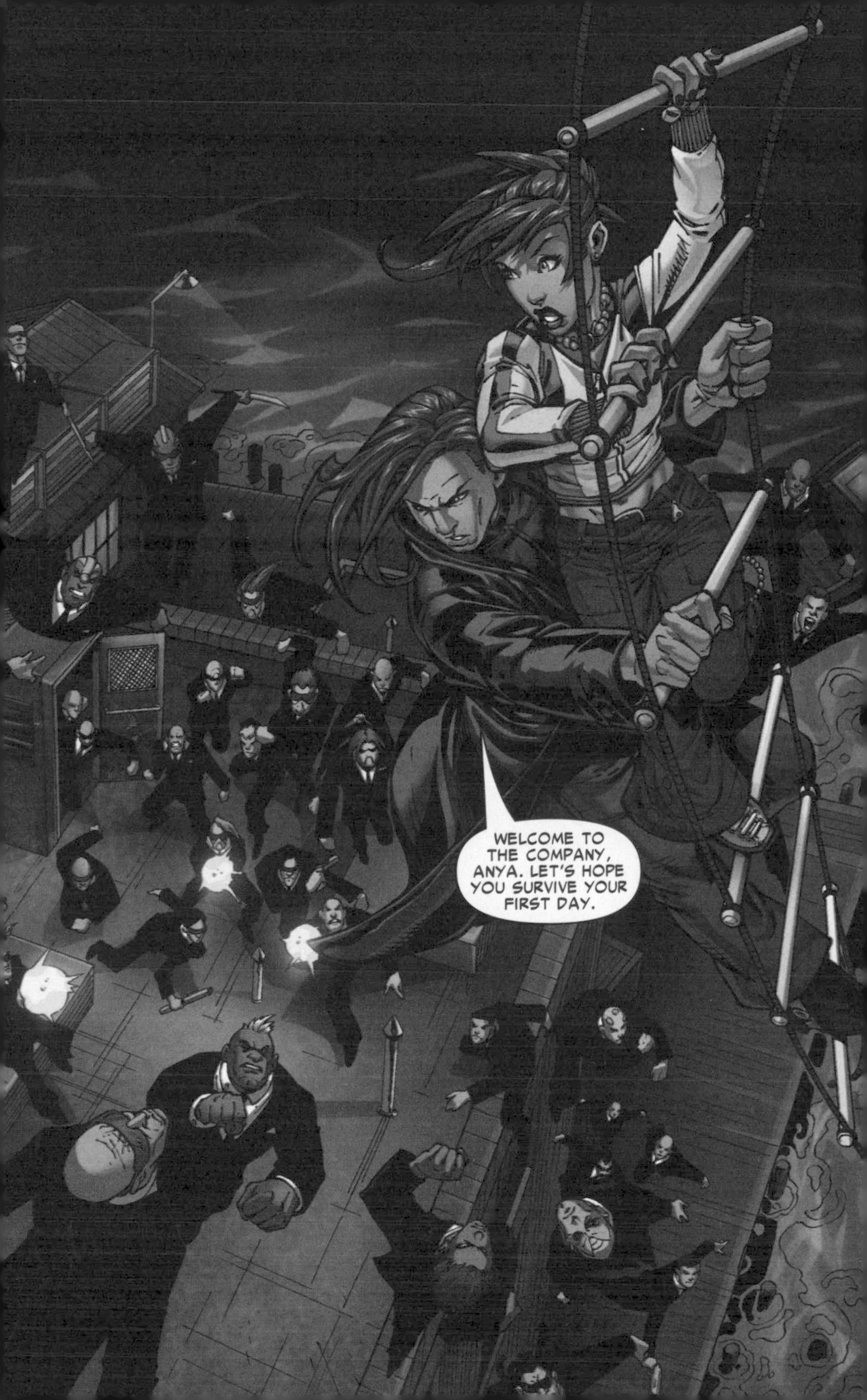
WELCOME TO THE COMPANY, ANYA. LET'S HOPE YOU SURVIVE YOUR FIRST DAY.

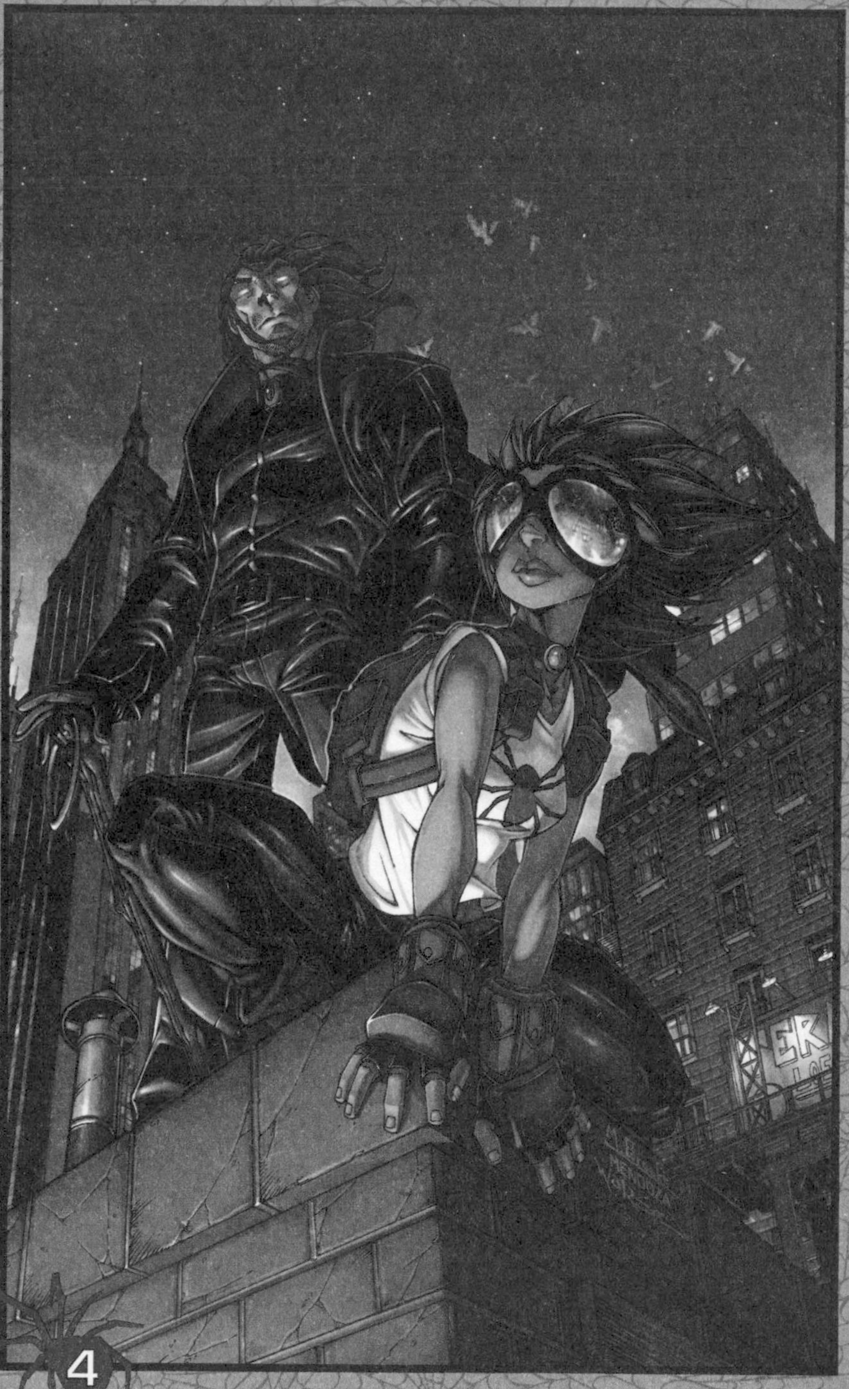

4

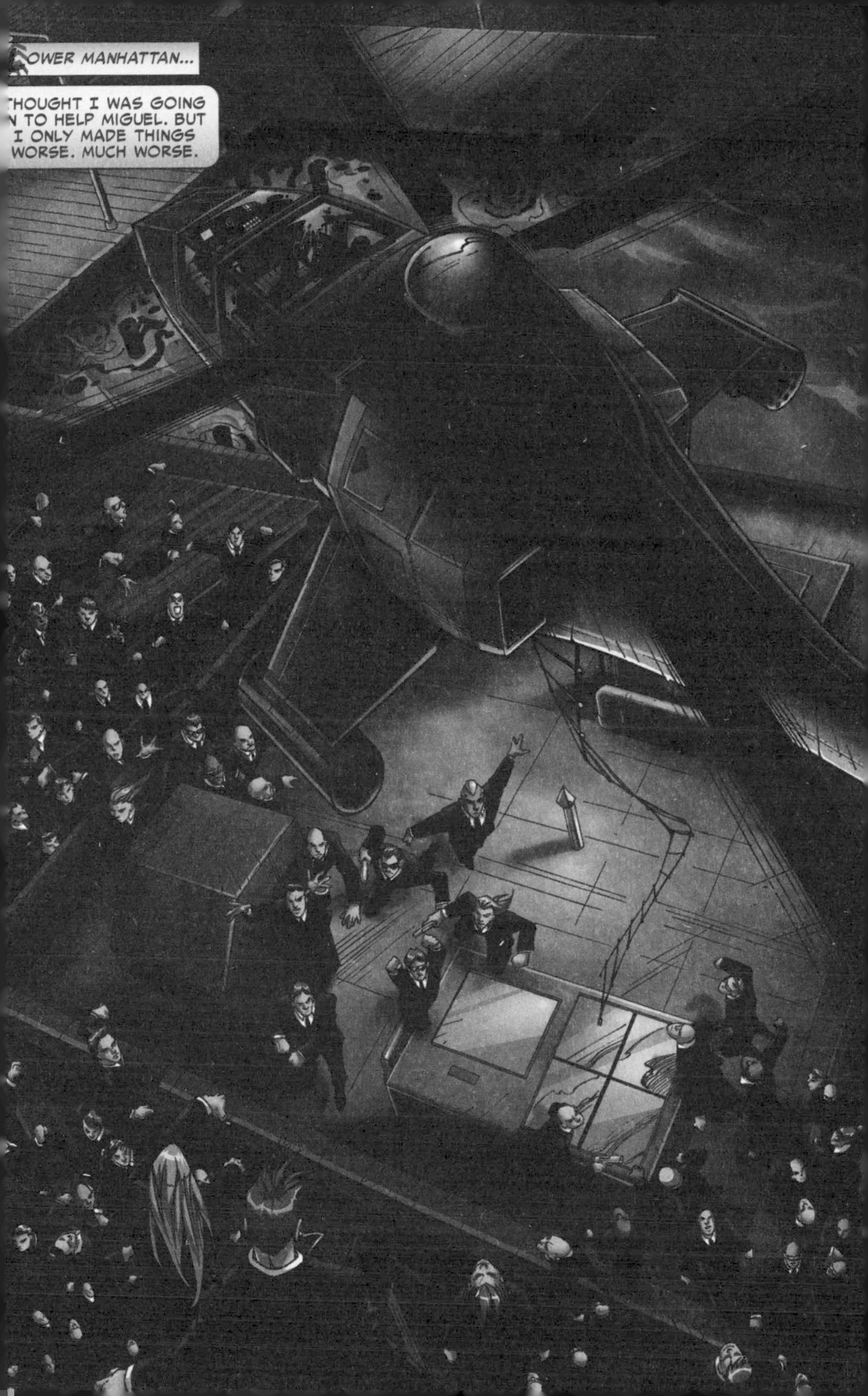
OWER MANHATTAN...
THOUGHT I WAS GOING
N TO HELP MIGUEL. BUT
I ONLY MADE THINGS
WORSE. MUCH WORSE.

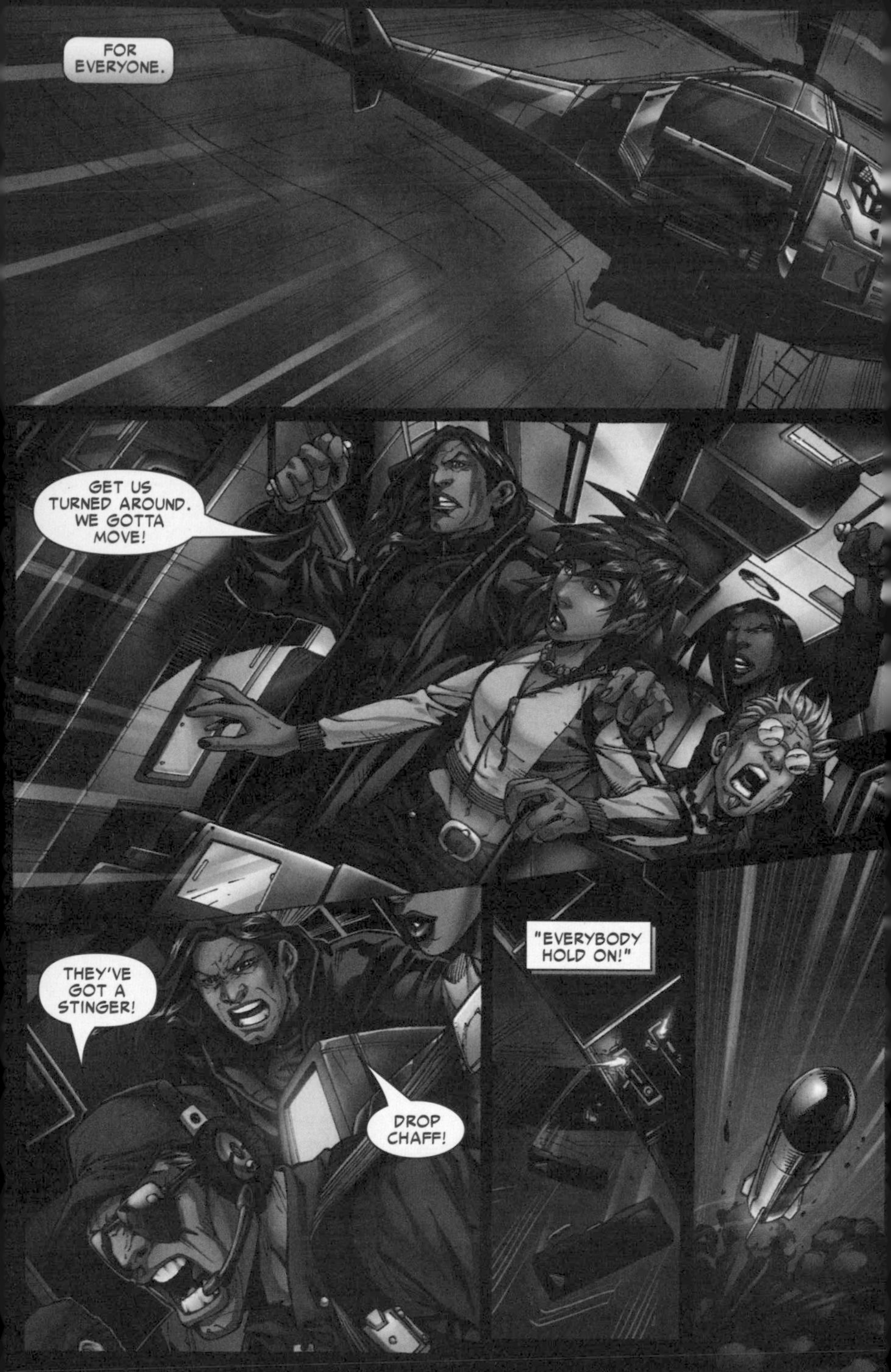
FOR EVERYONE.
GET US TURNED AROUND. WE GOTTA MOVE!
THEY'VE GOT A STINGER!
DROP CHAFF!
"EVERYBODY HOLD ON!"

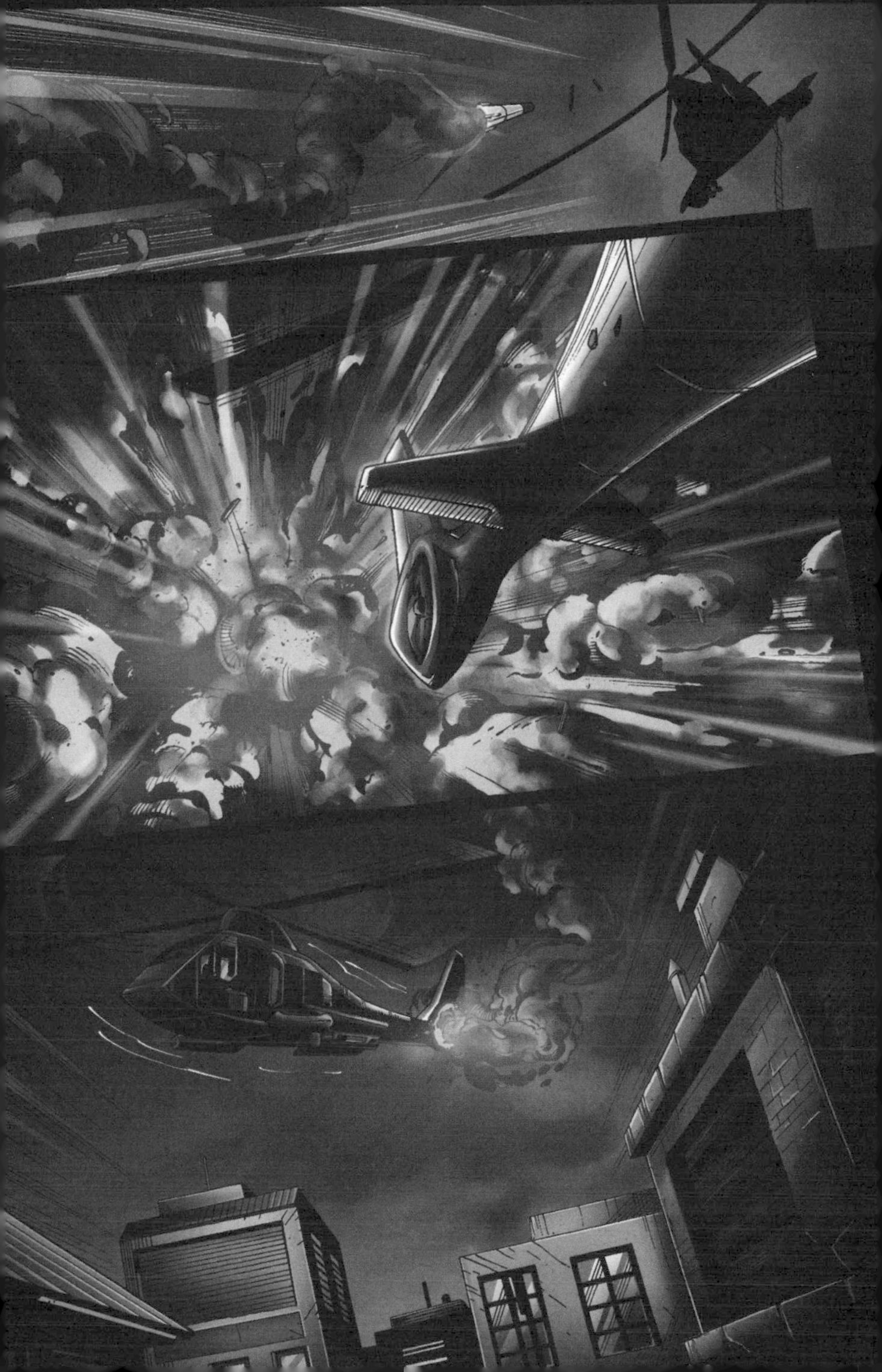

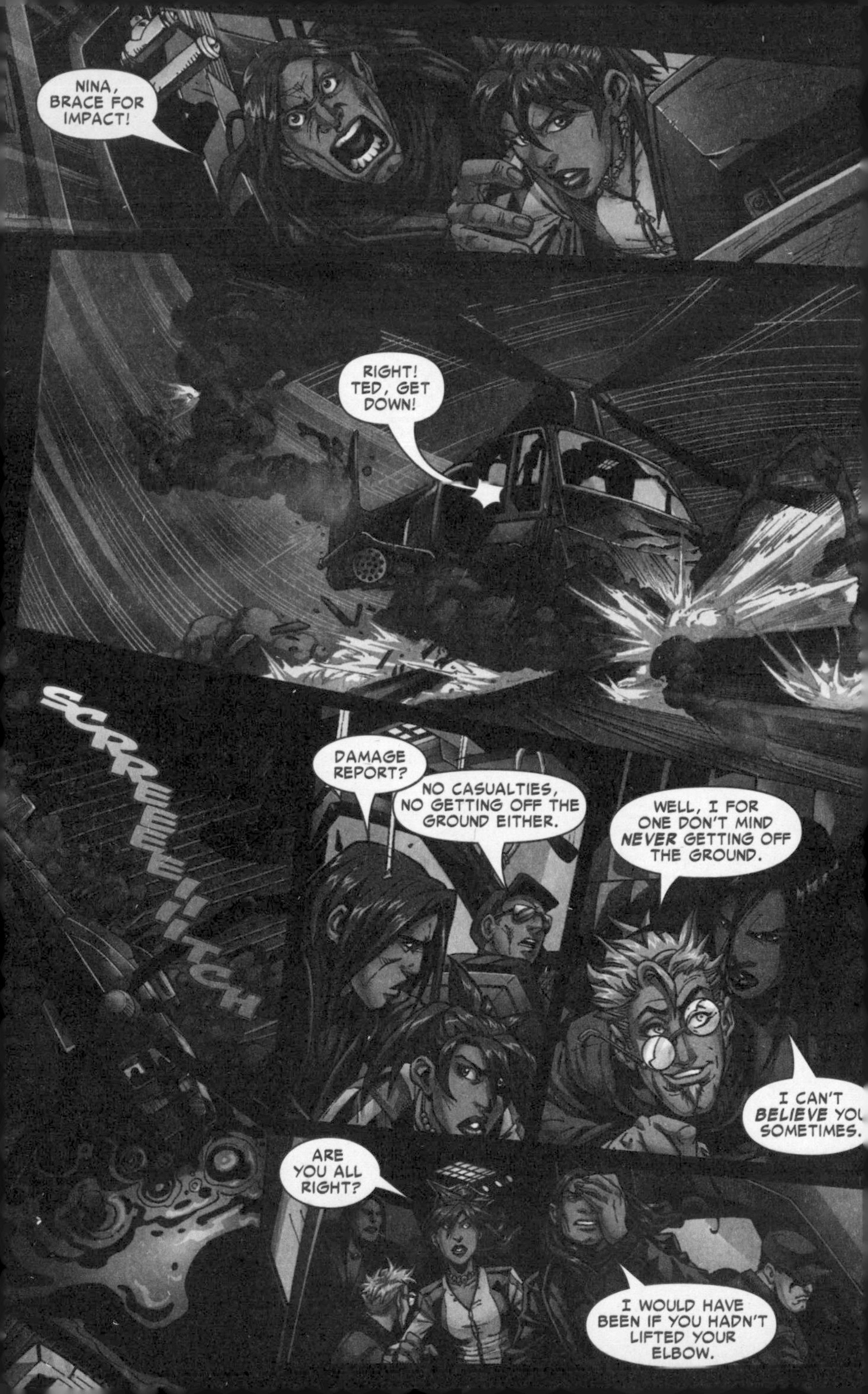
NINA, BRACE FOR IMPACT!
RIGHT! TED, GET DOWN!
SCREEE!!ITCH
DAMAGE REPORT?
NO CASUALTIES, NO GETTING OFF THE GROUND EITHER.
WELL, I FOR ONE DON'T MIND *NEVER* GETTING OFF THE GROUND.
I CAN'T *BELIEVE* YOU SOMETIMES.
ARE YOU ALL RIGHT?
I WOULD HAVE BEEN IF YOU HADN'T LIFTED YOUR ELBOW.

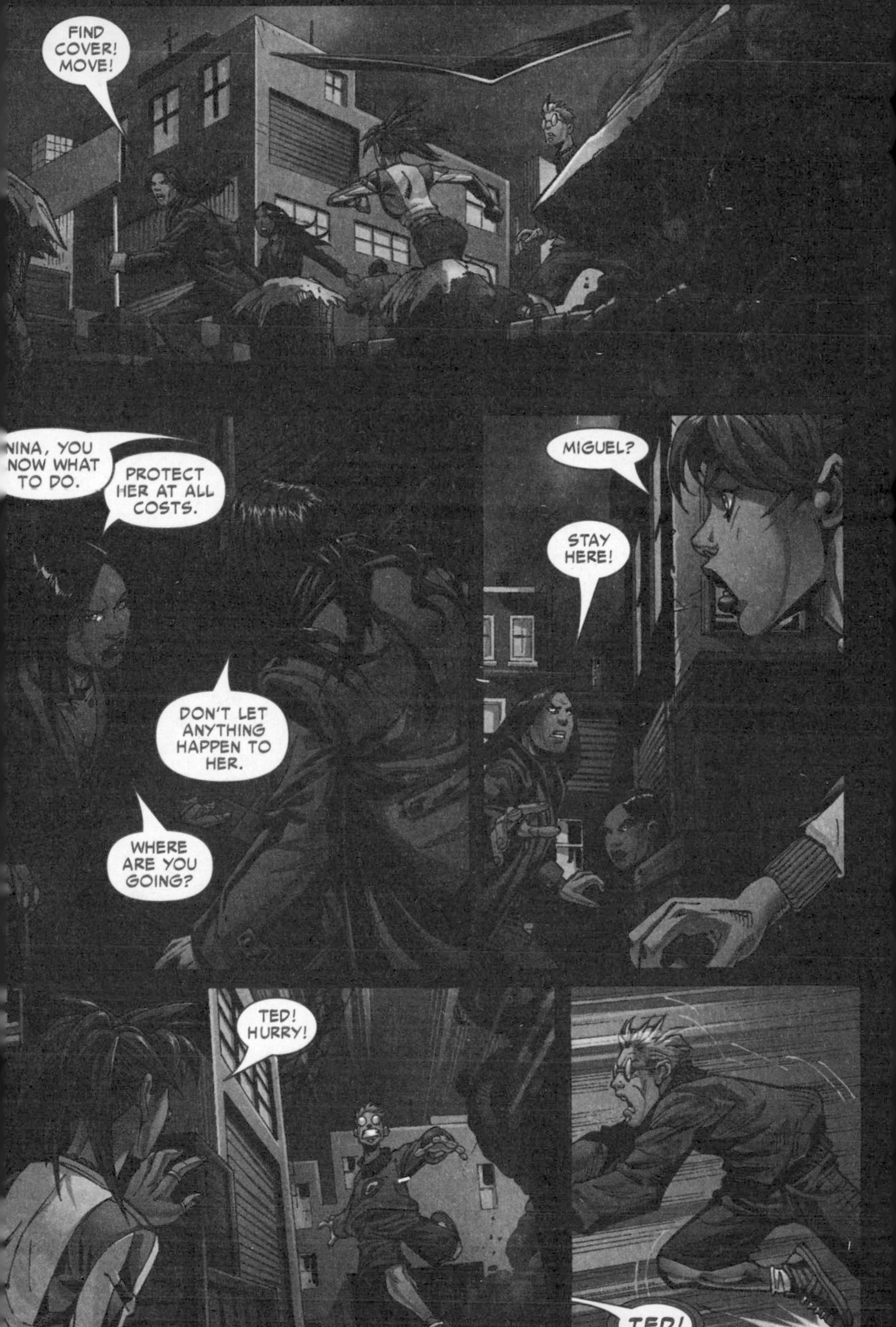
FIND COVER! MOVE!
NINA, YOU NOW WHAT TO DO.
PROTECT HER AT ALL COSTS.
DON'T LET ANYTHING HAPPEN TO HER.
WHERE ARE YOU GOING?
MIGUEL?
STAY HERE!
TED! HURRY!
TED!

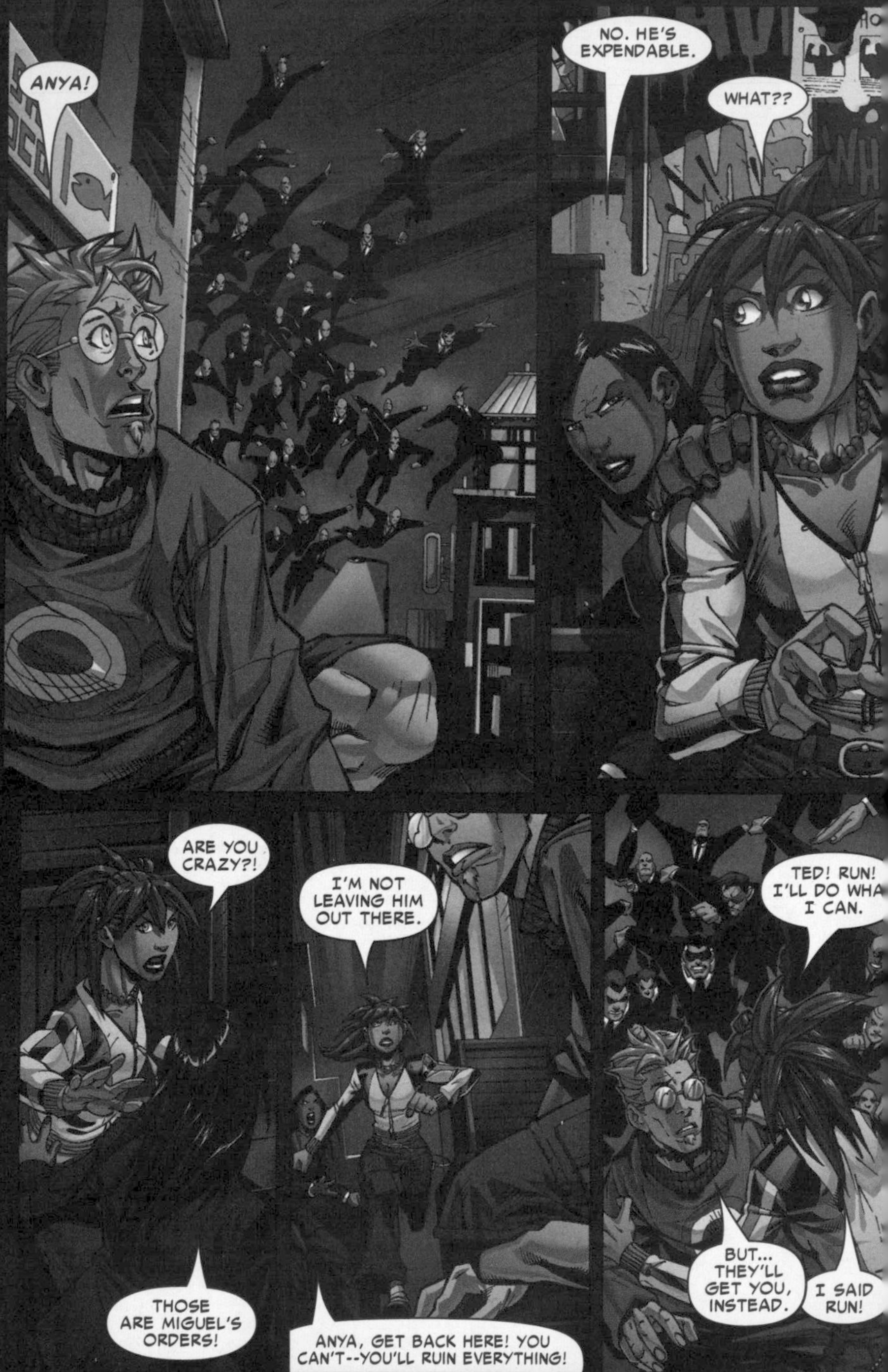
ANYA!
NO. HE'S EXPENDABLE.
WHAT??
ARE YOU CRAZY?!
THOSE ARE MIGUEL'S ORDERS!
I'M NOT LEAVING HIM OUT THERE.
ANYA, GET BACK HERE! YOU CAN'T--YOU'LL RUIN EVERYTHING!
TED! RUN! I'LL DO WHA I CAN.
BUT... THEY'LL GET YOU, INSTEAD.
I SAID RUN!

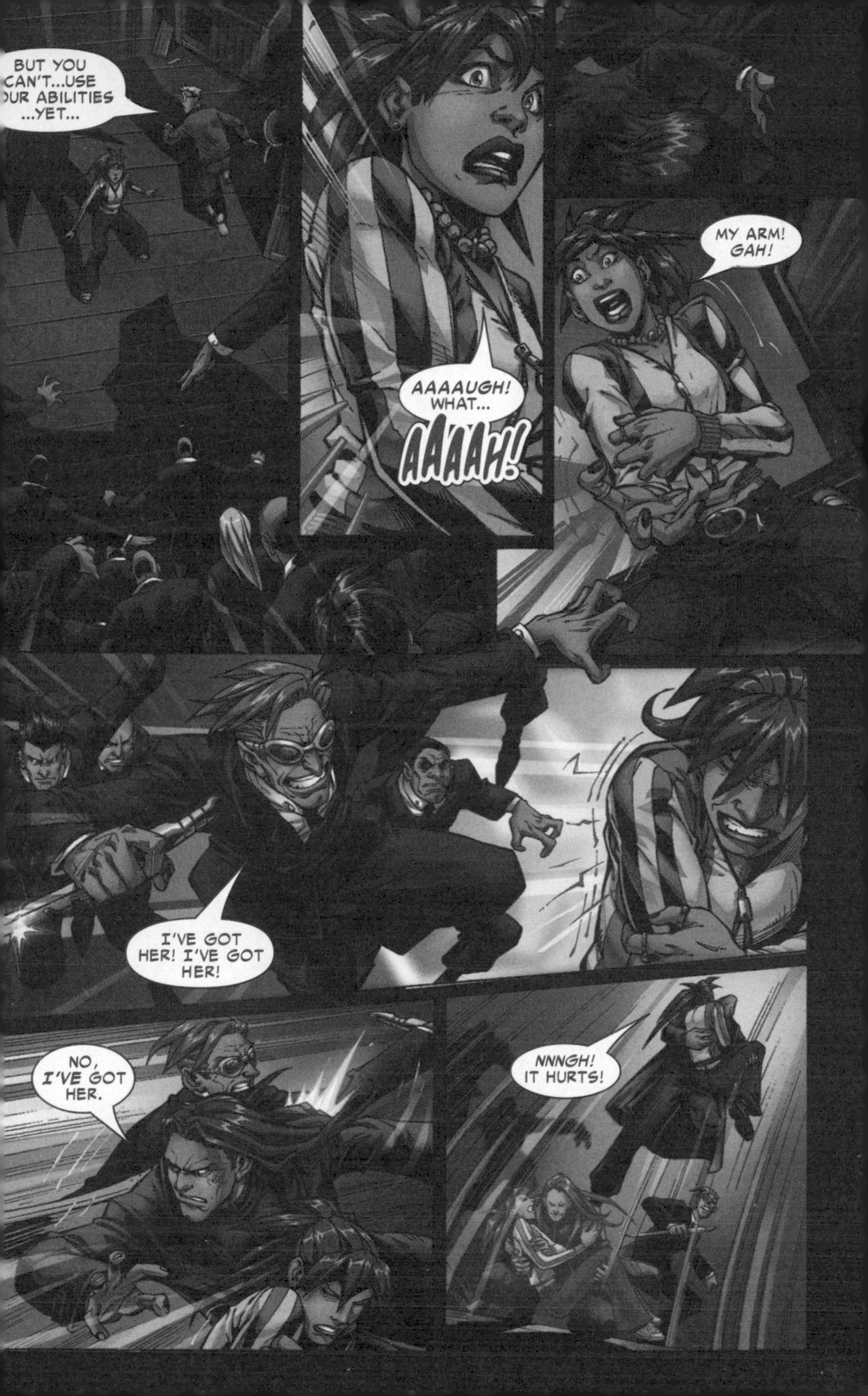

BUT YOU CAN'T...USE OUR ABILITIES ...YET...
AAAAUGH! WHAT...
AAAAH!
MY ARM! GAH!
I'VE GOT HER! I'VE GOT HER!
NO, I'VE GOT HER.
NNNGH! IT HURTS!

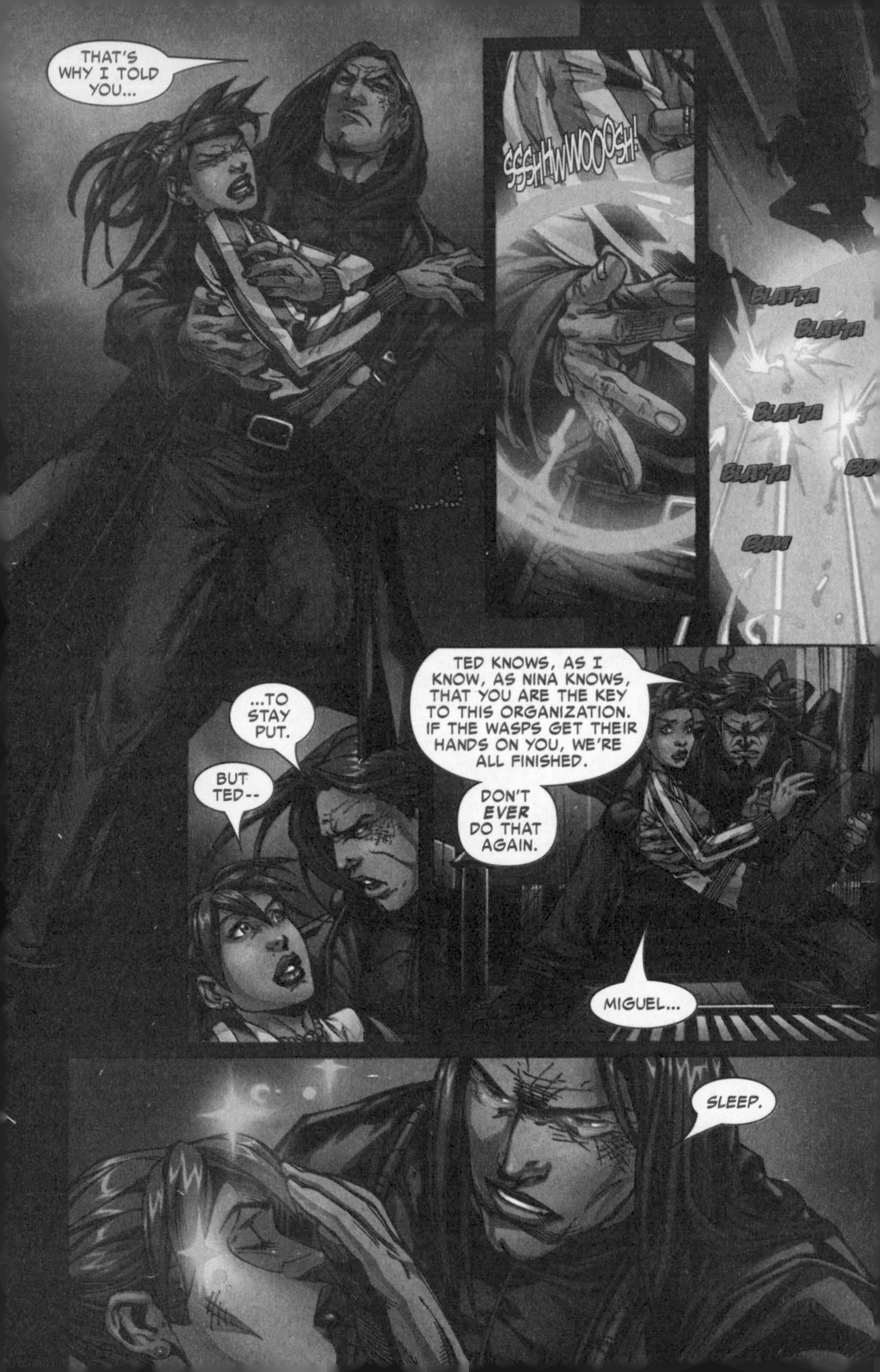
THAT'S WHY I TOLD YOU...
SSSHHWWOOOSH!
BLATTA
BLATTA
BLATTA
BLATTA
BAM
...TO STAY PUT.
BUT TED--
TED KNOWS, AS I KNOW, AS NINA KNOWS, THAT YOU ARE THE KEY TO THIS ORGANIZATION. IF THE WASPS GET THEIR HANDS ON YOU, WE'RE ALL FINISHED.
DON'T EVER DO THAT AGAIN.
MIGUEL...
SLEEP.

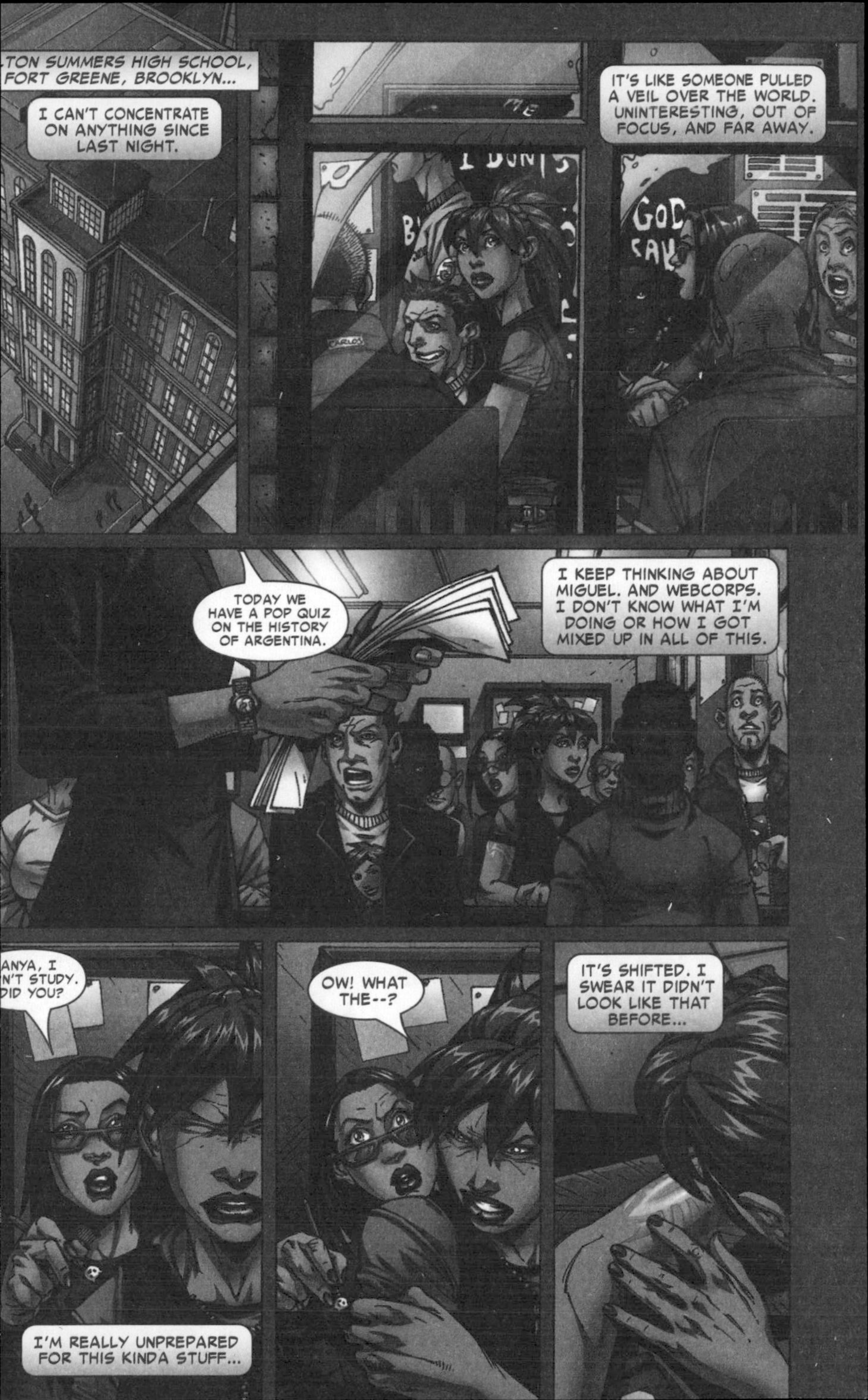

-TON SUMMERS HIGH SCHOOL, FORT GREENE, BROOKLYN...
I CAN'T CONCENTRATE ON ANYTHING SINCE LAST NIGHT.
IT'S LIKE SOMEONE PULLED A VEIL OVER THE WORLD. UNINTERESTING, OUT OF FOCUS, AND FAR AWAY.
TODAY WE HAVE A POP QUIZ ON THE HISTORY OF ARGENTINA.
I KEEP THINKING ABOUT MIGUEL. AND WEBCORPS. I DON'T KNOW WHAT I'M DOING OR HOW I GOT MIXED UP IN ALL OF THIS.
-ANYA, I -N'T STUDY. -DID YOU?
I'M REALLY UNPREPARED FOR THIS KINDA STUFF...
OW! WHAT THE--?
IT'S SHIFTED. I SWEAR IT DIDN'T LOOK LIKE THAT BEFORE...

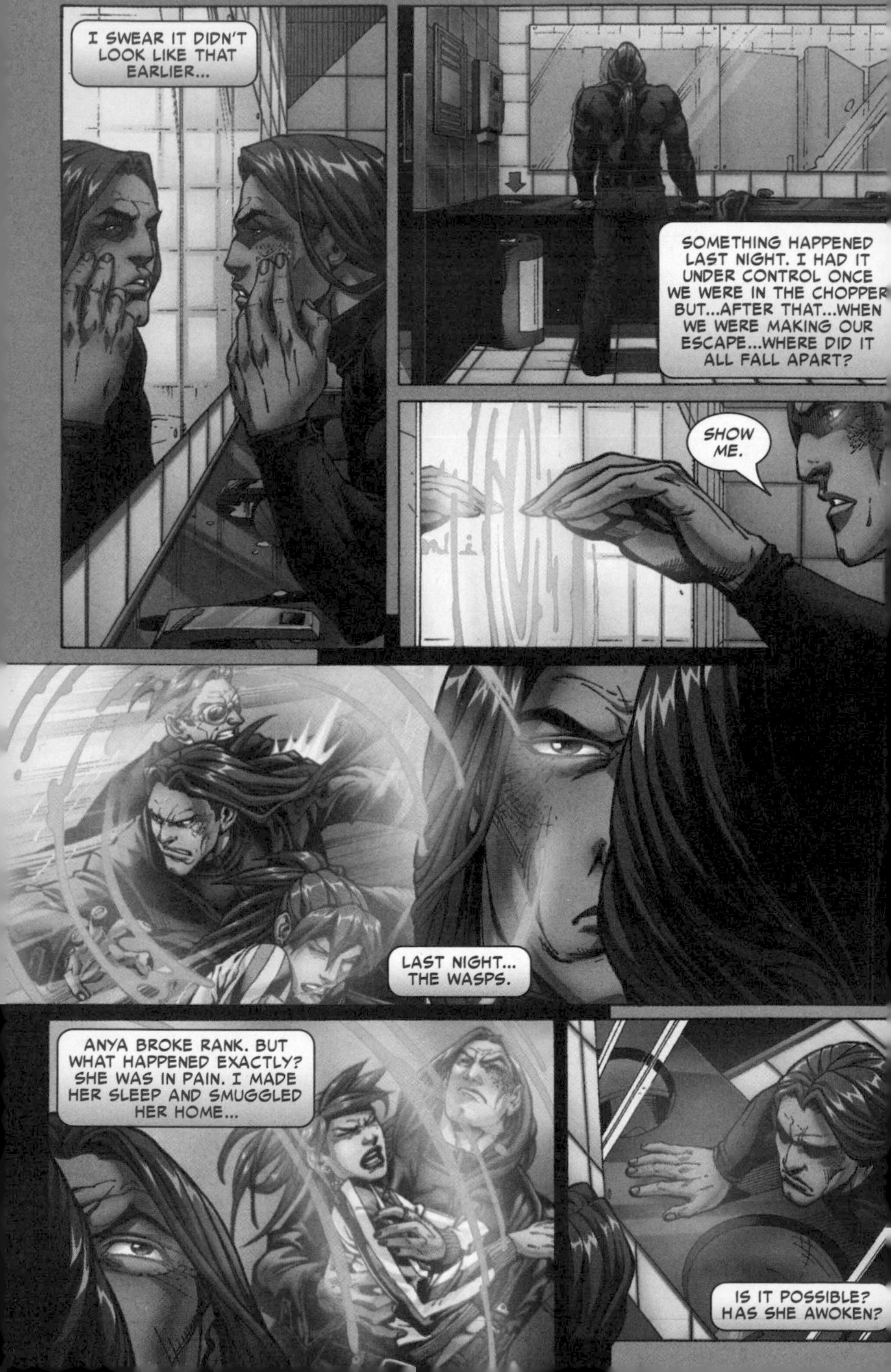
I SWEAR IT DIDN'T LOOK LIKE THAT EARLIER...
SOMETHING HAPPENED LAST NIGHT. I HAD IT UNDER CONTROL ONCE WE WERE IN THE CHOPPER BUT...AFTER THAT...WHEN WE WERE MAKING OUR ESCAPE...WHERE DID IT ALL FALL APART?
SHOW ME.
LAST NIGHT... THE WASPS.
ANYA BROKE RANK. BUT WHAT HAPPENED EXACTLY? SHE WAS IN PAIN. I MADE HER SLEEP AND SMUGGLED HER HOME...
IS IT POSSIBLE? HAS SHE AWOKEN?

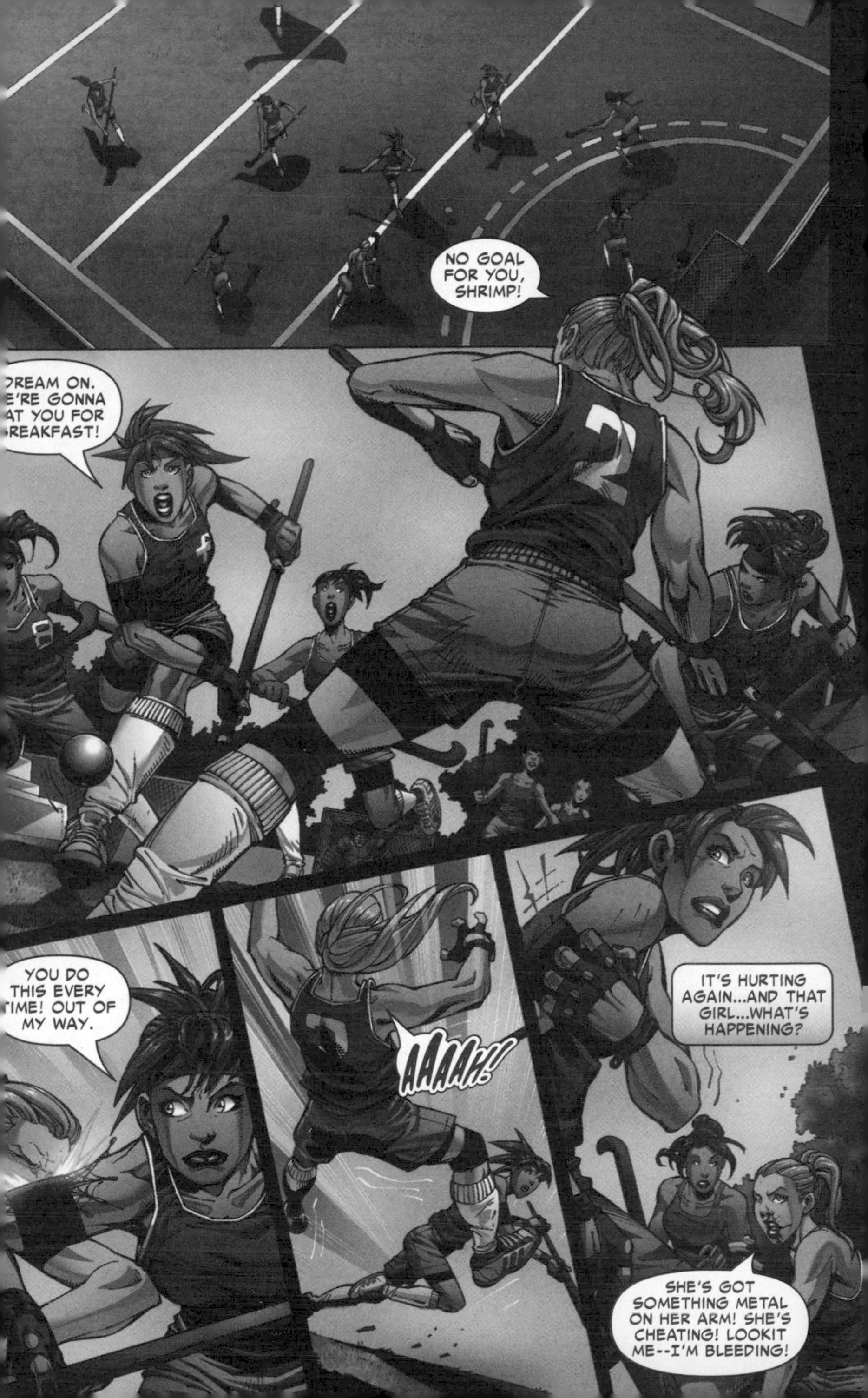
NO GOAL FOR YOU, SHRIMP!
DREAM ON. WE'RE GONNA EAT YOU FOR BREAKFAST!
YOU DO THIS EVERY TIME! OUT OF MY WAY.
AAAAH!
IT'S HURTING AGAIN...AND THAT GIRL...WHAT'S HAPPENING?
SHE'S GOT SOMETHING METAL ON HER ARM! SHE'S CHEATING! LOOKIT ME--I'M BLEEDING!

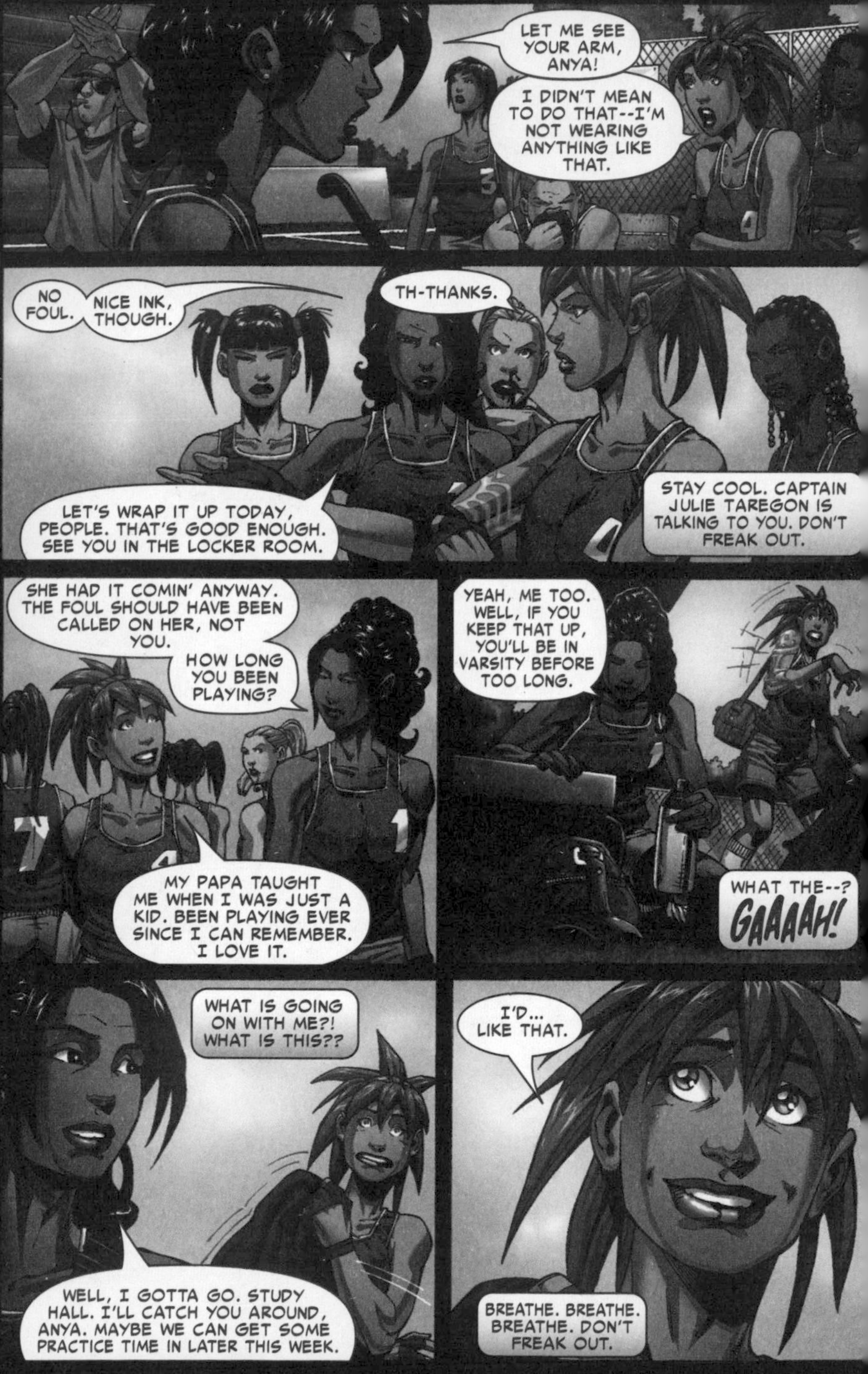

LET ME SEE YOUR ARM, ANYA!
I DIDN'T MEAN TO DO THAT--I'M NOT WEARING ANYTHING LIKE THAT.
NO FOUL.
NICE INK, THOUGH.
TH-THANKS.
LET'S WRAP IT UP TODAY, PEOPLE. THAT'S GOOD ENOUGH. SEE YOU IN THE LOCKER ROOM.
STAY COOL. CAPTAIN JULIE TAREGON IS TALKING TO YOU. DON'T FREAK OUT.
SHE HAD IT COMIN' ANYWAY. THE FOUL SHOULD HAVE BEEN CALLED ON HER, NOT YOU.
HOW LONG YOU BEEN PLAYING?
MY PAPA TAUGHT ME WHEN I WAS JUST A KID. BEEN PLAYING EVER SINCE I CAN REMEMBER. I LOVE IT.
YEAH, ME TOO. WELL, IF YOU KEEP THAT UP, YOU'LL BE IN VARSITY BEFORE TOO LONG.
WHAT THE--?
GAAAAH!
WHAT IS GOING ON WITH ME?! WHAT IS THIS??
WELL, I GOTTA GO. STUDY HALL. I'LL CATCH YOU AROUND, ANYA. MAYBE WE CAN GET SOME PRACTICE TIME IN LATER THIS WEEK.
I'D... LIKE THAT.
BREATHE. BREATHE. BREATHE. DON'T FREAK OUT.

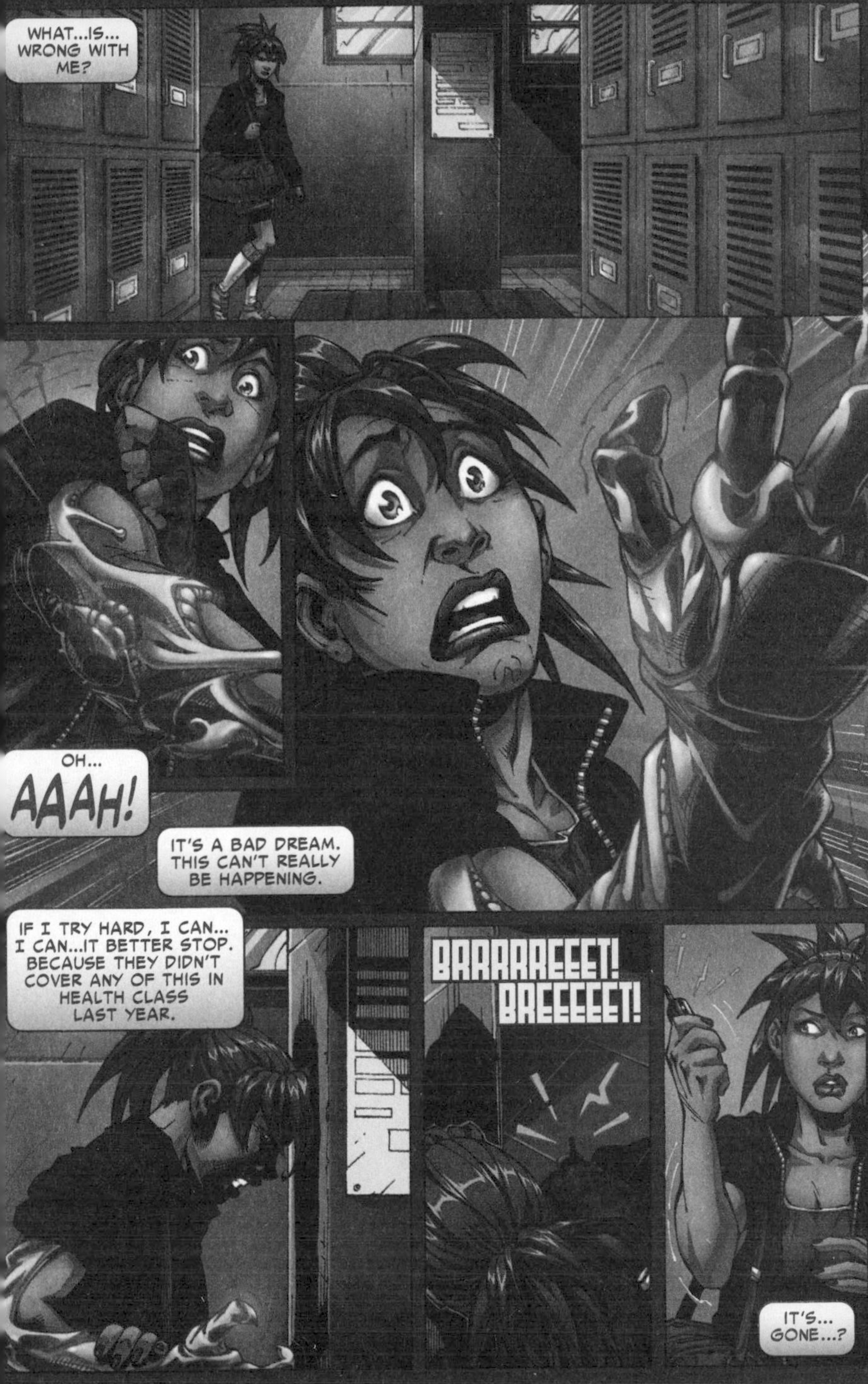
WHAT...IS... WRONG WITH ME?
OH... AAAH!
IT'S A BAD DREAM. THIS CAN'T REALLY BE HAPPENING.
IF I TRY HARD, I CAN... I CAN...IT BETTER STOP. BECAUSE THEY DIDN'T COVER ANY OF THIS IN HEALTH CLASS LAST YEAR.
BRRRRREEET! BREEEEET!
IT'S... GONE...?

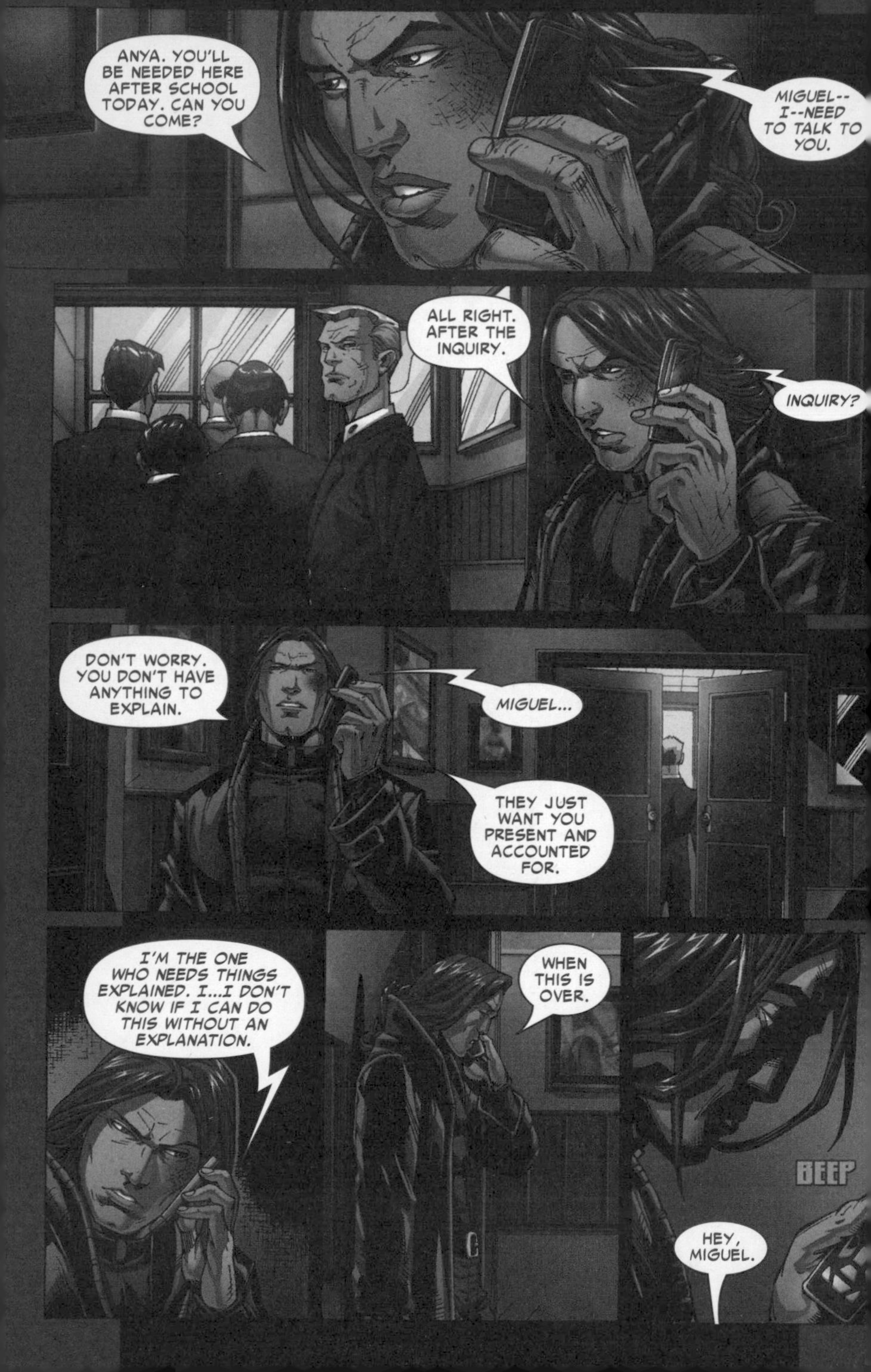
ANYA. YOU'LL BE NEEDED HERE AFTER SCHOOL TODAY. CAN YOU COME?
MIGUEL-- I--NEED TO TALK TO YOU.
ALL RIGHT. AFTER THE INQUIRY.
INQUIRY?
DON'T WORRY. YOU DON'T HAVE ANYTHING TO EXPLAIN.
MIGUEL...
THEY JUST WANT YOU PRESENT AND ACCOUNTED FOR.
I'M THE ONE WHO NEEDS THINGS EXPLAINED. I...I DON'T KNOW IF I CAN DO THIS WITHOUT AN EXPLANATION.
WHEN THIS IS OVER.
BEEP
HEY, MIGUEL.

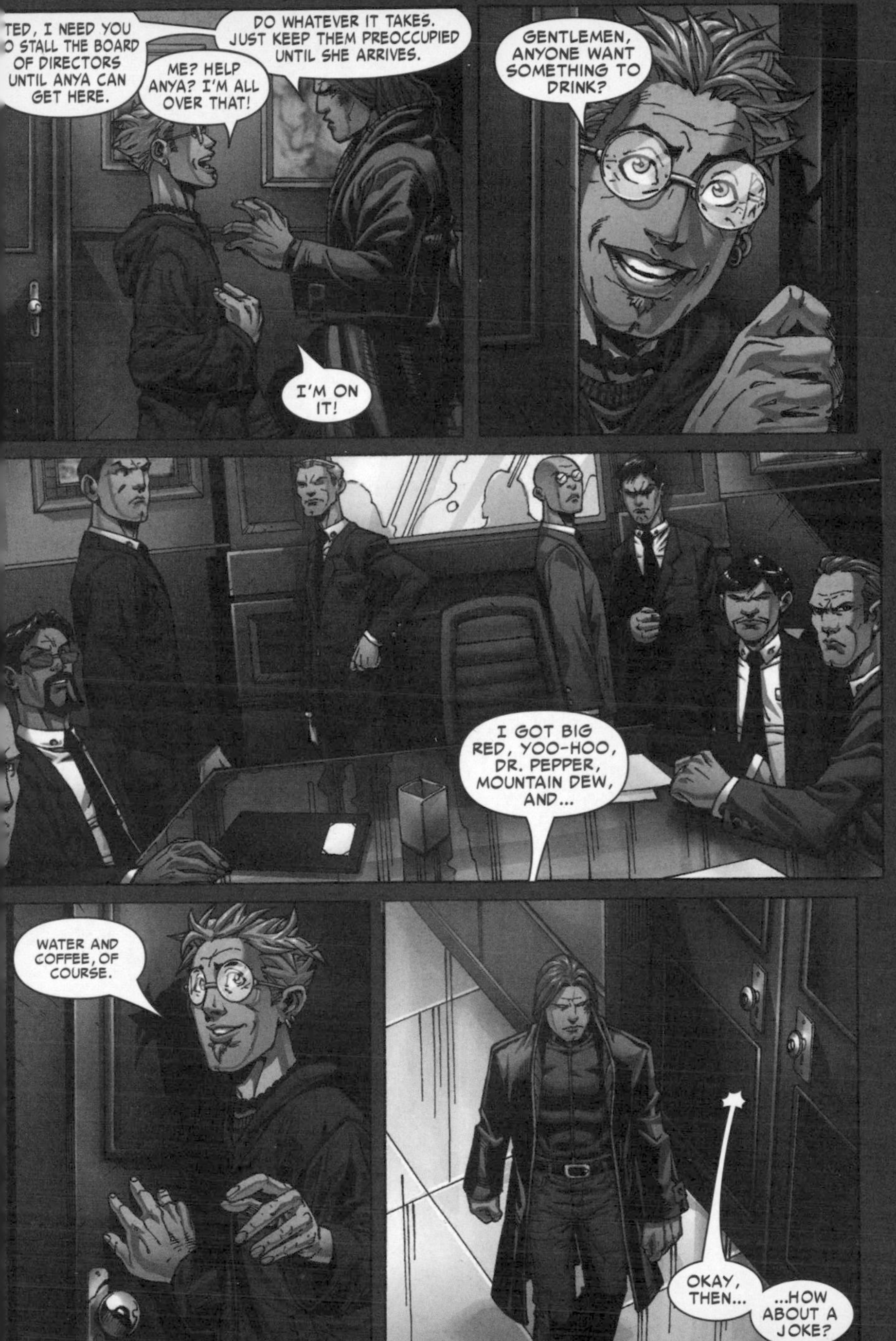
TED, I NEED YOU O STALL THE BOARD OF DIRECTORS UNTIL ANYA CAN GET HERE.
ME? HELP ANYA? I'M ALL OVER THAT!
DO WHATEVER IT TAKES. JUST KEEP THEM PREOCCUPIED UNTIL SHE ARRIVES.
I'M ON IT!
GENTLEMEN, ANYONE WANT SOMETHING TO DRINK?
I GOT BIG RED, YOO-HOO, DR. PEPPER, MOUNTAIN DEW, AND...
WATER AND COFFEE, OF COURSE.
OKAY, THEN...
...HOW ABOUT A JOKE?

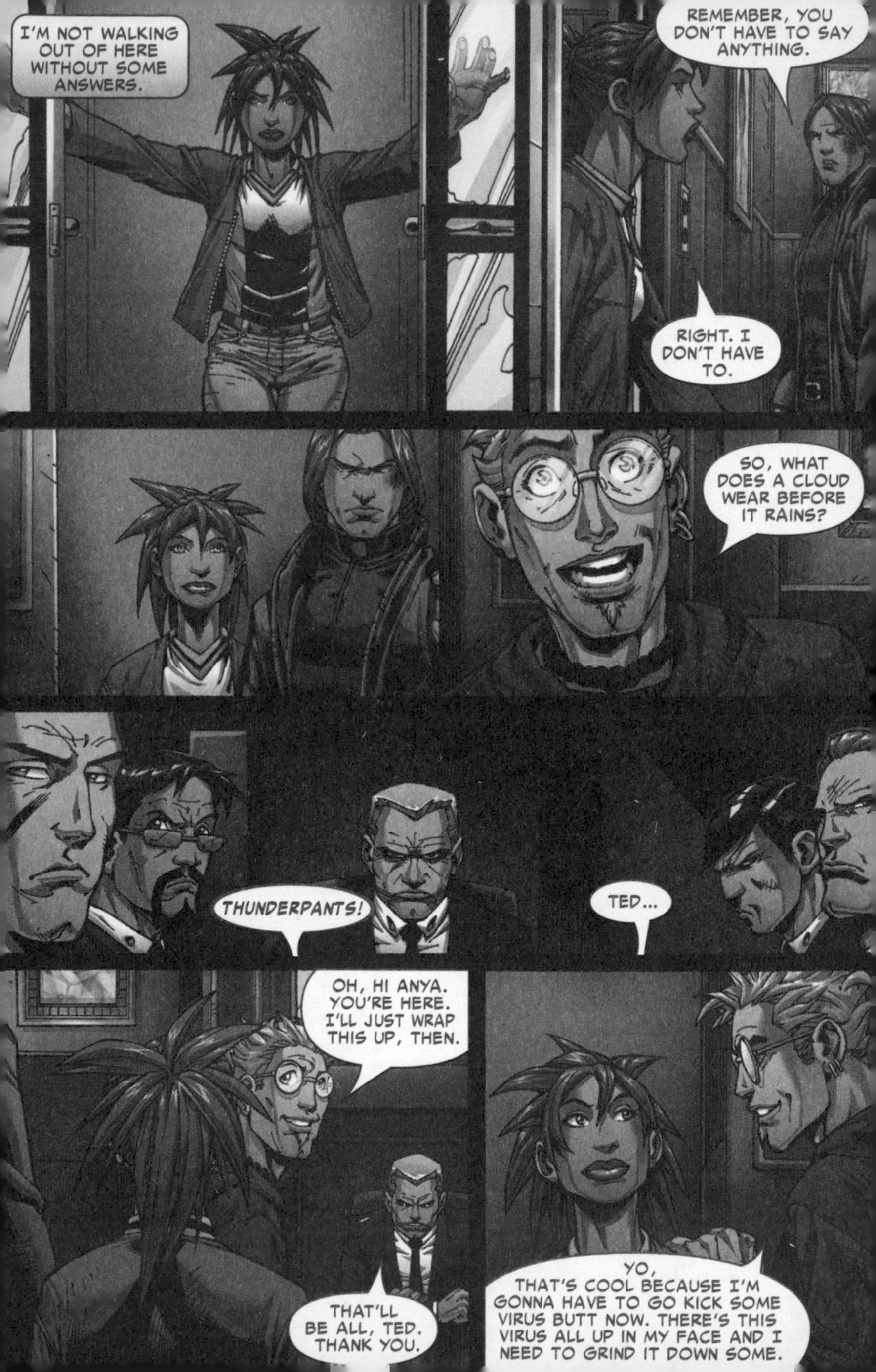
I'M NOT WALKING OUT OF HERE WITHOUT SOME ANSWERS.
REMEMBER, YOU DON'T HAVE TO SAY ANYTHING.
RIGHT. I DON'T HAVE TO.
SO, WHAT DOES A CLOUD WEAR BEFORE IT RAINS?
THUNDERPANTS!
TED...
OH, HI ANYA. YOU'RE HERE. I'LL JUST WRAP THIS UP, THEN.
THAT'LL BE ALL, TED. THANK YOU.
YO, THAT'S COOL BECAUSE I'M GONNA HAVE TO GO KICK SOME VIRUS BUTT NOW. THERE'S THIS VIRUS ALL UP IN MY FACE AND I NEED TO GRIND IT DOWN SOME.

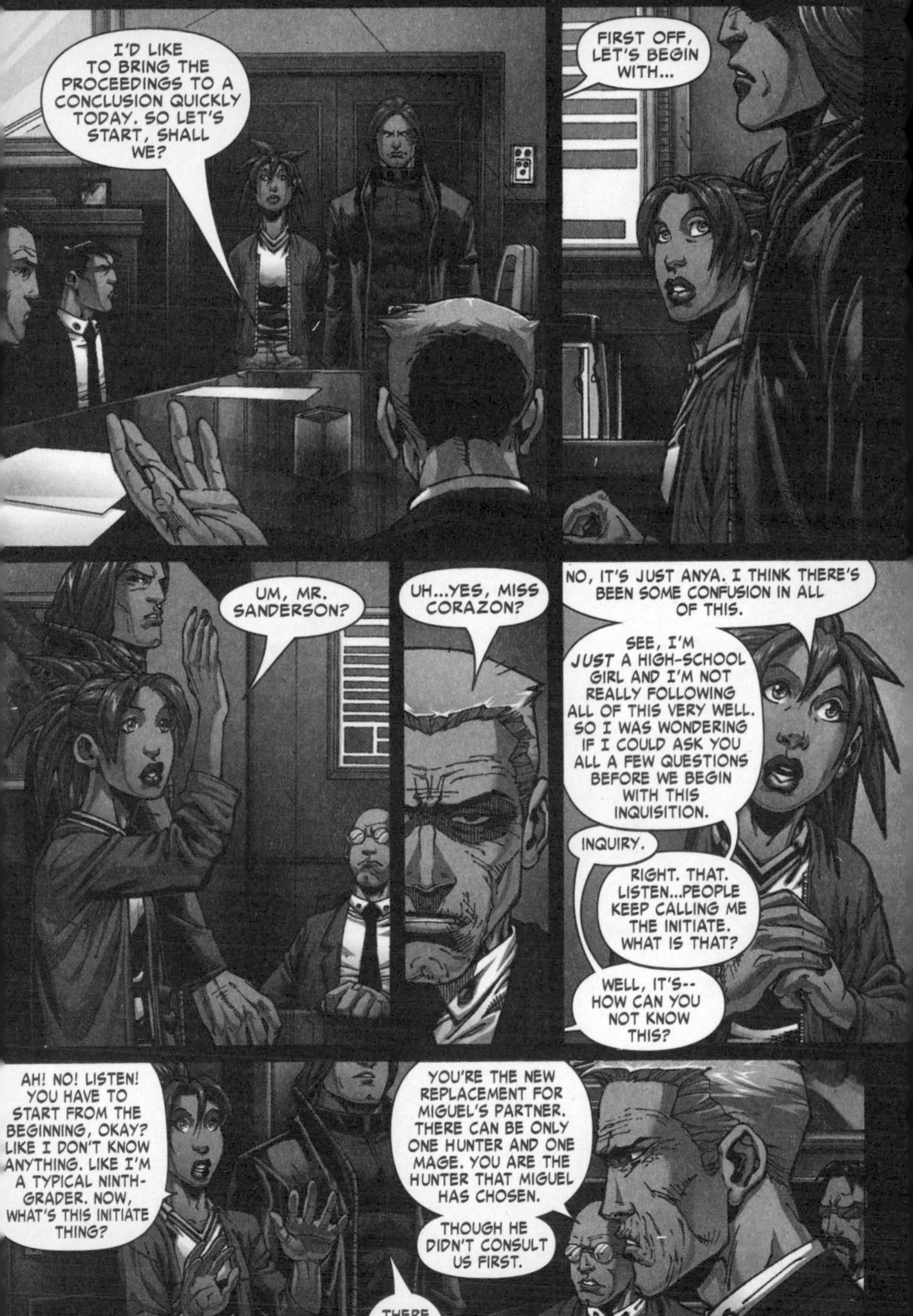
I'D LIKE TO BRING THE PROCEEDINGS TO A CONCLUSION QUICKLY TODAY. SO LET'S START, SHALL WE?
FIRST OFF, LET'S BEGIN WITH...
UM, MR. SANDERSON?
UH...YES, MISS CORAZON?
NO, IT'S JUST ANYA. I THINK THERE'S BEEN SOME CONFUSION IN ALL OF THIS.
SEE, I'M JUST A HIGH-SCHOOL GIRL AND I'M NOT REALLY FOLLOWING ALL OF THIS VERY WELL. SO I WAS WONDERING IF I COULD ASK YOU ALL A FEW QUESTIONS BEFORE WE BEGIN WITH THIS INQUISITION.
INQUIRY.
RIGHT. THAT. LISTEN...PEOPLE KEEP CALLING ME THE INITIATE. WHAT IS THAT?
WELL, IT'S-- HOW CAN YOU NOT KNOW THIS?
AH! NO! LISTEN! YOU HAVE TO START FROM THE BEGINNING, OKAY? LIKE I DON'T KNOW ANYTHING. LIKE I'M A TYPICAL NINTH-GRADER. NOW, WHAT'S THIS INITIATE THING?
YOU'RE THE NEW REPLACEMENT FOR MIGUEL'S PARTNER. THERE CAN BE ONLY ONE HUNTER AND ONE MAGE. YOU ARE THE HUNTER THAT MIGUEL HAS CHOSEN.
THOUGH HE DIDN'T CONSULT US FIRST.
THERE WASN'T TIME.

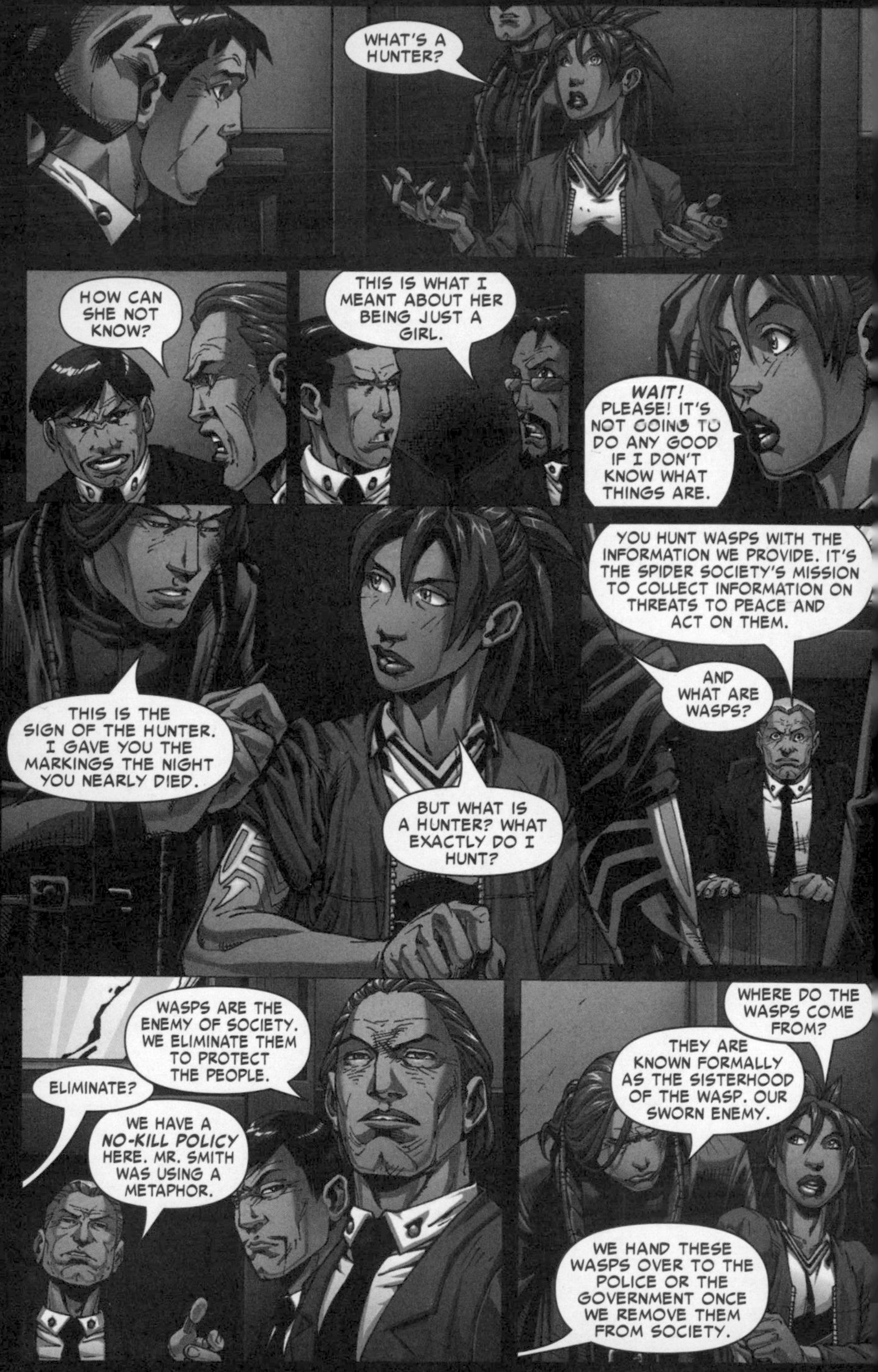
WHAT'S A HUNTER?
HOW CAN SHE NOT KNOW?
THIS IS WHAT I MEANT ABOUT HER BEING JUST A GIRL.
WAIT! PLEASE! IT'S NOT GOING TO DO ANY GOOD IF I DON'T KNOW WHAT THINGS ARE.
THIS IS THE SIGN OF THE HUNTER. I GAVE YOU THE MARKINGS THE NIGHT YOU NEARLY DIED.
BUT WHAT IS A HUNTER? WHAT EXACTLY DO I HUNT?
YOU HUNT WASPS WITH THE INFORMATION WE PROVIDE. IT'S THE SPIDER SOCIETY'S MISSION TO COLLECT INFORMATION ON THREATS TO PEACE AND ACT ON THEM.
AND WHAT ARE WASPS?
WASPS ARE THE ENEMY OF SOCIETY. WE ELIMINATE THEM TO PROTECT THE PEOPLE.
ELIMINATE?
WE HAVE A *NO-KILL POLICY* HERE. MR. SMITH WAS USING A METAPHOR.
WHERE DO THE WASPS COME FROM?
THEY ARE KNOWN FORMALLY AS THE SISTERHOOD OF THE WASP. OUR SWORN ENEMY.
WE HAND THESE WASPS OVER TO THE POLICE OR THE GOVERNMENT ONCE WE REMOVE THEM FROM SOCIETY.

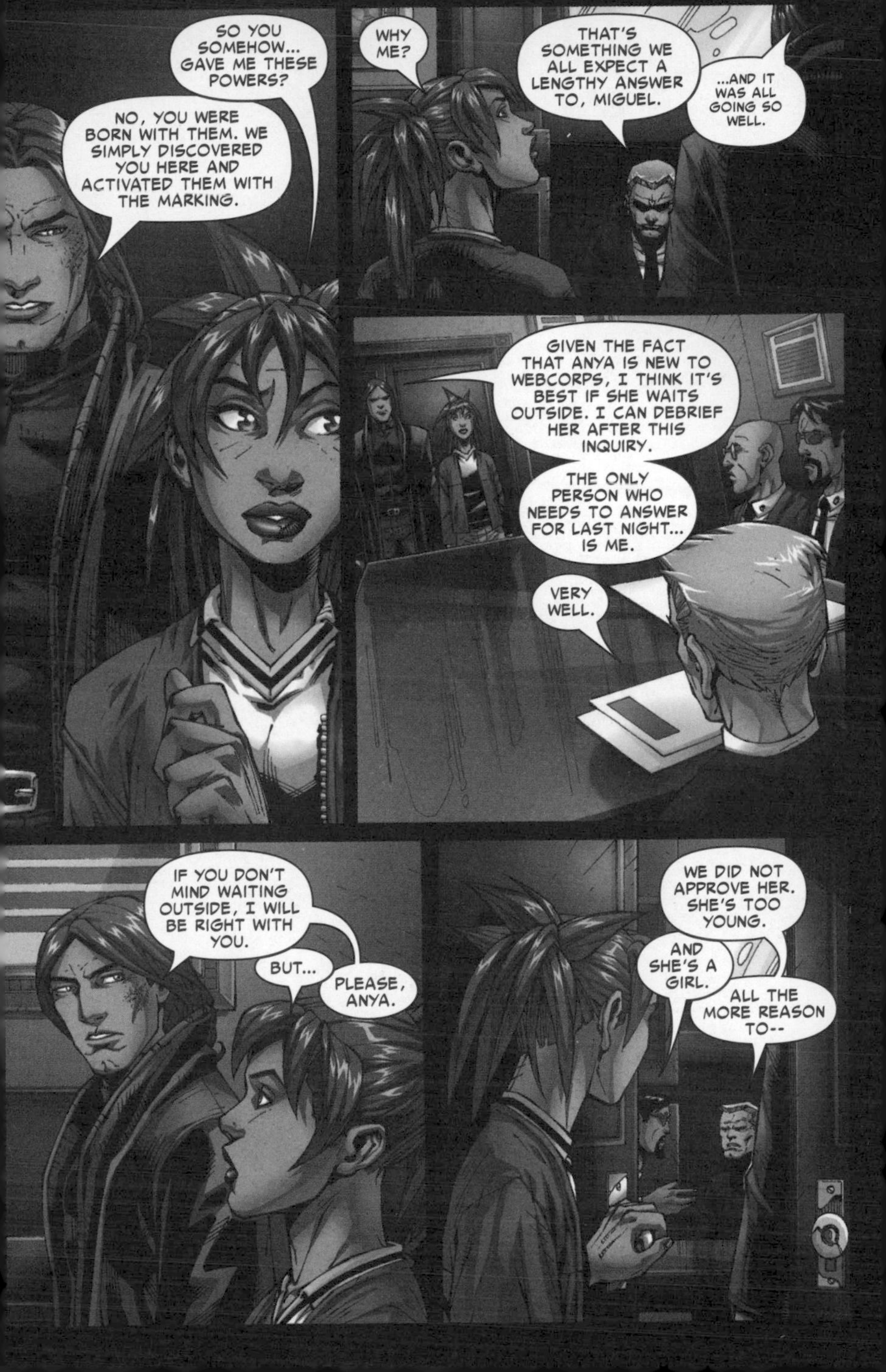
SO YOU SOMEHOW... GAVE ME THESE POWERS?
NO, YOU WERE BORN WITH THEM. WE SIMPLY DISCOVERED YOU HERE AND ACTIVATED THEM WITH THE MARKING.
WHY ME?
THAT'S SOMETHING WE ALL EXPECT A LENGTHY ANSWER TO, MIGUEL.
...AND IT WAS ALL GOING SO WELL.
GIVEN THE FACT THAT ANYA IS NEW TO WEBCORPS, I THINK IT'S BEST IF SHE WAITS OUTSIDE. I CAN DEBRIEF HER AFTER THIS INQUIRY.
THE ONLY PERSON WHO NEEDS TO ANSWER FOR LAST NIGHT... IS ME.
VERY WELL.
IF YOU DON'T MIND WAITING OUTSIDE, I WILL BE RIGHT WITH YOU.
BUT...
PLEASE, ANYA.
WE DID NOT APPROVE HER. SHE'S TOO YOUNG.
AND SHE'S A GIRL.
ALL THE MORE REASON TO--

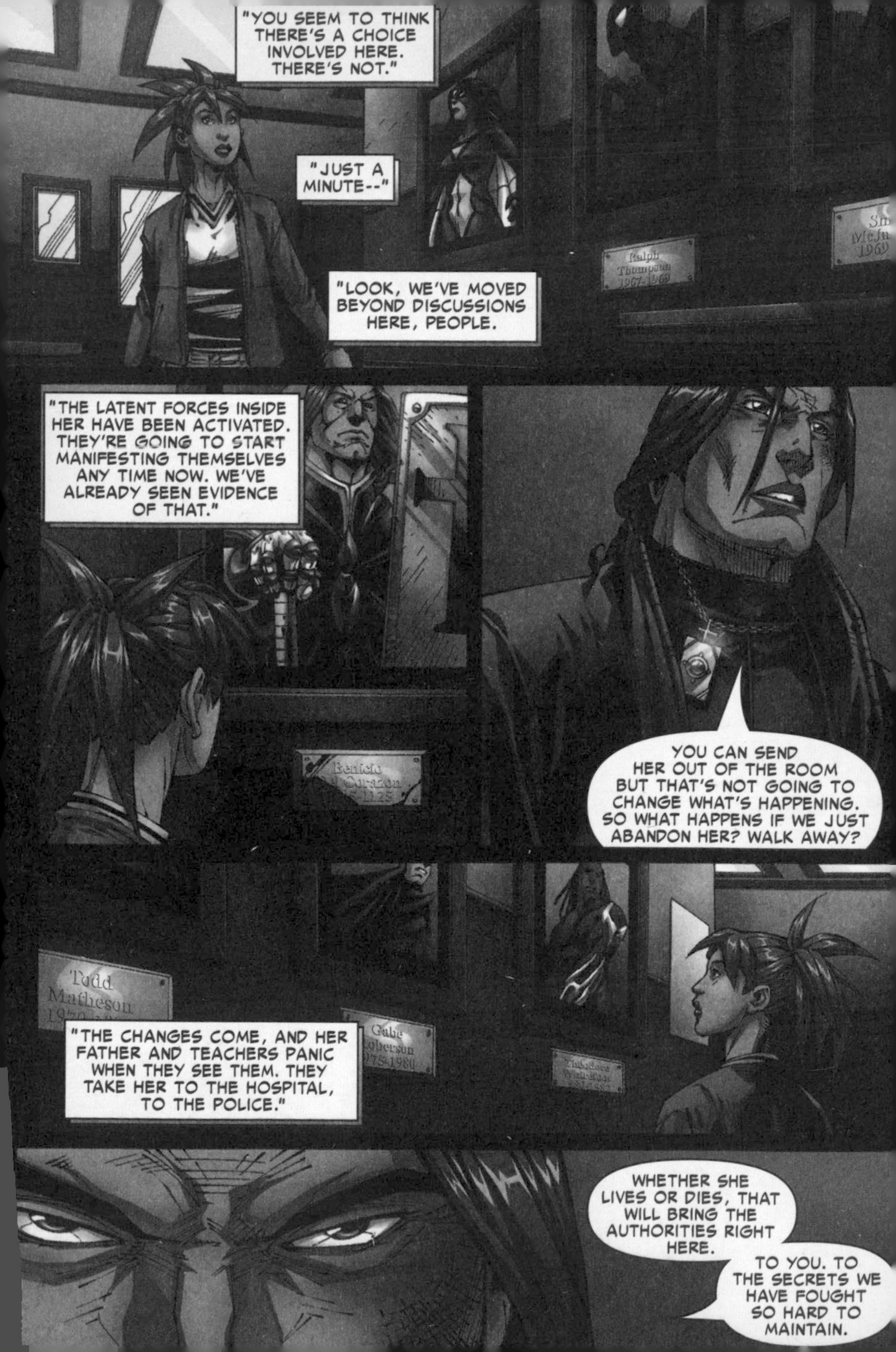

"YOU SEEM TO THINK THERE'S A CHOICE INVOLVED HERE. THERE'S NOT."
"JUST A MINUTE--"
"LOOK, WE'VE MOVED BEYOND DISCUSSIONS HERE, PEOPLE.
Ralph Thompson
"THE LATENT FORCES INSIDE HER HAVE BEEN ACTIVATED. THEY'RE GOING TO START MANIFESTING THEMSELVES ANY TIME NOW. WE'VE ALREADY SEEN EVIDENCE OF THAT."
YOU CAN SEND HER OUT OF THE ROOM BUT THAT'S NOT GOING TO CHANGE WHAT'S HAPPENING. SO WHAT HAPPENS IF WE JUST ABANDON HER? WALK AWAY?
Todd Matheson
"THE CHANGES COME, AND HER FATHER AND TEACHERS PANIC WHEN THEY SEE THEM. THEY TAKE HER TO THE HOSPITAL, TO THE POLICE."
WHETHER SHE LIVES OR DIES, THAT WILL BRING THE AUTHORITIES RIGHT HERE.
TO YOU. TO THE SECRETS WE HAVE FOUGHT SO HARD TO MAINTAIN.

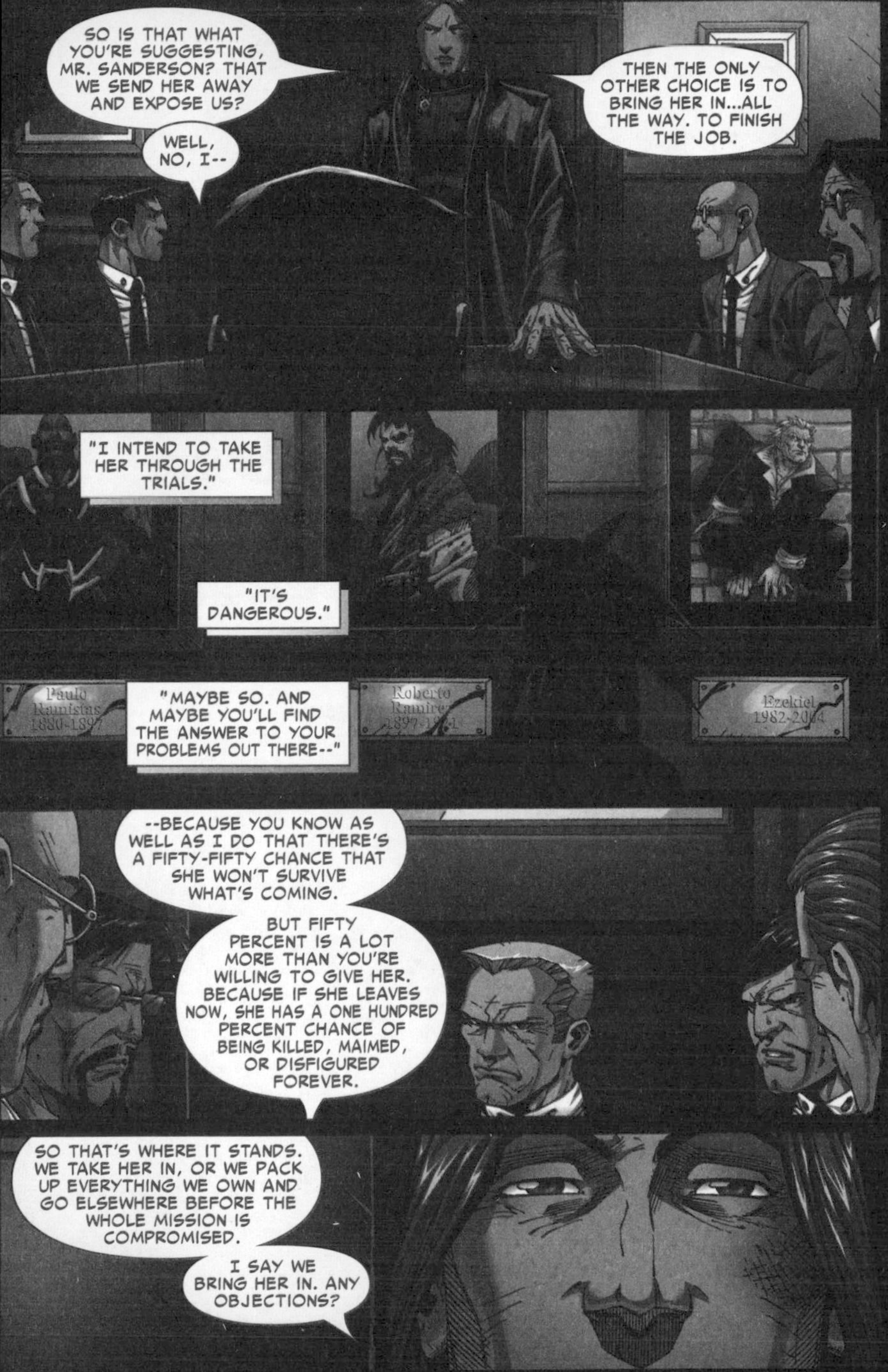
SO IS THAT WHAT YOU'RE SUGGESTING, MR. SANDERSON? THAT WE SEND HER AWAY AND EXPOSE US?
WELL, NO, I--
THEN THE ONLY OTHER CHOICE IS TO BRING HER IN...ALL THE WAY. TO FINISH THE JOB.
"I INTEND TO TAKE HER THROUGH THE TRIALS."
"IT'S DANGEROUS."
"MAYBE SO. AND MAYBE YOU'LL FIND THE ANSWER TO YOUR PROBLEMS OUT THERE--"
Ezekiel
1982-2004
--BECAUSE YOU KNOW AS WELL AS I DO THAT THERE'S A FIFTY-FIFTY CHANCE THAT SHE WON'T SURVIVE WHAT'S COMING.
BUT FIFTY PERCENT IS A LOT MORE THAN YOU'RE WILLING TO GIVE HER. BECAUSE IF SHE LEAVES NOW, SHE HAS A ONE HUNDRED PERCENT CHANCE OF BEING KILLED, MAIMED, OR DISFIGURED FOREVER.
SO THAT'S WHERE IT STANDS. WE TAKE HER IN, OR WE PACK UP EVERYTHING WE OWN AND GO ELSEWHERE BEFORE THE WHOLE MISSION IS COMPROMISED.
I SAY WE BRING HER IN. ANY OBJECTIONS?

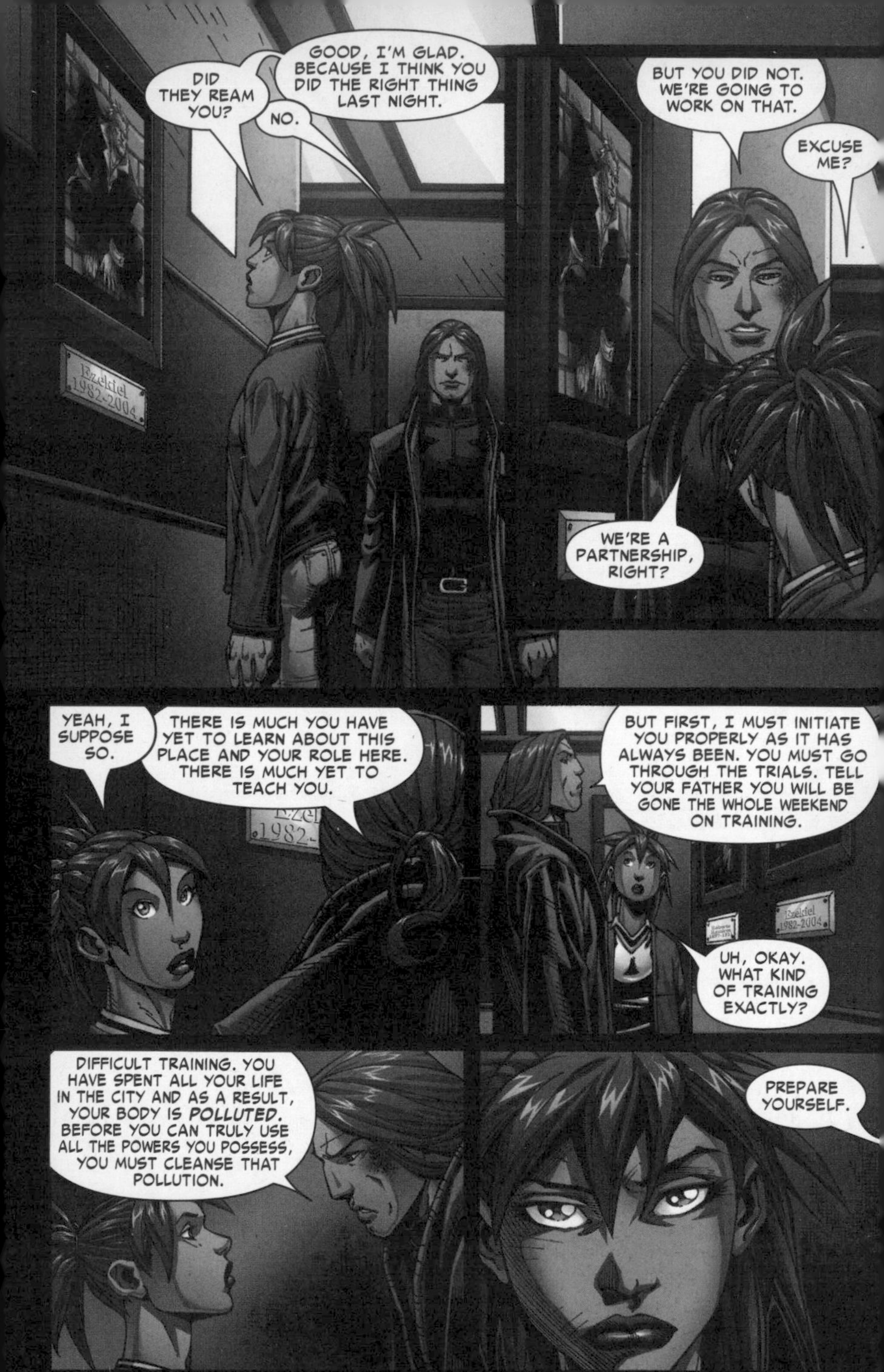
DID THEY REAM YOU?
NO.
GOOD, I'M GLAD. BECAUSE I THINK YOU DID THE RIGHT THING LAST NIGHT.
Ezekiel 1982-2004
BUT YOU DID NOT. WE'RE GOING TO WORK ON THAT.
EXCUSE ME?
WE'RE A PARTNERSHIP, RIGHT?
YEAH, I SUPPOSE SO.
THERE IS MUCH YOU HAVE YET TO LEARN ABOUT THIS PLACE AND YOUR ROLE HERE. THERE IS MUCH YET TO TEACH YOU.
BUT FIRST, I MUST INITIATE YOU PROPERLY AS IT HAS ALWAYS BEEN. YOU MUST GO THROUGH THE TRIALS. TELL YOUR FATHER YOU WILL BE GONE THE WHOLE WEEKEND ON TRAINING.
Ezekiel 1982-2004
UH, OKAY. WHAT KIND OF TRAINING EXACTLY?
DIFFICULT TRAINING. YOU HAVE SPENT ALL YOUR LIFE IN THE CITY AND AS A RESULT, YOUR BODY IS *POLLUTED.* BEFORE YOU CAN TRULY USE ALL THE POWERS YOU POSSESS, YOU MUST CLEANSE THAT POLLUTION.
PREPARE YOURSELF.

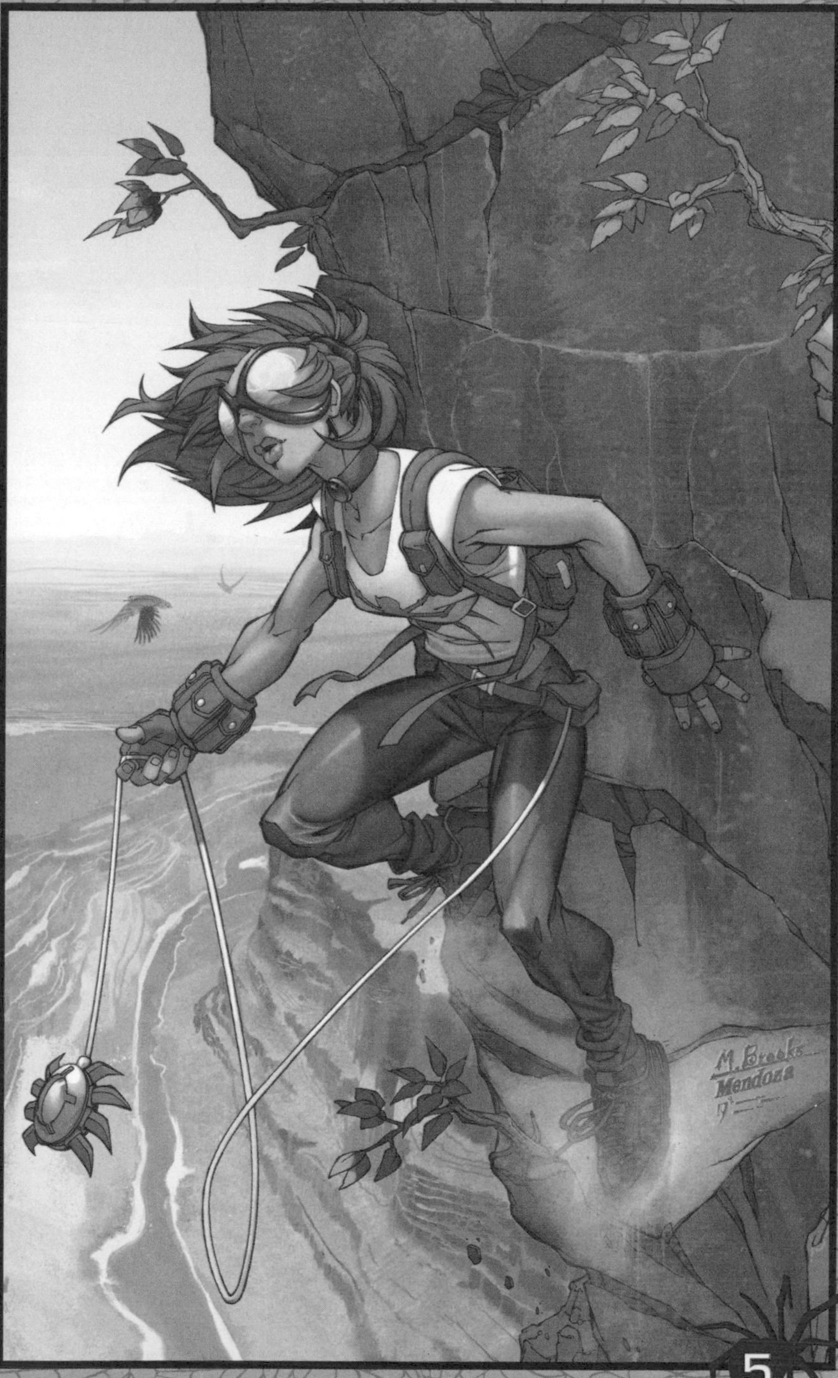
M. Brooks
Mendoza

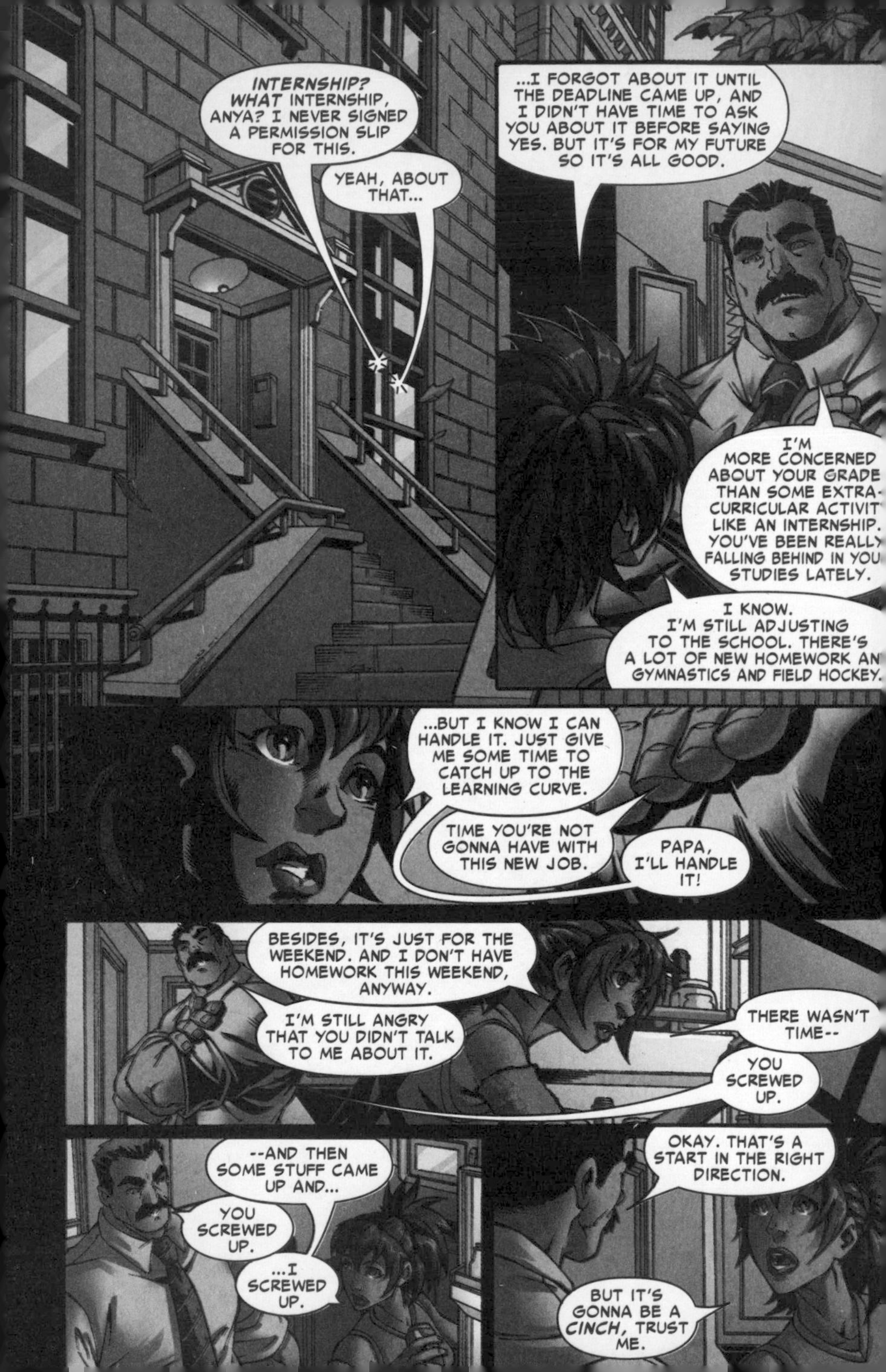
INTERNSHIP? WHAT INTERNSHIP, ANYA? I NEVER SIGNED A PERMISSION SLIP FOR THIS.
YEAH, ABOUT THAT...
...I FORGOT ABOUT IT UNTIL THE DEADLINE CAME UP, AND I DIDN'T HAVE TIME TO ASK YOU ABOUT IT BEFORE SAYING YES. BUT IT'S FOR MY FUTURE SO IT'S ALL GOOD.
I'M MORE CONCERNED ABOUT YOUR GRADE THAN SOME EXTRA-CURRICULAR ACTIVIT LIKE AN INTERNSHIP. YOU'VE BEEN REALLY FALLING BEHIND IN YOU STUDIES LATELY.
I KNOW. I'M STILL ADJUSTING TO THE SCHOOL. THERE'S A LOT OF NEW HOMEWORK AN GYMNASTICS AND FIELD HOCKEY.
...BUT I KNOW I CAN HANDLE IT. JUST GIVE ME SOME TIME TO CATCH UP TO THE LEARNING CURVE.
TIME YOU'RE NOT GONNA HAVE WITH THIS NEW JOB.
PAPA, I'LL HANDLE IT!
BESIDES, IT'S JUST FOR THE WEEKEND. AND I DON'T HAVE HOMEWORK THIS WEEKEND, ANYWAY.
I'M STILL ANGRY THAT YOU DIDN'T TALK TO ME ABOUT IT.
THERE WASN'T TIME--
YOU SCREWED UP.
--AND THEN SOME STUFF CAME UP AND...
YOU SCREWED UP.
...I SCREWED UP.
OKAY. THAT'S A START IN THE RIGHT DIRECTION.
BUT IT'S GONNA BE A CINCH, TRUST ME.

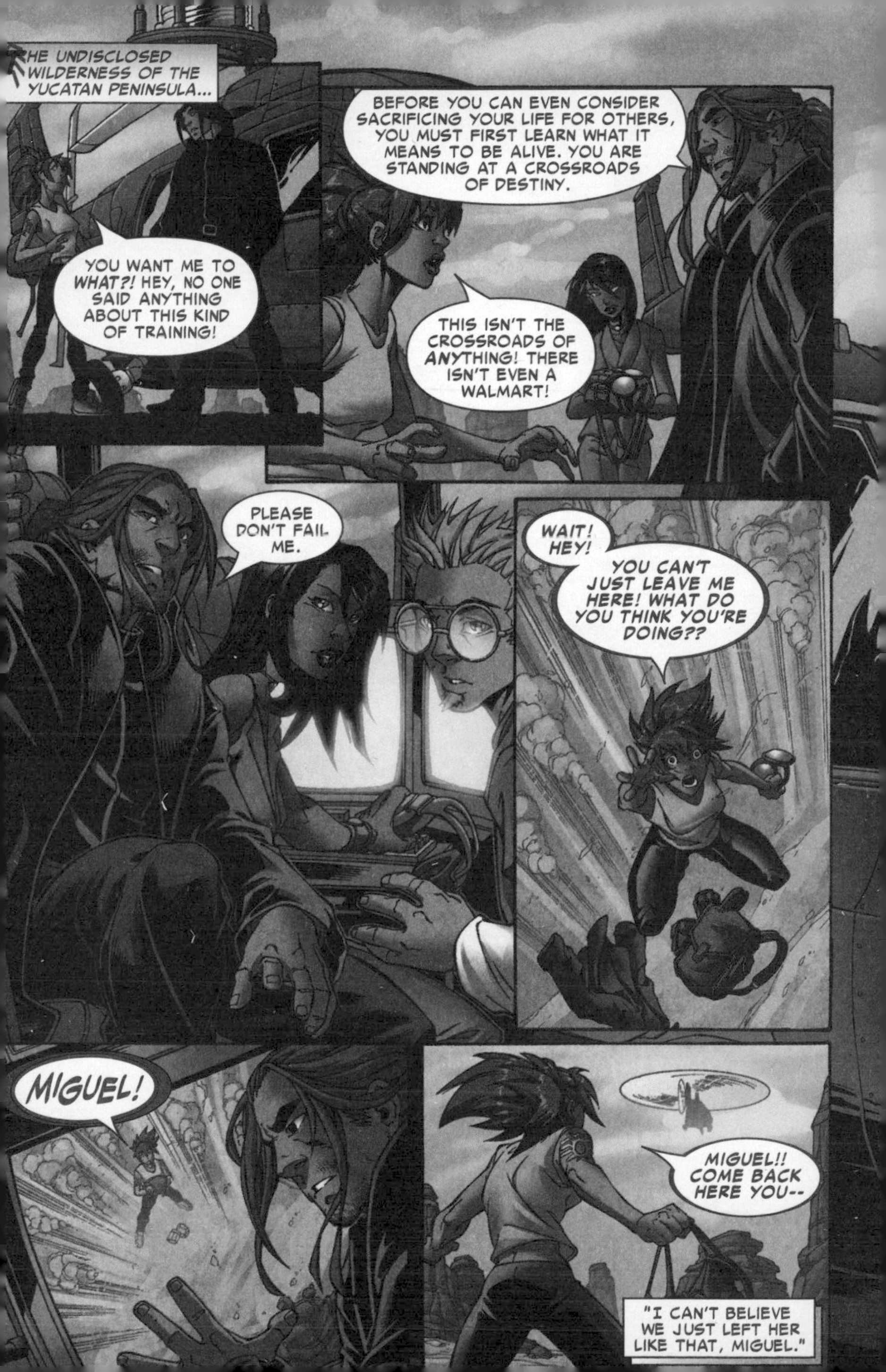
THE UNDISCLOSED WILDERNESS OF THE YUCATAN PENINSULA...
YOU WANT ME TO WHAT?! HEY, NO ONE SAID ANYTHING ABOUT THIS KIND OF TRAINING!
BEFORE YOU CAN EVEN CONSIDER SACRIFICING YOUR LIFE FOR OTHERS, YOU MUST FIRST LEARN WHAT IT MEANS TO BE ALIVE. YOU ARE STANDING AT A CROSSROADS OF DESTINY.
THIS ISN'T THE CROSSROADS OF ANYTHING! THERE ISN'T EVEN A WALMART!
PLEASE DON'T FAIL ME.
WAIT! HEY!
YOU CAN'T JUST LEAVE ME HERE! WHAT DO YOU THINK YOU'RE DOING??
MIGUEL!
MIGUEL!! COME BACK HERE YOU--
"I CAN'T BELIEVE WE JUST LEFT HER LIKE THAT, MIGUEL."

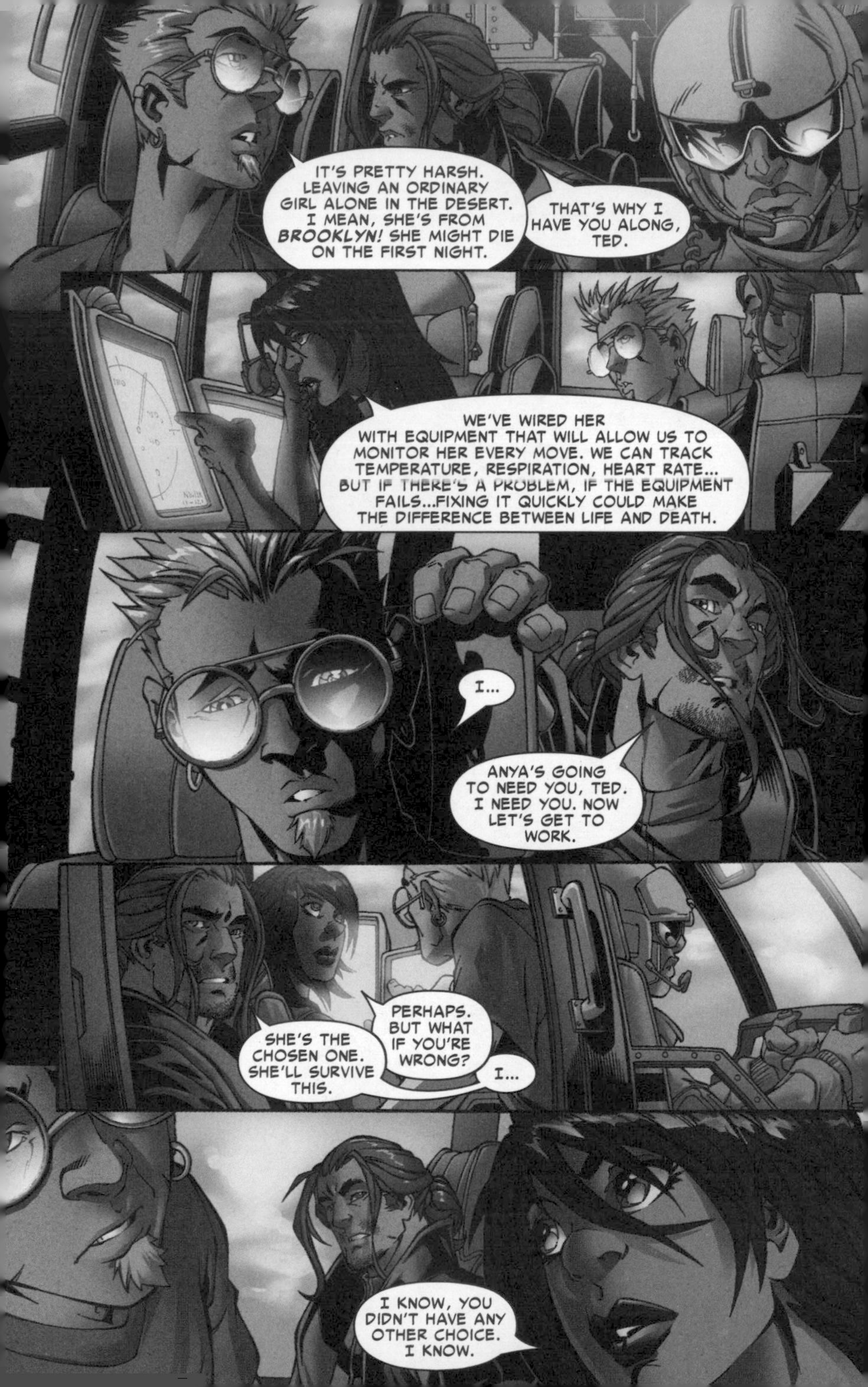
IT'S PRETTY HARSH. LEAVING AN ORDINARY GIRL ALONE IN THE DESERT. I MEAN, SHE'S FROM BROOKLYN! SHE MIGHT DIE ON THE FIRST NIGHT.
THAT'S WHY I HAVE YOU ALONG, TED.
WE'VE WIRED HER WITH EQUIPMENT THAT WILL ALLOW US TO MONITOR HER EVERY MOVE. WE CAN TRACK TEMPERATURE, RESPIRATION, HEART RATE... BUT IF THERE'S A PROBLEM, IF THE EQUIPMENT FAILS...FIXING IT QUICKLY COULD MAKE THE DIFFERENCE BETWEEN LIFE AND DEATH.
I...
ANYA'S GOING TO NEED YOU, TED. I NEED YOU. NOW LET'S GET TO WORK.
SHE'S THE CHOSEN ONE. SHE'LL SURVIVE THIS.
PERHAPS. BUT WHAT IF YOU'RE WRONG?
I...
I KNOW, YOU DIDN'T HAVE ANY OTHER CHOICE. I KNOW.

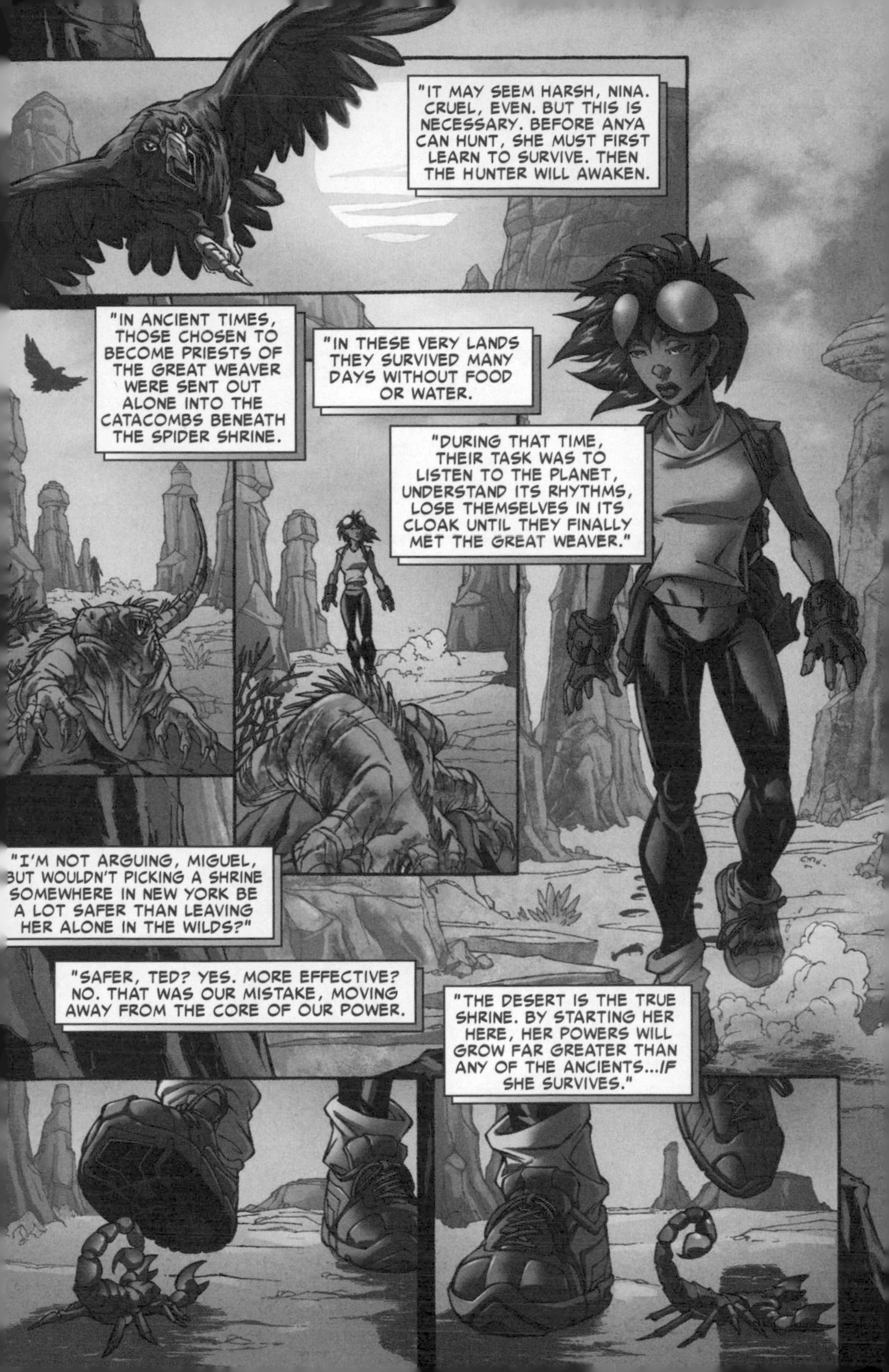
"IT MAY SEEM HARSH, NINA. CRUEL, EVEN. BUT THIS IS NECESSARY. BEFORE ANYA CAN HUNT, SHE MUST FIRST LEARN TO SURVIVE. THEN THE HUNTER WILL AWAKEN.
"IN ANCIENT TIMES, THOSE CHOSEN TO BECOME PRIESTS OF THE GREAT WEAVER WERE SENT OUT ALONE INTO THE CATACOMBS BENEATH THE SPIDER SHRINE.
"IN THESE VERY LANDS THEY SURVIVED MANY DAYS WITHOUT FOOD OR WATER.
"DURING THAT TIME, THEIR TASK WAS TO LISTEN TO THE PLANET, UNDERSTAND ITS RHYTHMS, LOSE THEMSELVES IN ITS CLOAK UNTIL THEY FINALLY MET THE GREAT WEAVER."
"I'M NOT ARGUING, MIGUEL, BUT WOULDN'T PICKING A SHRINE SOMEWHERE IN NEW YORK BE A LOT SAFER THAN LEAVING HER ALONE IN THE WILDS?"
"SAFER, TED? YES. MORE EFFECTIVE? NO. THAT WAS OUR MISTAKE, MOVING AWAY FROM THE CORE OF OUR POWER.
"THE DESERT IS THE TRUE SHRINE. BY STARTING HER HERE, HER POWERS WILL GROW FAR GREATER THAN ANY OF THE ANCIENTS...*IF* SHE SURVIVES."

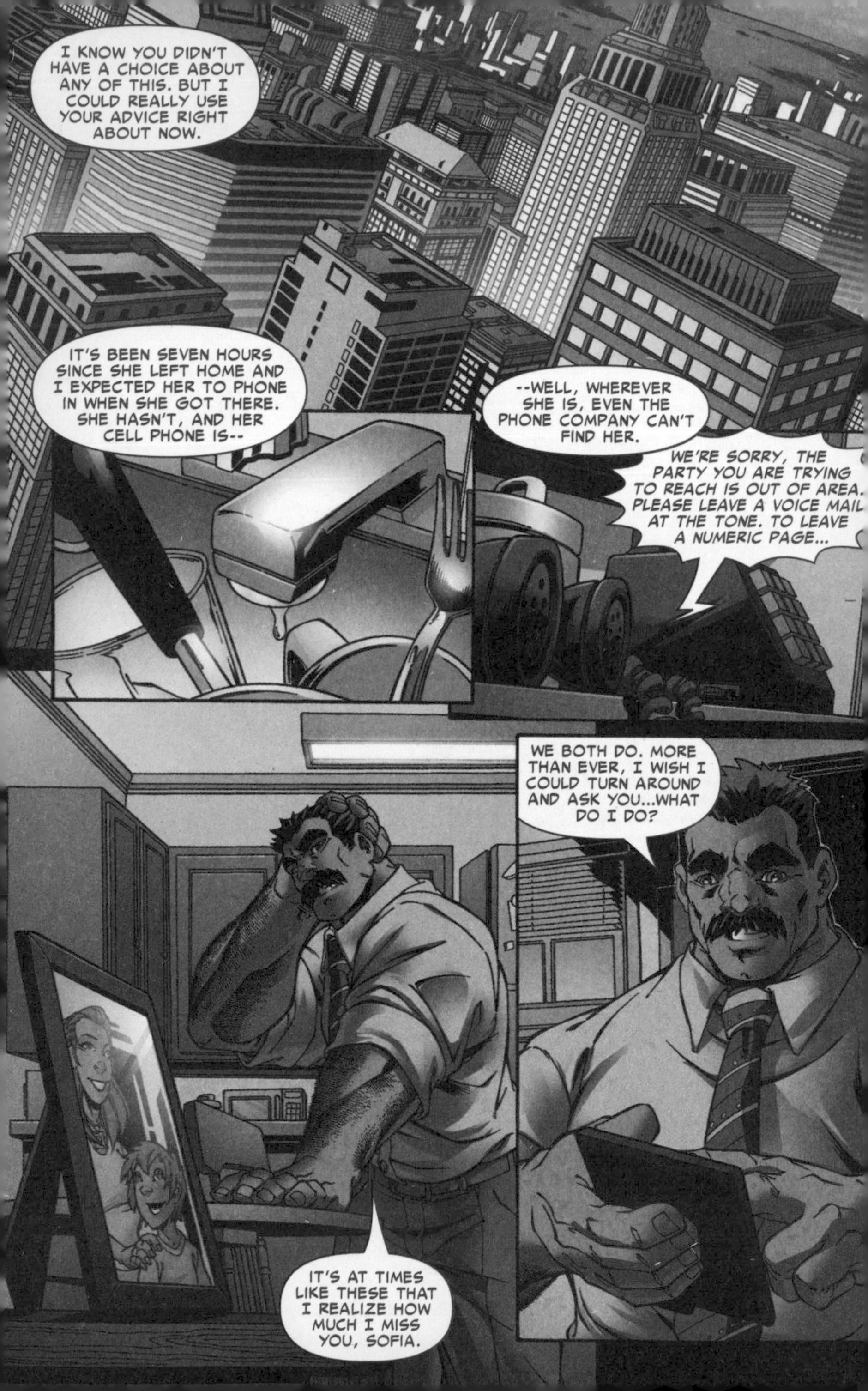
I KNOW YOU DIDN'T HAVE A CHOICE ABOUT ANY OF THIS. BUT I COULD REALLY USE YOUR ADVICE RIGHT ABOUT NOW.
IT'S BEEN SEVEN HOURS SINCE SHE LEFT HOME AND I EXPECTED HER TO PHONE IN WHEN SHE GOT THERE. SHE HASN'T, AND HER CELL PHONE IS--
--WELL, WHEREVER SHE IS, EVEN THE PHONE COMPANY CAN'T FIND HER.
WE'RE SORRY, THE PARTY YOU ARE TRYING TO REACH IS OUT OF AREA. PLEASE LEAVE A VOICE MAIL AT THE TONE. TO LEAVE A NUMERIC PAGE...
IT'S AT TIMES LIKE THESE THAT I REALIZE HOW MUCH I MISS YOU, SOFIA.
WE BOTH DO. MORE THAN EVER, I WISH I COULD TURN AROUND AND ASK YOU...WHAT DO I DO?

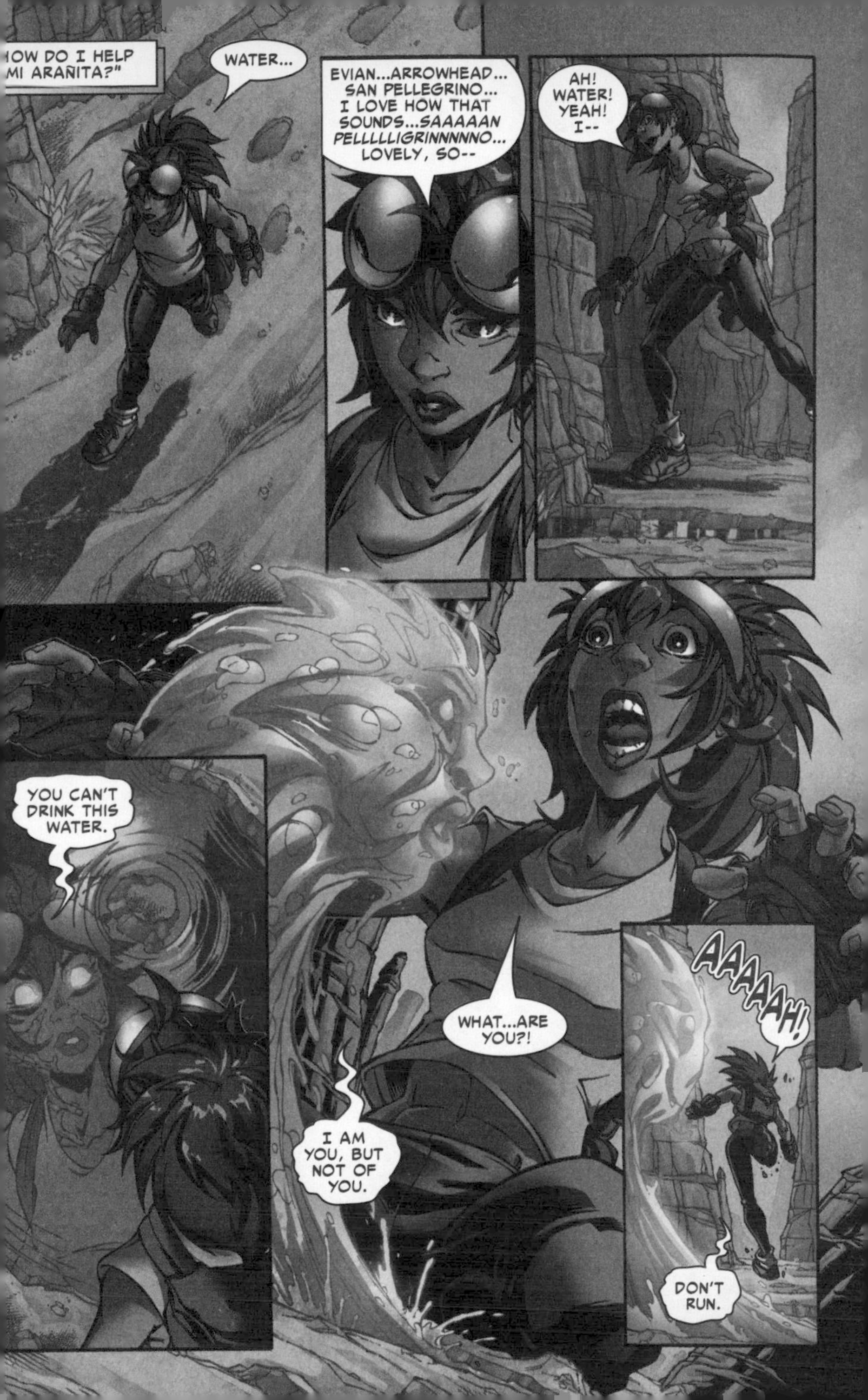
HOW DO I HELP MI ARAÑITA?"
WATER...
EVIAN...ARROWHEAD... SAN PELLEGRINO... I LOVE HOW THAT SOUNDS...SAAAAAN PELLLLLIGRINNNNNO... LOVELY, SO--
AH! WATER! YEAH! I--
YOU CAN'T DRINK THIS WATER.
WHAT...ARE YOU?!
I AM YOU, BUT NOT OF YOU.
AAAAAAH!
DON'T RUN.

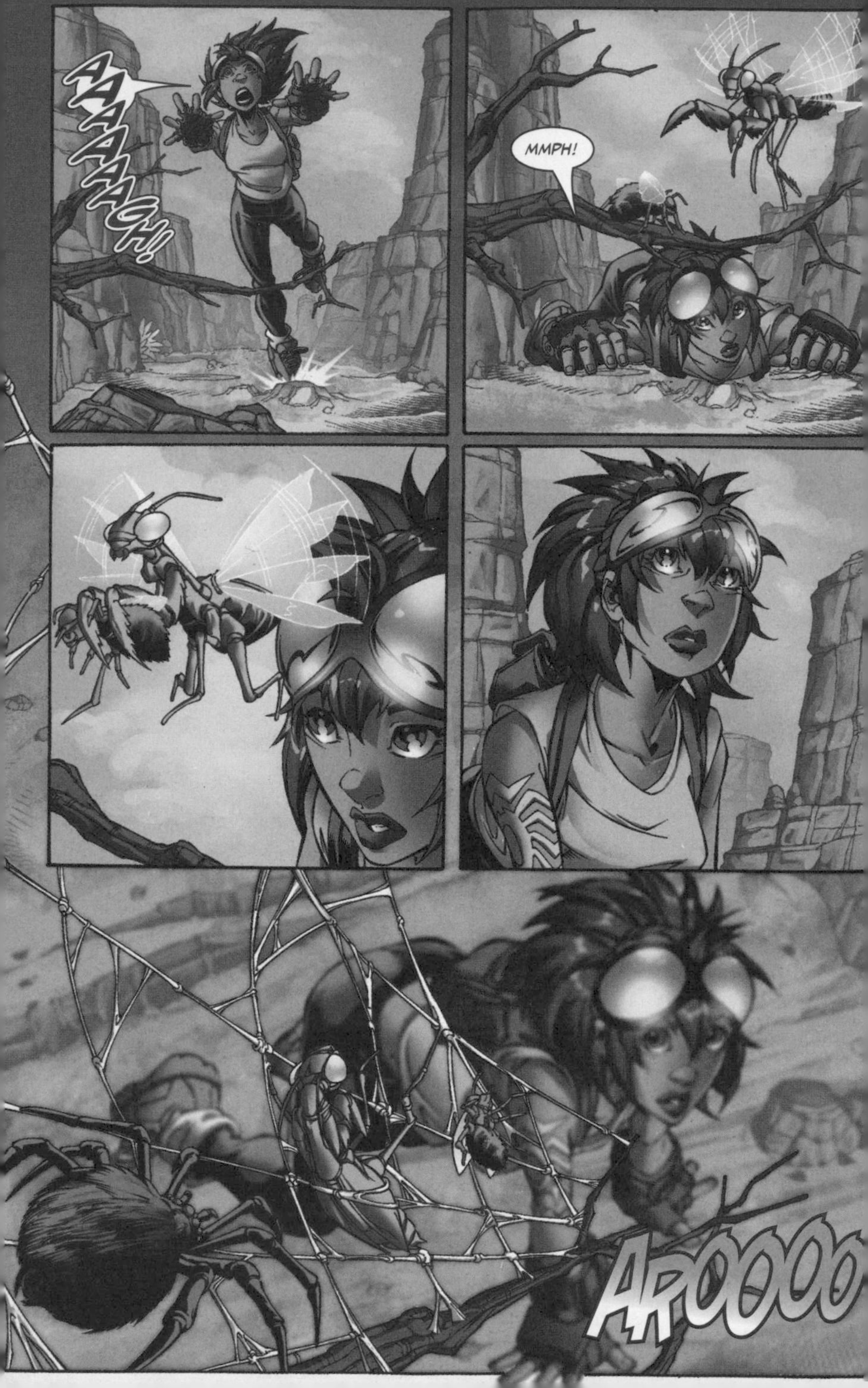
AAAAAAGH!
MMPH!
AROOOO

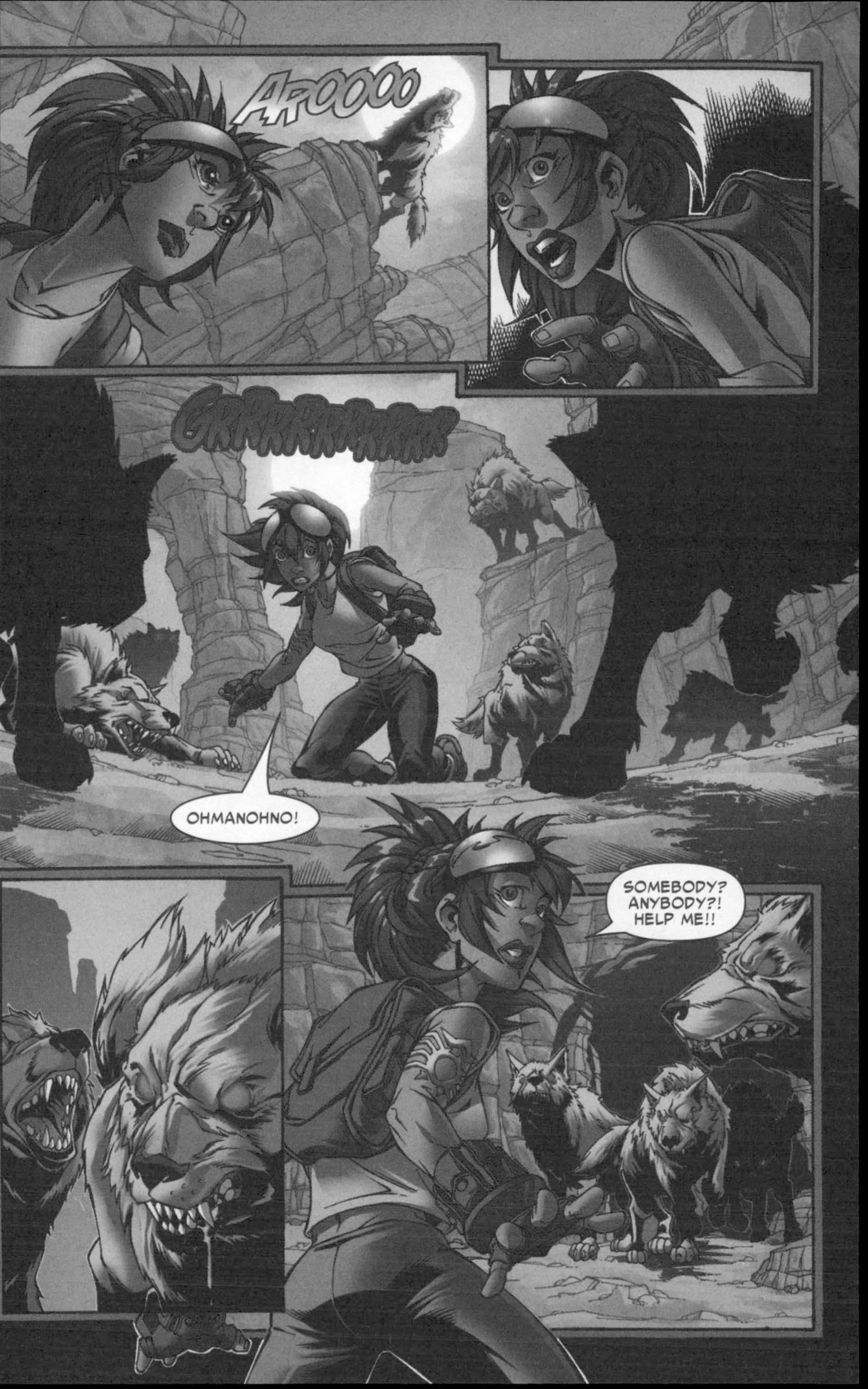
AROOOO
GRRRRRRRRRRR
OHMANOHNO!
SOMEBODY? ANYBODY?! HELP ME!!

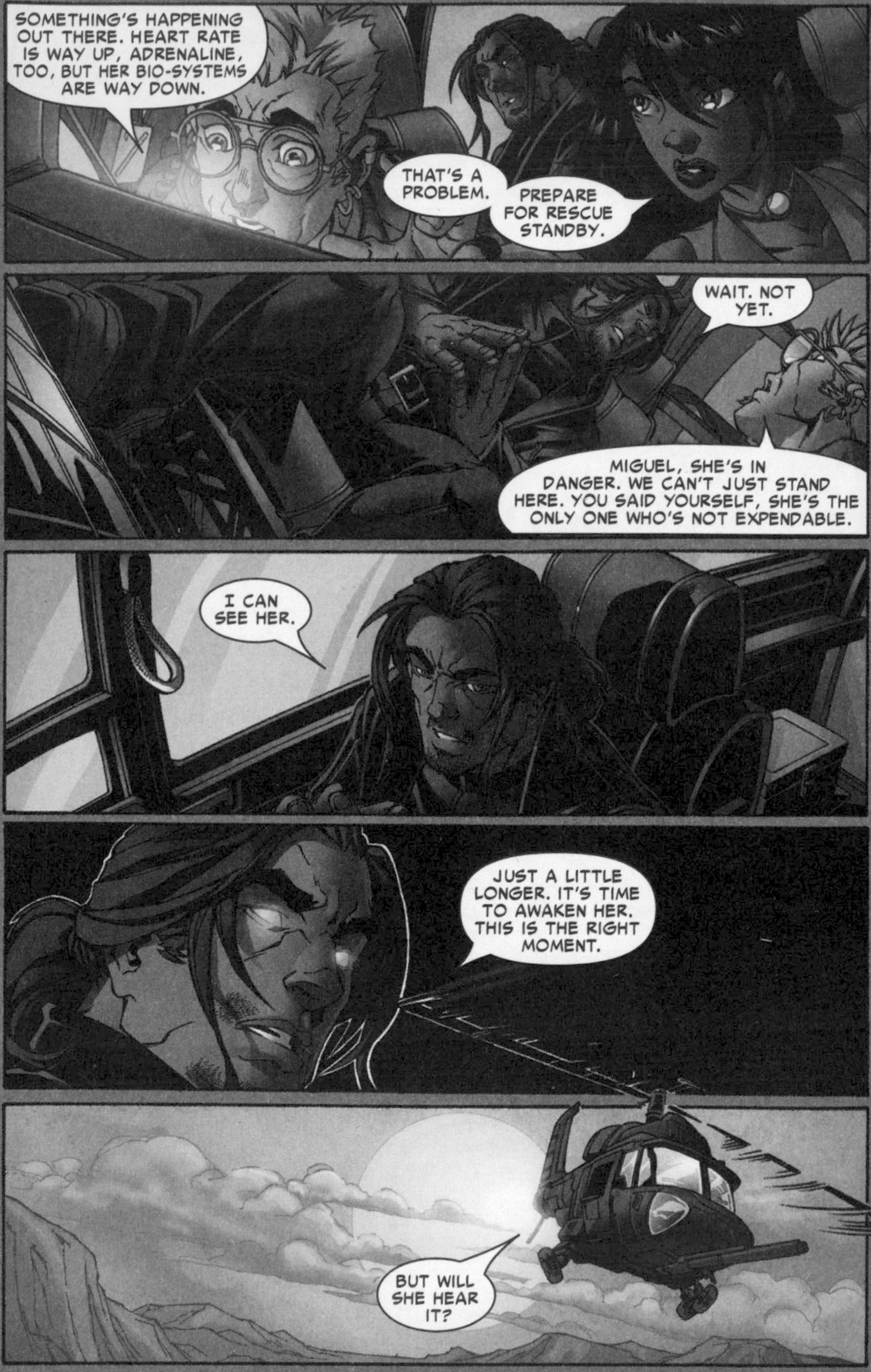
SOMETHING'S HAPPENING OUT THERE. HEART RATE IS WAY UP, ADRENALINE, TOO, BUT HER BIO-SYSTEMS ARE WAY DOWN.
THAT'S A PROBLEM.
PREPARE FOR RESCUE STANDBY.
WAIT. NOT YET.
MIGUEL, SHE'S IN DANGER. WE CAN'T JUST STAND HERE. YOU SAID YOURSELF, SHE'S THE ONLY ONE WHO'S NOT EXPENDABLE.
I CAN SEE HER.
JUST A LITTLE LONGER. IT'S TIME TO AWAKEN HER. THIS IS THE RIGHT MOMENT.
BUT WILL SHE HEAR IT?

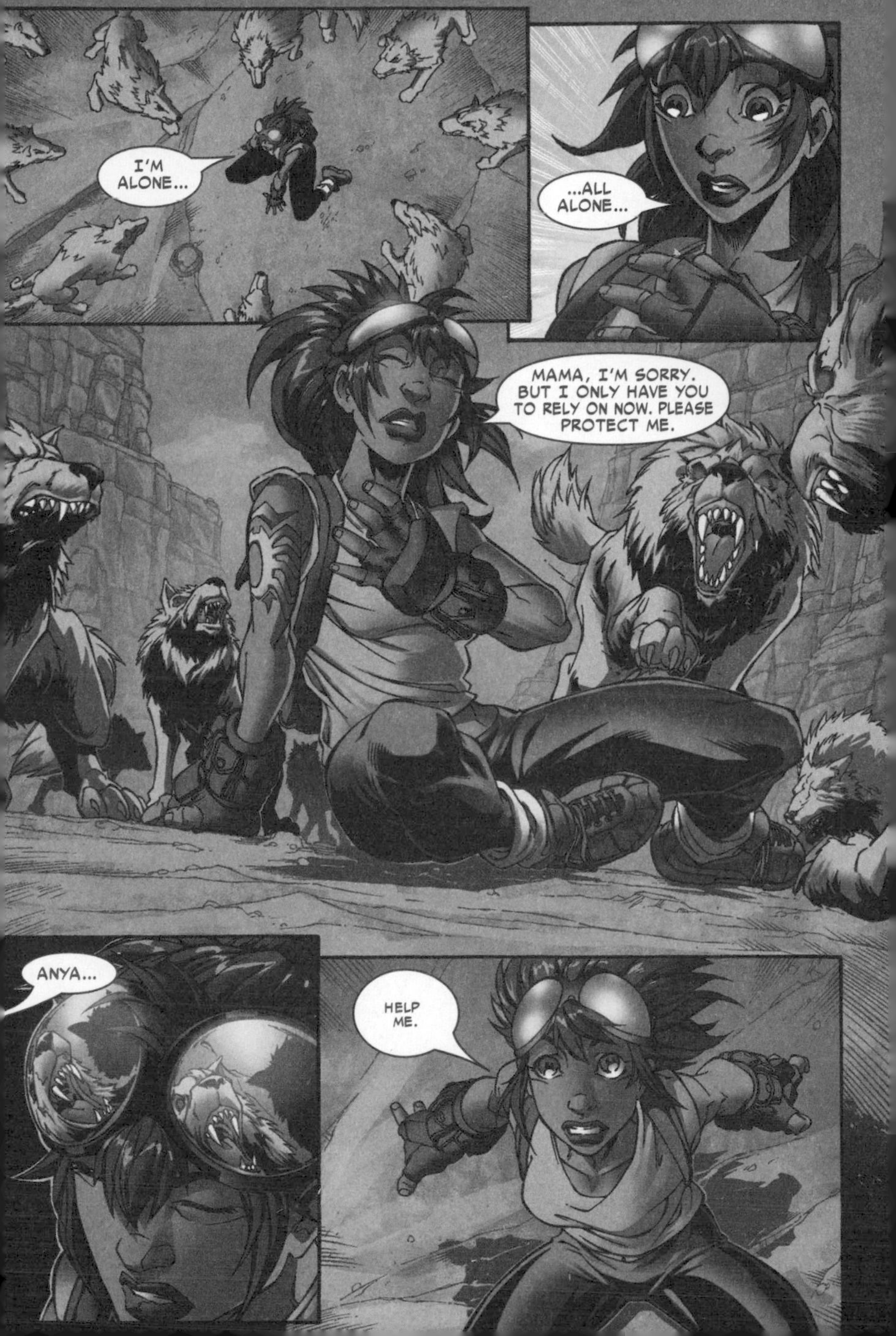
I'M ALONE...
...ALL ALONE...
MAMA, I'M SORRY. BUT I ONLY HAVE YOU TO RELY ON NOW. PLEASE PROTECT ME.
ANYA...
HELP ME.

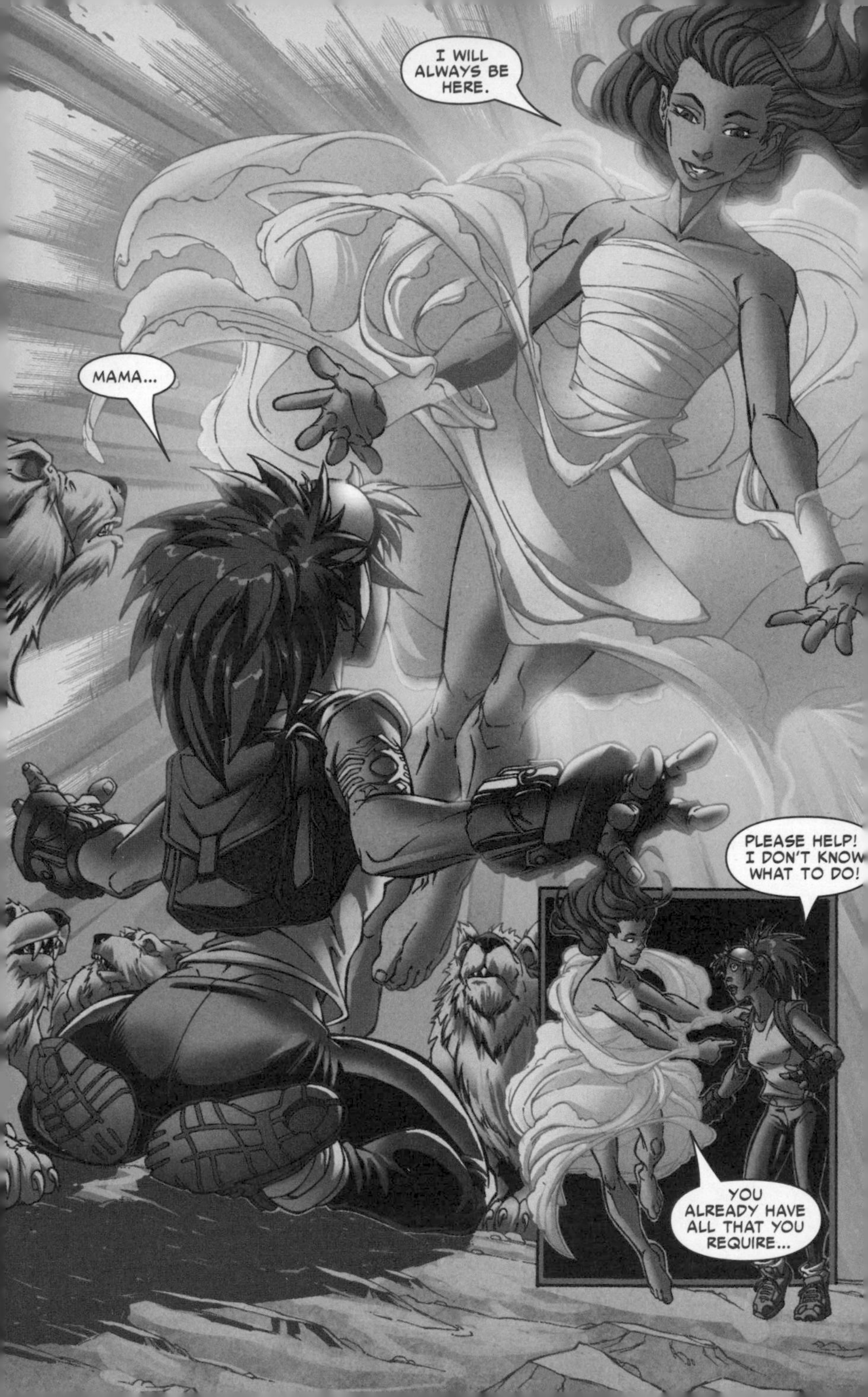
I WILL ALWAYS BE HERE.
MAMA...
PLEASE HELP! I DON'T KNOW WHAT TO DO!
YOU ALREADY HAVE ALL THAT YOU REQUIRE...

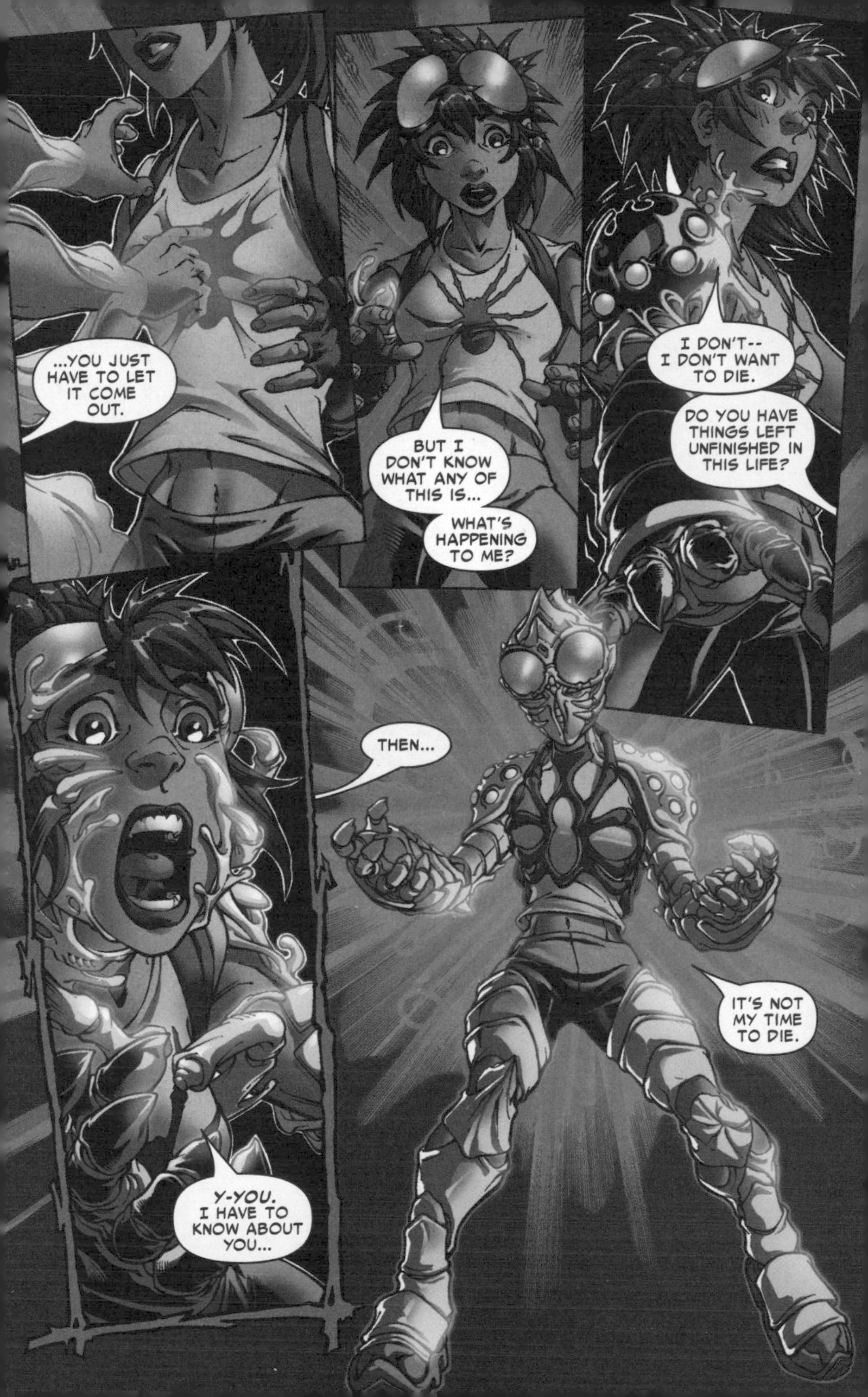

...YOU JUST HAVE TO LET IT COME OUT.
BUT I DON'T KNOW WHAT ANY OF THIS IS...
WHAT'S HAPPENING TO ME?
I DON'T-- I DON'T WANT TO DIE.
DO YOU HAVE THINGS LEFT UNFINISHED IN THIS LIFE?
Y-YOU. I HAVE TO KNOW ABOUT YOU...
THEN...
IT'S NOT MY TIME TO DIE.

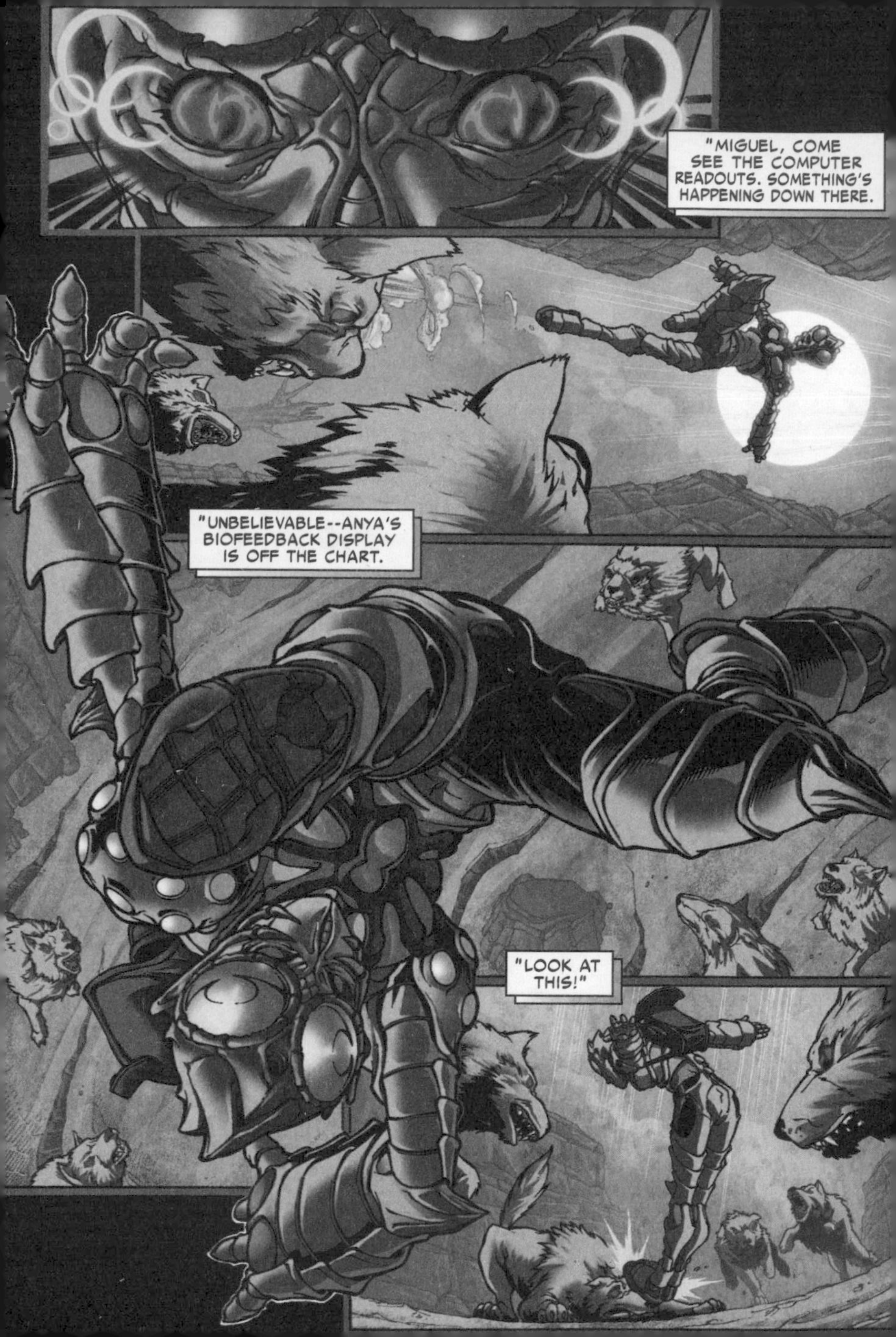
"MIGUEL, COME SEE THE COMPUTER READOUTS. SOMETHING'S HAPPENING DOWN THERE.
"UNBELIEVABLE--ANYA'S BIOFEEDBACK DISPLAY IS OFF THE CHART.
"LOOK AT THIS!"

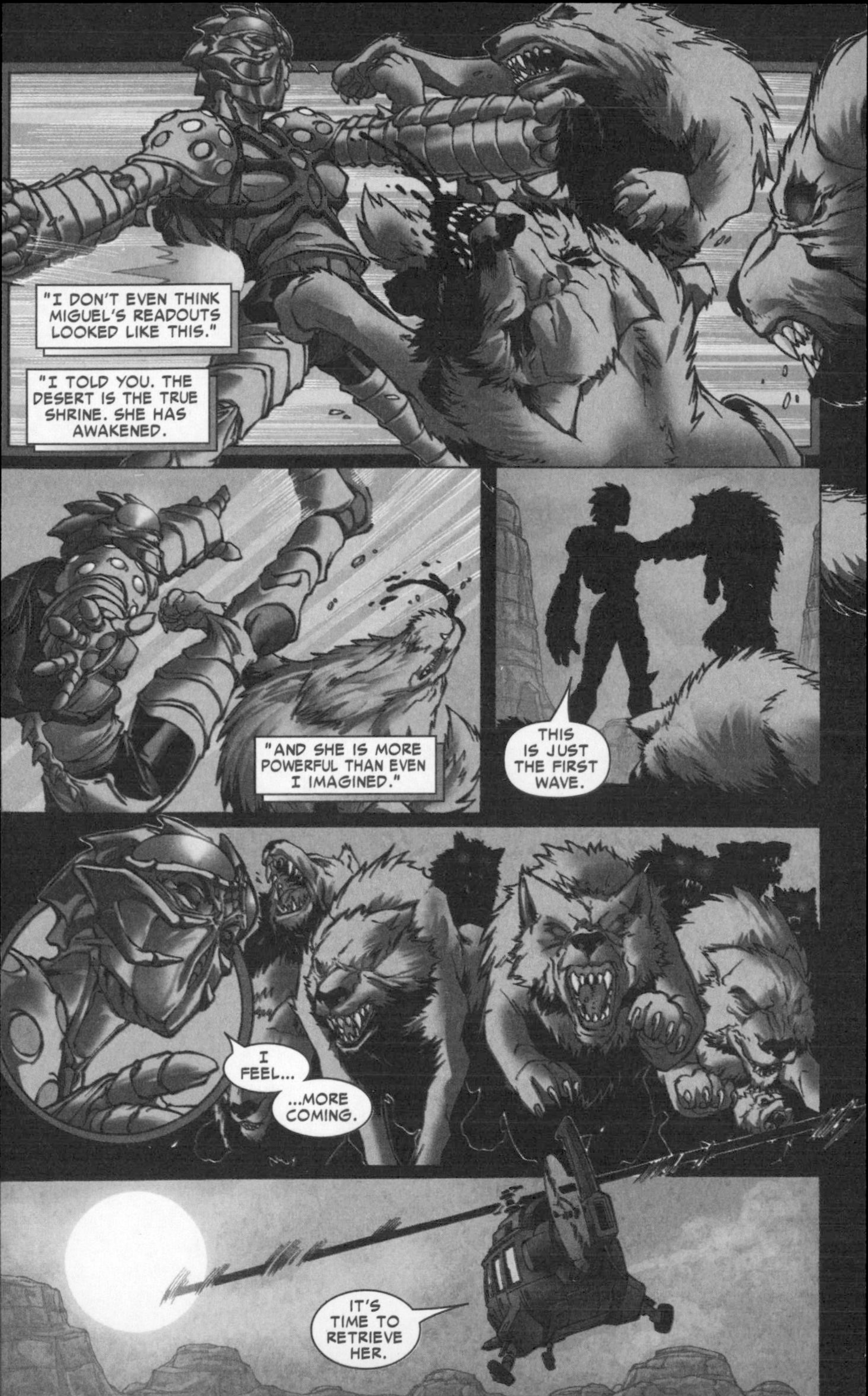
"I DON'T EVEN THINK MIGUEL'S READOUTS LOOKED LIKE THIS."
"I TOLD YOU. THE DESERT IS THE TRUE SHRINE. SHE HAS AWAKENED.
"AND SHE IS MORE POWERFUL THAN EVEN I IMAGINED."
THIS IS JUST THE FIRST WAVE.
I FEEL...
...MORE COMING.
IT'S TIME TO RETRIEVE HER.

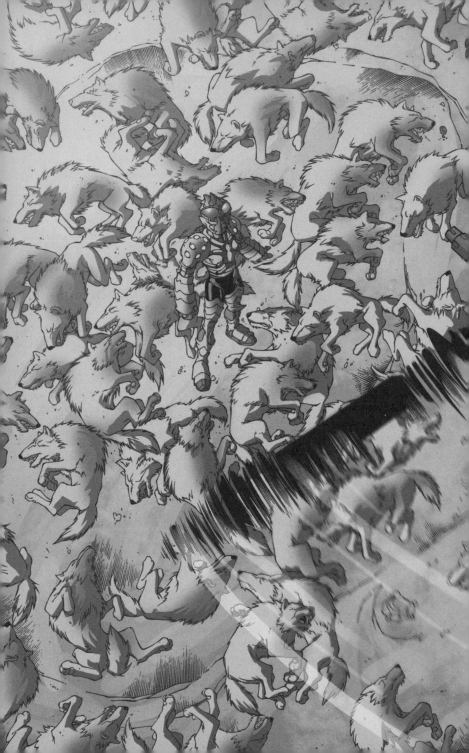

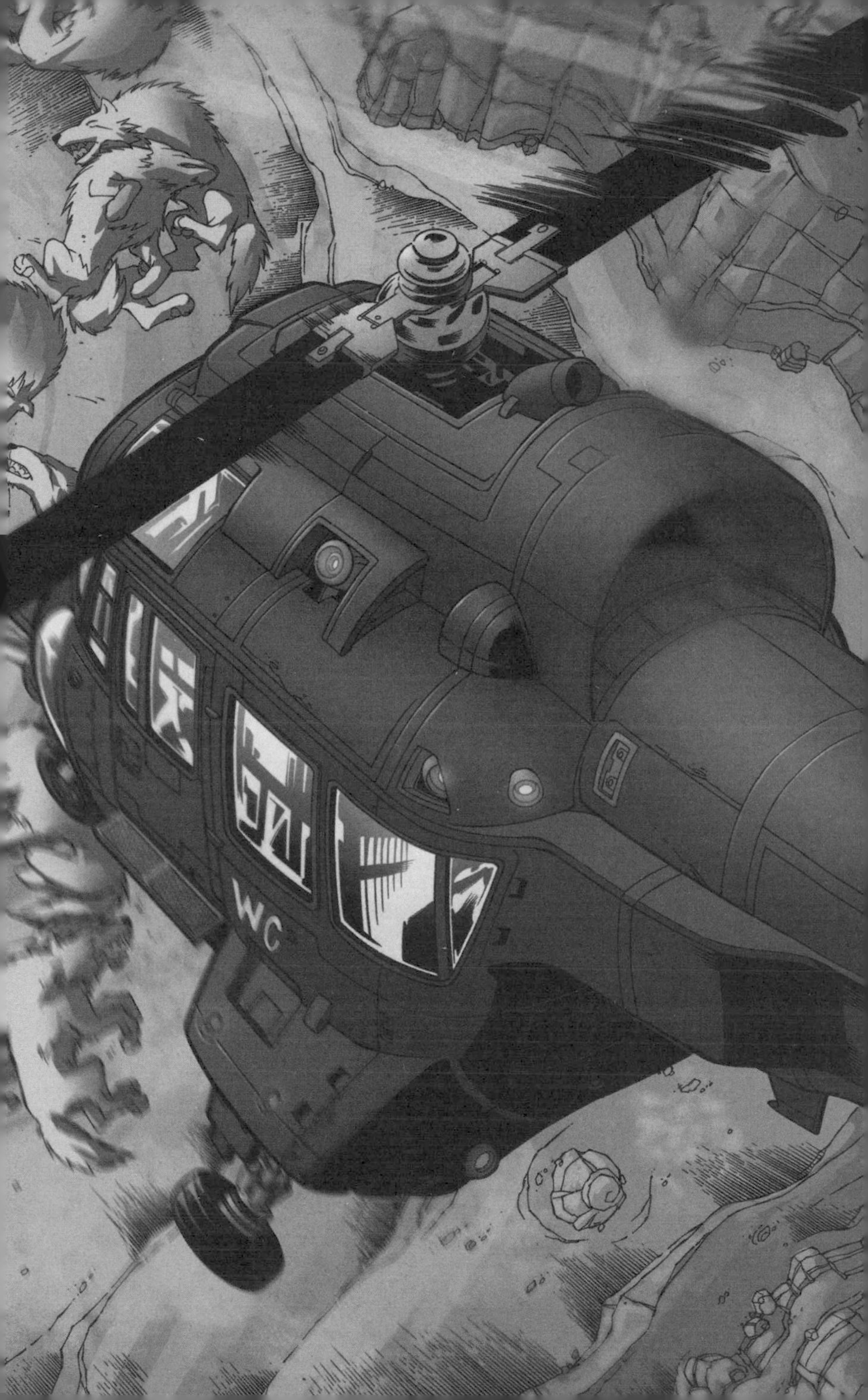
WC

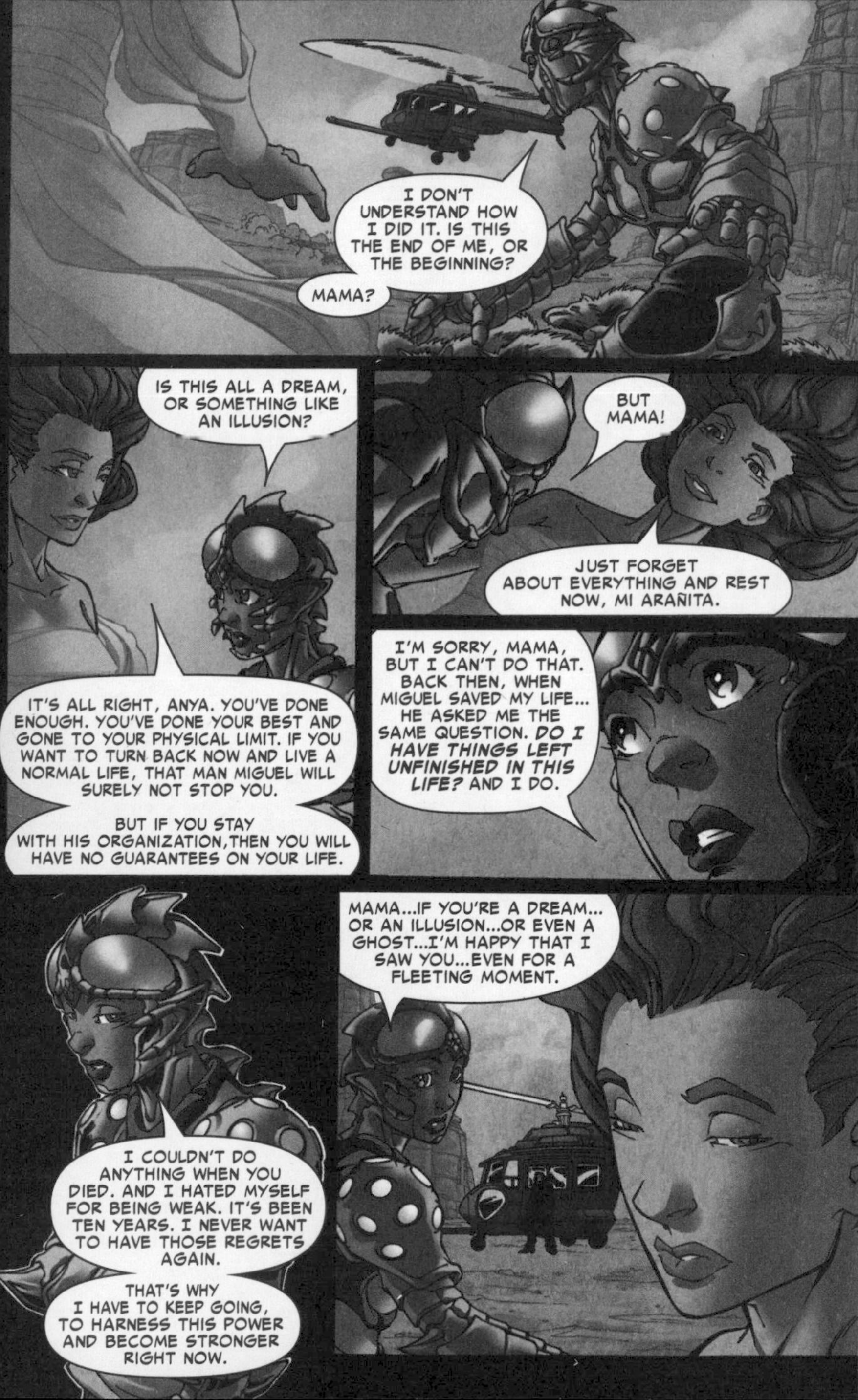

I DON'T UNDERSTAND HOW I DID IT. IS THIS THE END OF ME, OR THE BEGINNING?
MAMA?
IS THIS ALL A DREAM, OR SOMETHING LIKE AN ILLUSION?
IT'S ALL RIGHT, ANYA. YOU'VE DONE ENOUGH. YOU'VE DONE YOUR BEST AND GONE TO YOUR PHYSICAL LIMIT. IF YOU WANT TO TURN BACK NOW AND LIVE A NORMAL LIFE, THAT MAN MIGUEL WILL SURELY NOT STOP YOU.
BUT IF YOU STAY WITH HIS ORGANIZATION,THEN YOU WILL HAVE NO GUARANTEES ON YOUR LIFE.
BUT MAMA!
JUST FORGET ABOUT EVERYTHING AND REST NOW, MI ARAÑITA.
I'M SORRY, MAMA, BUT I CAN'T DO THAT. BACK THEN, WHEN MIGUEL SAVED MY LIFE... HE ASKED ME THE SAME QUESTION. *DO I HAVE THINGS LEFT UNFINISHED IN THIS LIFE?* AND I DO.
I COULDN'T DO ANYTHING WHEN YOU DIED. AND I HATED MYSELF FOR BEING WEAK. IT'S BEEN TEN YEARS. I NEVER WANT TO HAVE THOSE REGRETS AGAIN.
THAT'S WHY I HAVE TO KEEP GOING, TO HARNESS THIS POWER AND BECOME STRONGER RIGHT NOW.
MAMA...IF YOU'RE A DREAM... OR AN ILLUSION...OR EVEN A GHOST...I'M HAPPY THAT I SAW YOU...EVEN FOR A FLEETING MOMENT.

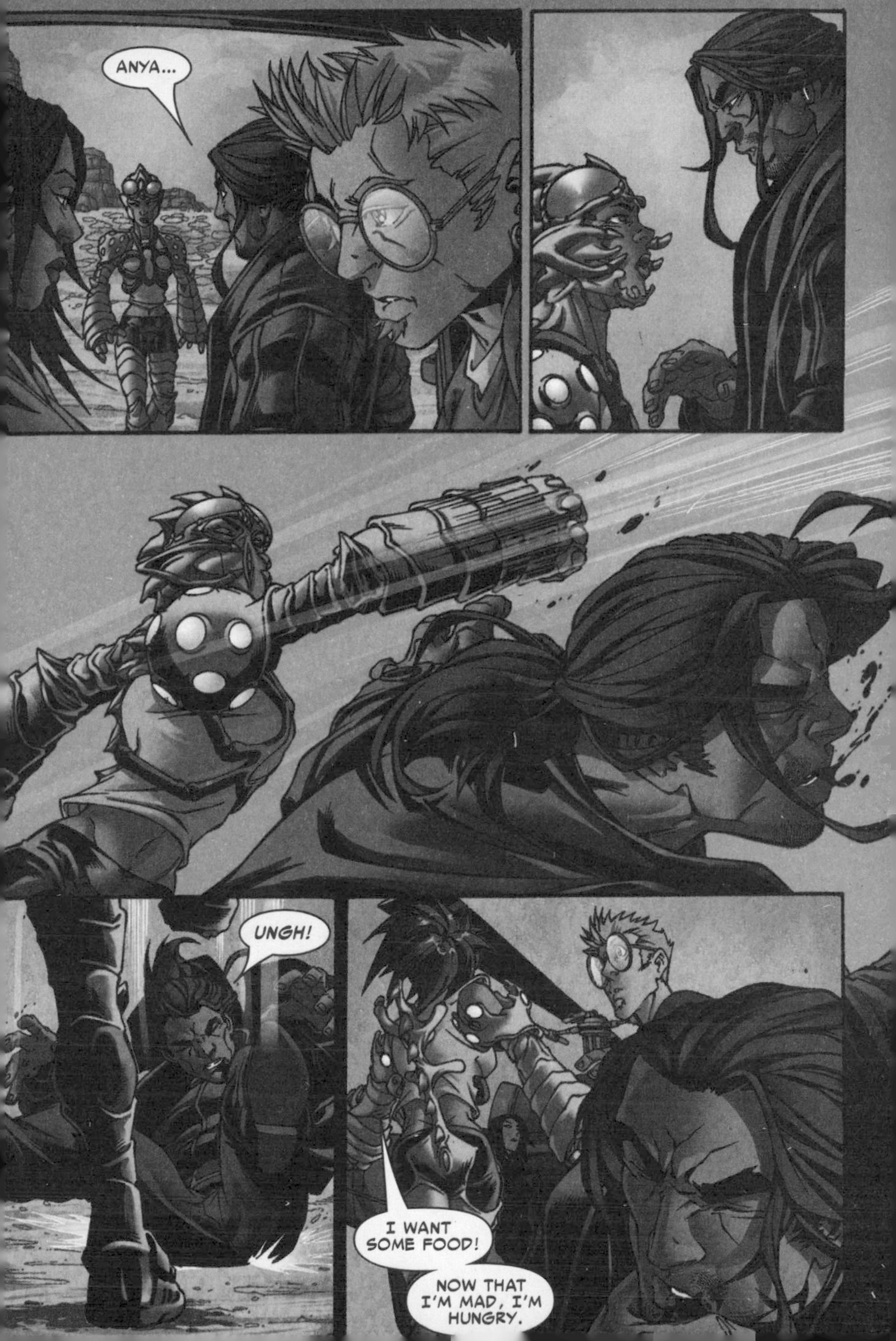
ANYA...
UNGH!
I WANT SOME FOOD!
NOW THAT I'M MAD, I'M HUNGRY.

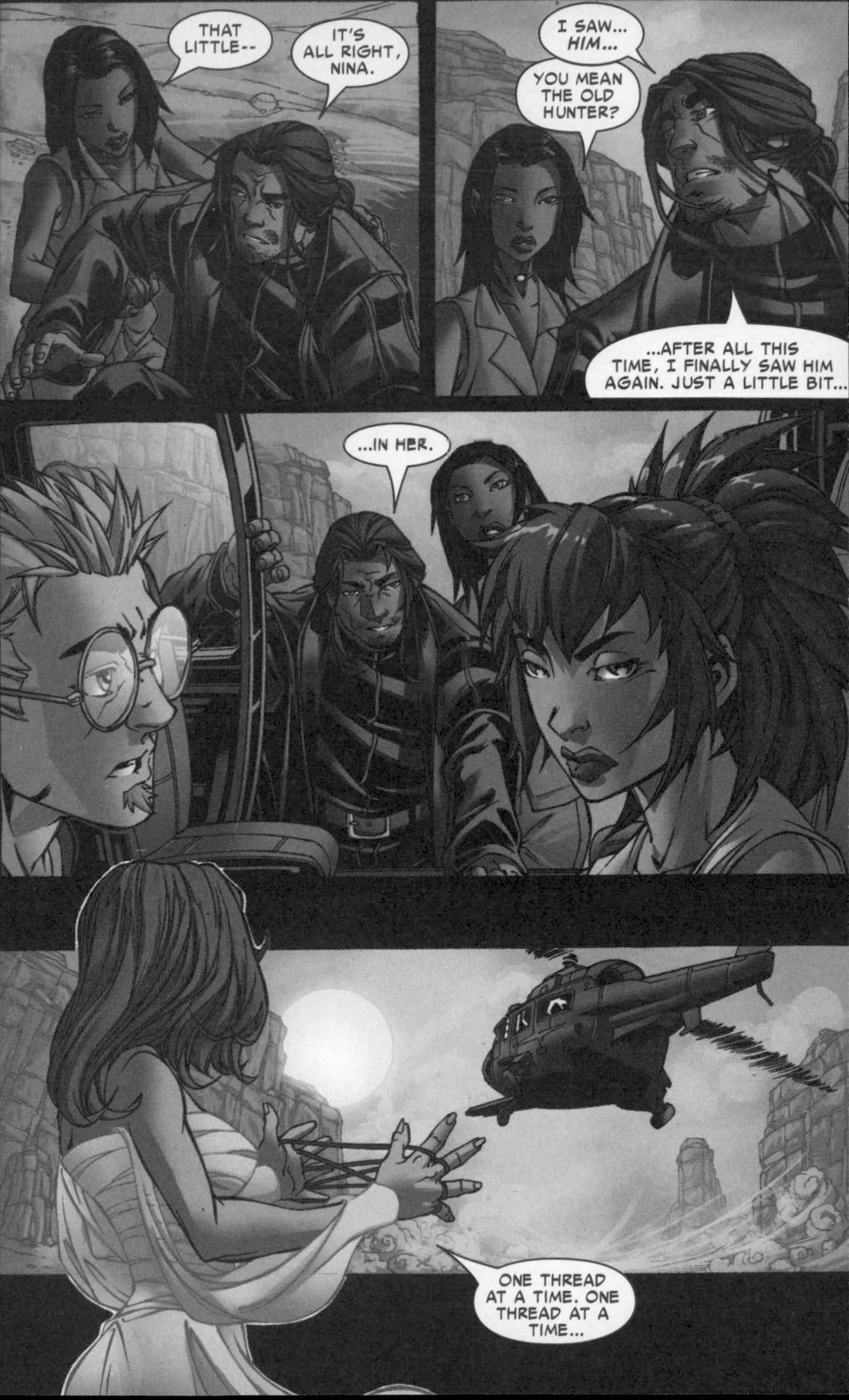
THAT LITTLE--
IT'S ALL RIGHT, NINA.
I SAW... HIM...
YOU MEAN THE OLD HUNTER?
...AFTER ALL THIS TIME, I FINALLY SAW HIM AGAIN. JUST A LITTLE BIT...
...IN HER.
ONE THREAD AT A TIME. ONE THREAD AT A TIME...

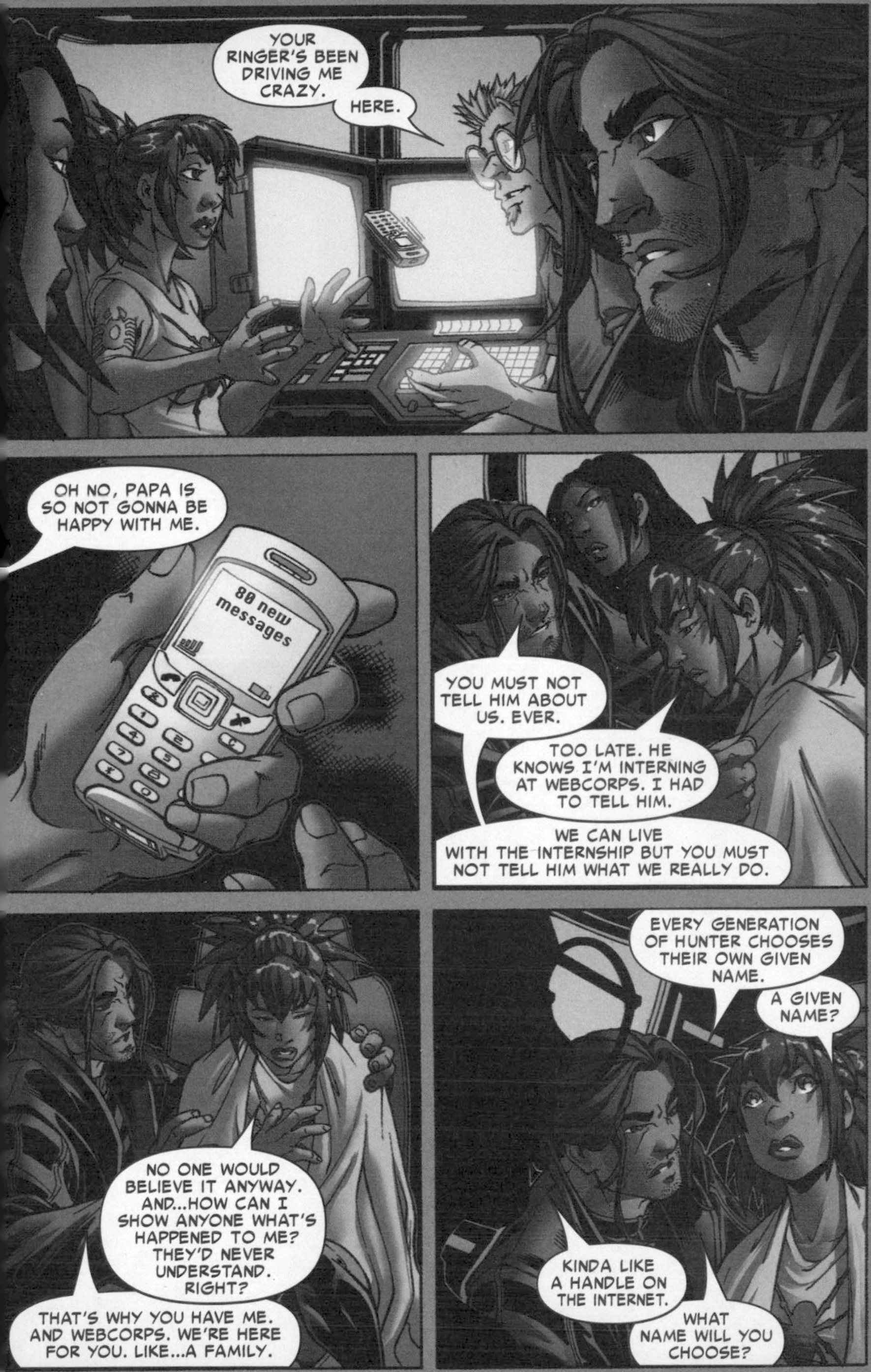
YOUR RINGER'S BEEN DRIVING ME CRAZY.
HERE.
OH NO, PAPA IS SO NOT GONNA BE HAPPY WITH ME.
80 new messages
YOU MUST NOT TELL HIM ABOUT US. EVER.
TOO LATE. HE KNOWS I'M INTERNING AT WEBCORPS. I HAD TO TELL HIM.
WE CAN LIVE WITH THE INTERNSHIP BUT YOU MUST NOT TELL HIM WHAT WE REALLY DO.
NO ONE WOULD BELIEVE IT ANYWAY. AND...HOW CAN I SHOW ANYONE WHAT'S HAPPENED TO ME? THEY'D NEVER UNDERSTAND. RIGHT?
THAT'S WHY YOU HAVE ME. AND WEBCORPS. WE'RE HERE FOR YOU. LIKE...A FAMILY.
EVERY GENERATION OF HUNTER CHOOSES THEIR OWN GIVEN NAME.
A GIVEN NAME?
KINDA LIKE A HANDLE ON THE INTERNET.
WHAT NAME WILL YOU CHOOSE?

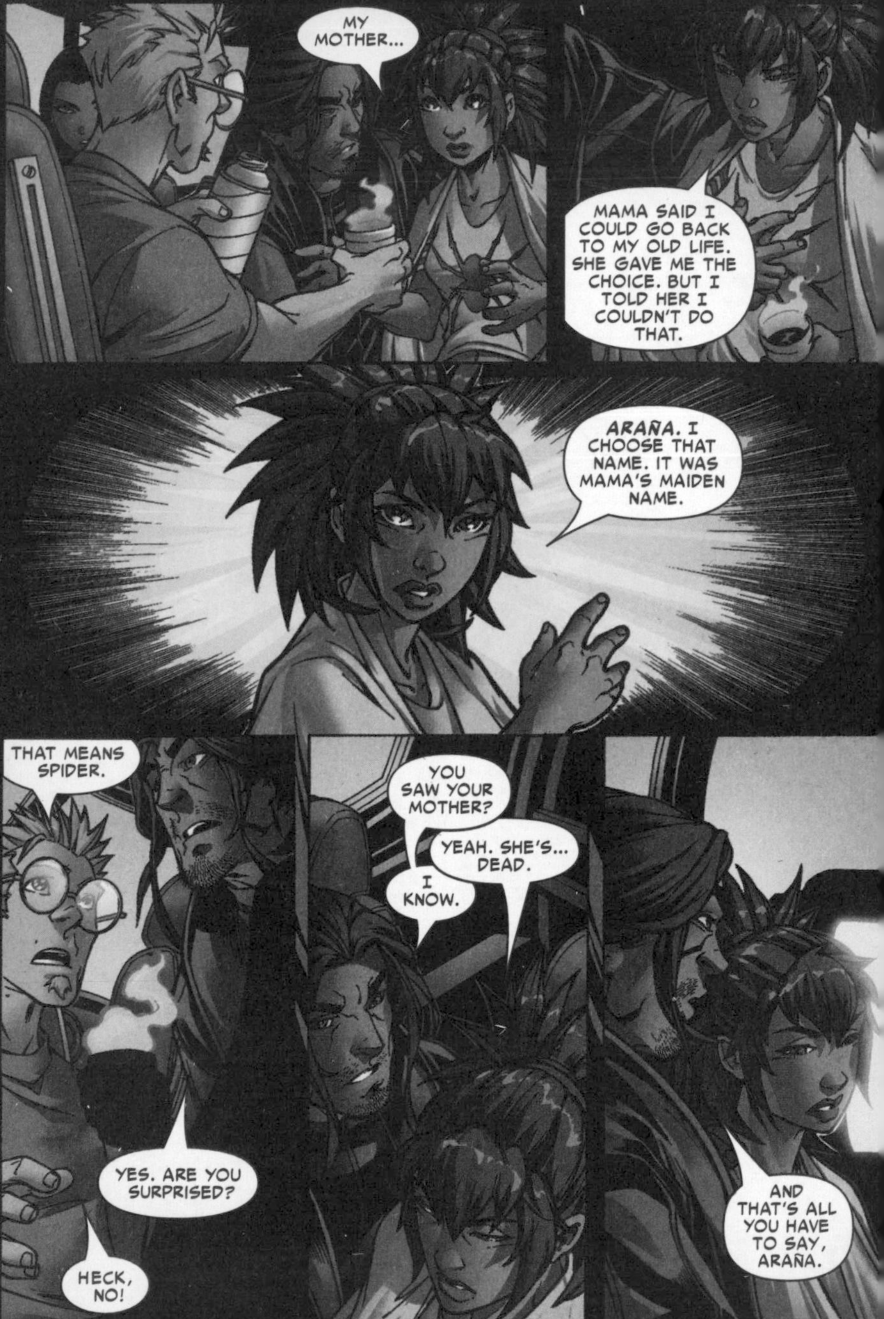
MY MOTHER...
MAMA SAID I COULD GO BACK TO MY OLD LIFE. SHE GAVE ME THE CHOICE. BUT I TOLD HER I COULDN'T DO THAT.
ARAÑA. I CHOOSE THAT NAME. IT WAS MAMA'S MAIDEN NAME.
THAT MEANS SPIDER.
YES. ARE YOU SURPRISED?
HECK, NO!
YOU SAW YOUR MOTHER?
YEAH. SHE'S... DEAD.
I KNOW.
AND THAT'S ALL YOU HAVE TO SAY, ARAÑA.

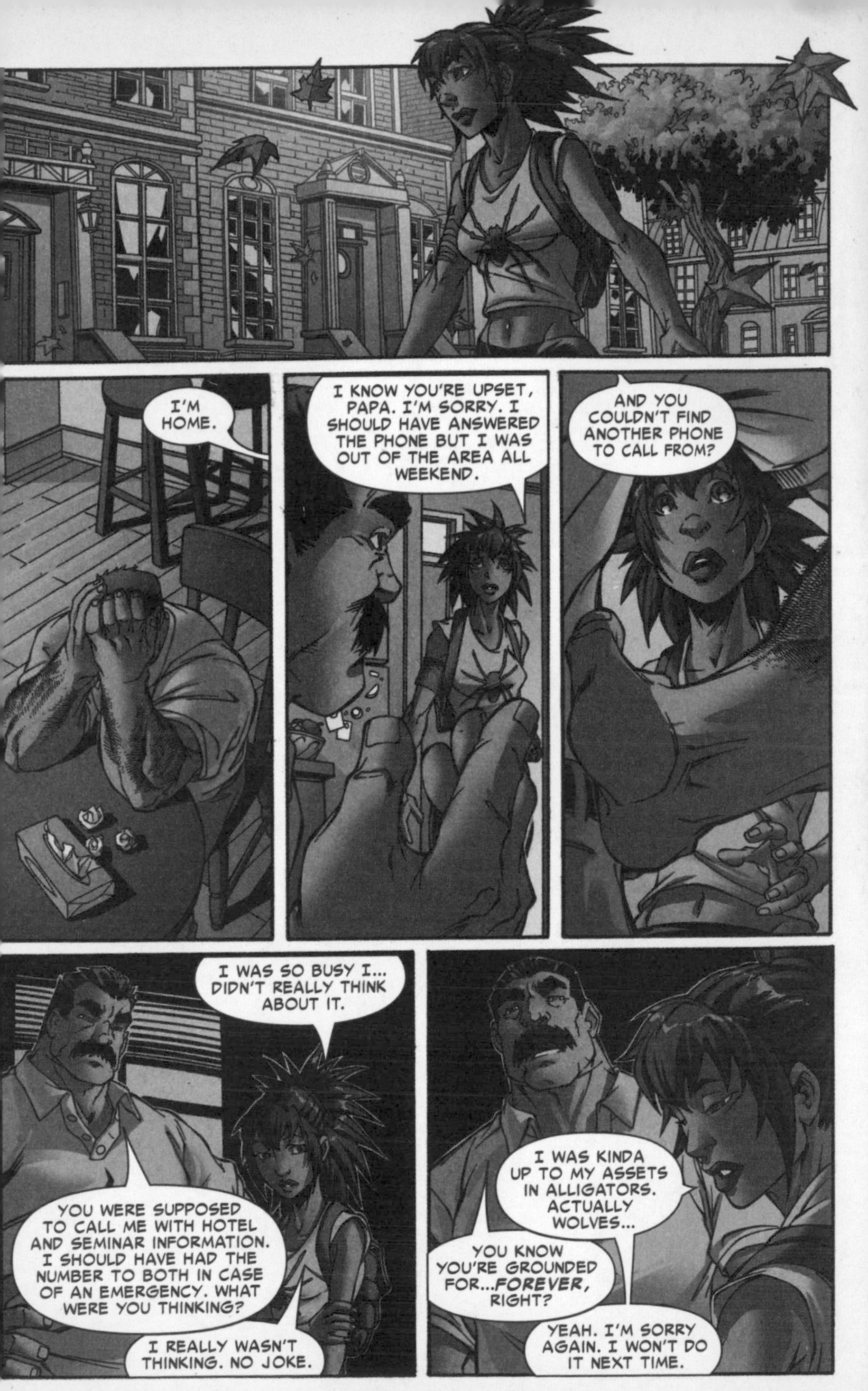
I'M HOME.
I KNOW YOU'RE UPSET, PAPA. I'M SORRY. I SHOULD HAVE ANSWERED THE PHONE BUT I WAS OUT OF THE AREA ALL WEEKEND.
AND YOU COULDN'T FIND ANOTHER PHONE TO CALL FROM?
I WAS SO BUSY I... DIDN'T REALLY THINK ABOUT IT.
YOU WERE SUPPOSED TO CALL ME WITH HOTEL AND SEMINAR INFORMATION. I SHOULD HAVE HAD THE NUMBER TO BOTH IN CASE OF AN EMERGENCY. WHAT WERE YOU THINKING?
I REALLY WASN'T THINKING. NO JOKE.
I WAS KINDA UP TO MY ASSETS IN ALLIGATORS. ACTUALLY WOLVES...
YOU KNOW YOU'RE GROUNDED FOR...*FOREVER*, RIGHT?
YEAH. I'M SORRY AGAIN. I WON'T DO IT NEXT TIME.

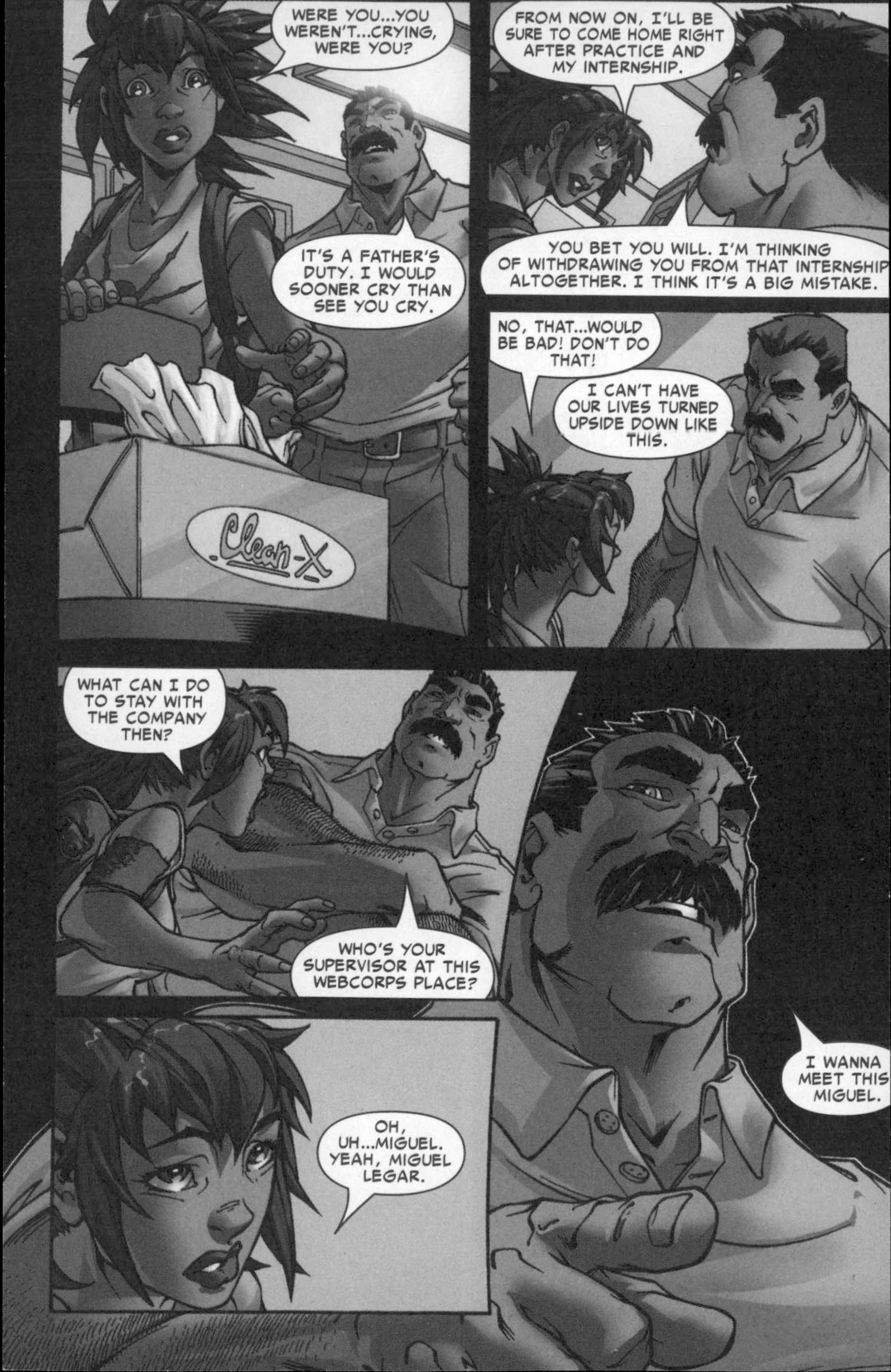
WERE YOU...YOU WEREN'T...CRYING, WERE YOU?
IT'S A FATHER'S DUTY. I WOULD SOONER CRY THAN SEE YOU CRY.
Clean-X
FROM NOW ON, I'LL BE SURE TO COME HOME RIGHT AFTER PRACTICE AND MY INTERNSHIP.
YOU BET YOU WILL. I'M THINKING OF WITHDRAWING YOU FROM THAT INTERNSHIP ALTOGETHER. I THINK IT'S A BIG MISTAKE.
NO, THAT...WOULD BE BAD! DON'T DO THAT!
I CAN'T HAVE OUR LIVES TURNED UPSIDE DOWN LIKE THIS.
WHAT CAN I DO TO STAY WITH THE COMPANY THEN?
WHO'S YOUR SUPERVISOR AT THIS WEBCORPS PLACE?
OH, UH...MIGUEL. YEAH, MIGUEL LEGAR.
I WANNA MEET THIS MIGUEL.

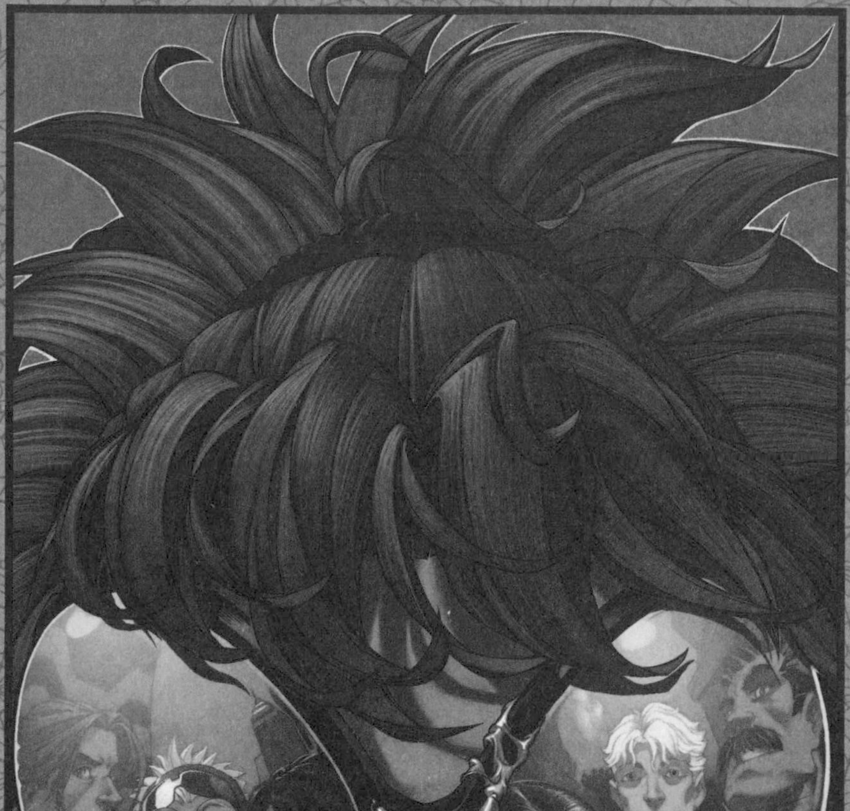
M. Brooks
MENDOZA
6

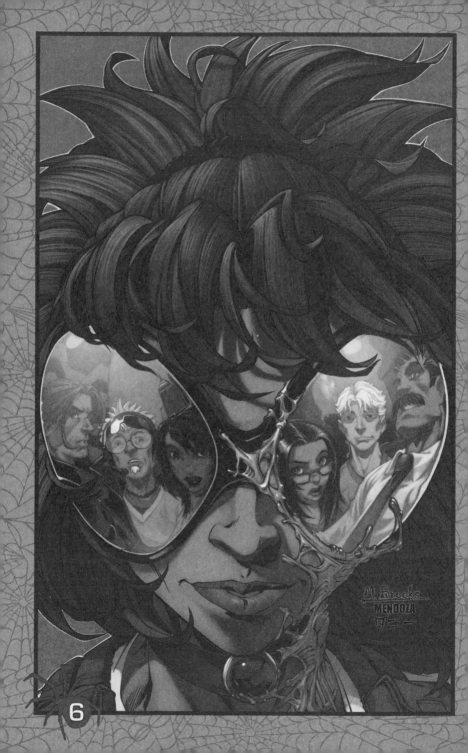

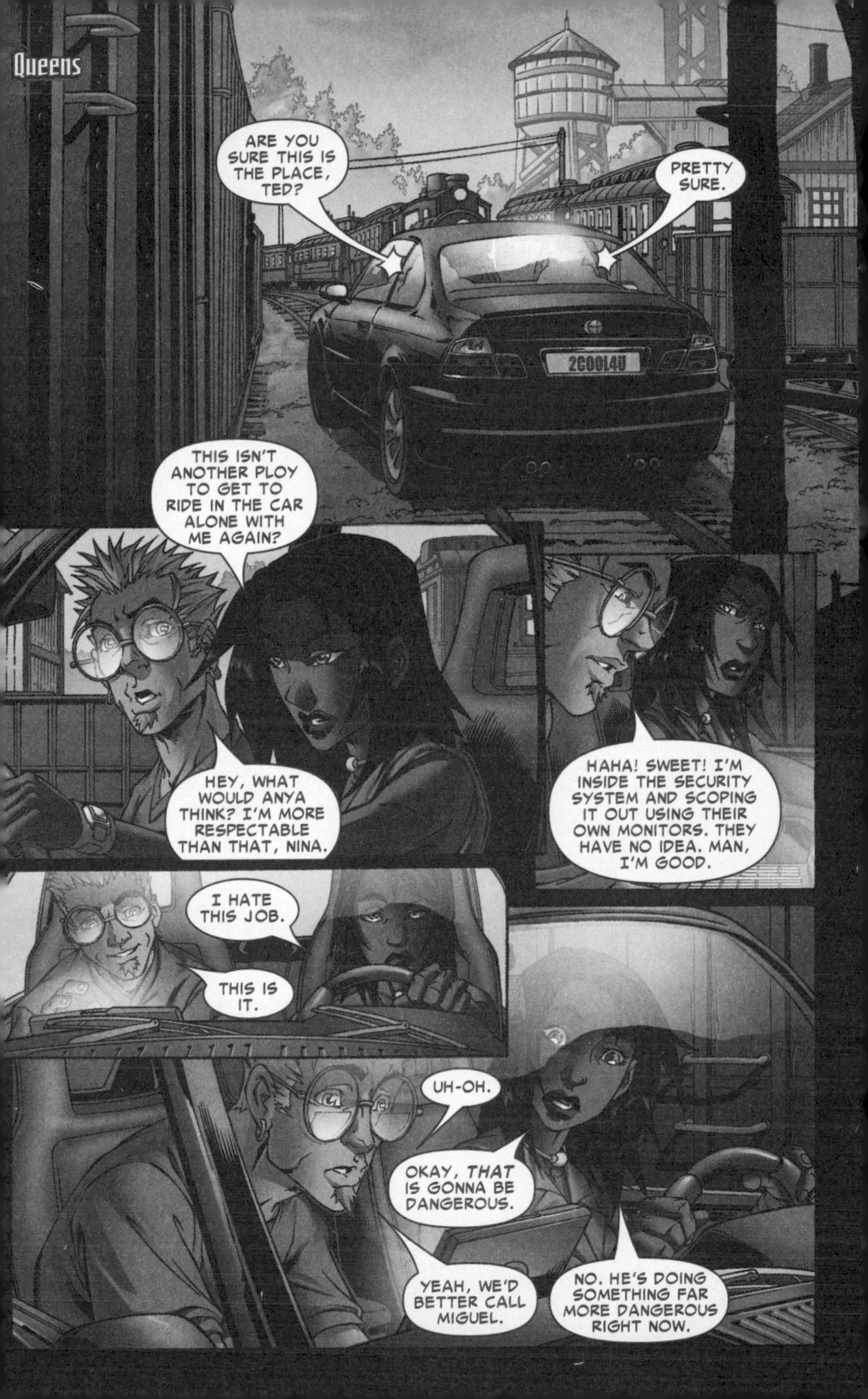
Queens
ARE YOU SURE THIS IS THE PLACE, TED?
PRETTY SURE.
2COOL4U
THIS ISN'T ANOTHER PLOY TO GET TO RIDE IN THE CAR ALONE WITH ME AGAIN?
HEY, WHAT WOULD ANYA THINK? I'M MORE RESPECTABLE THAN THAT, NINA.
HAHA! SWEET! I'M INSIDE THE SECURITY SYSTEM AND SCOPING IT OUT USING THEIR OWN MONITORS. THEY HAVE NO IDEA. MAN, I'M GOOD.
I HATE THIS JOB.
THIS IS IT.
UH-OH.
OKAY, *THAT* IS GONNA BE DANGEROUS.
YEAH, WE'D BETTER CALL MIGUEL.
NO. HE'S DOING SOMETHING FAR MORE DANGEROUS RIGHT NOW.

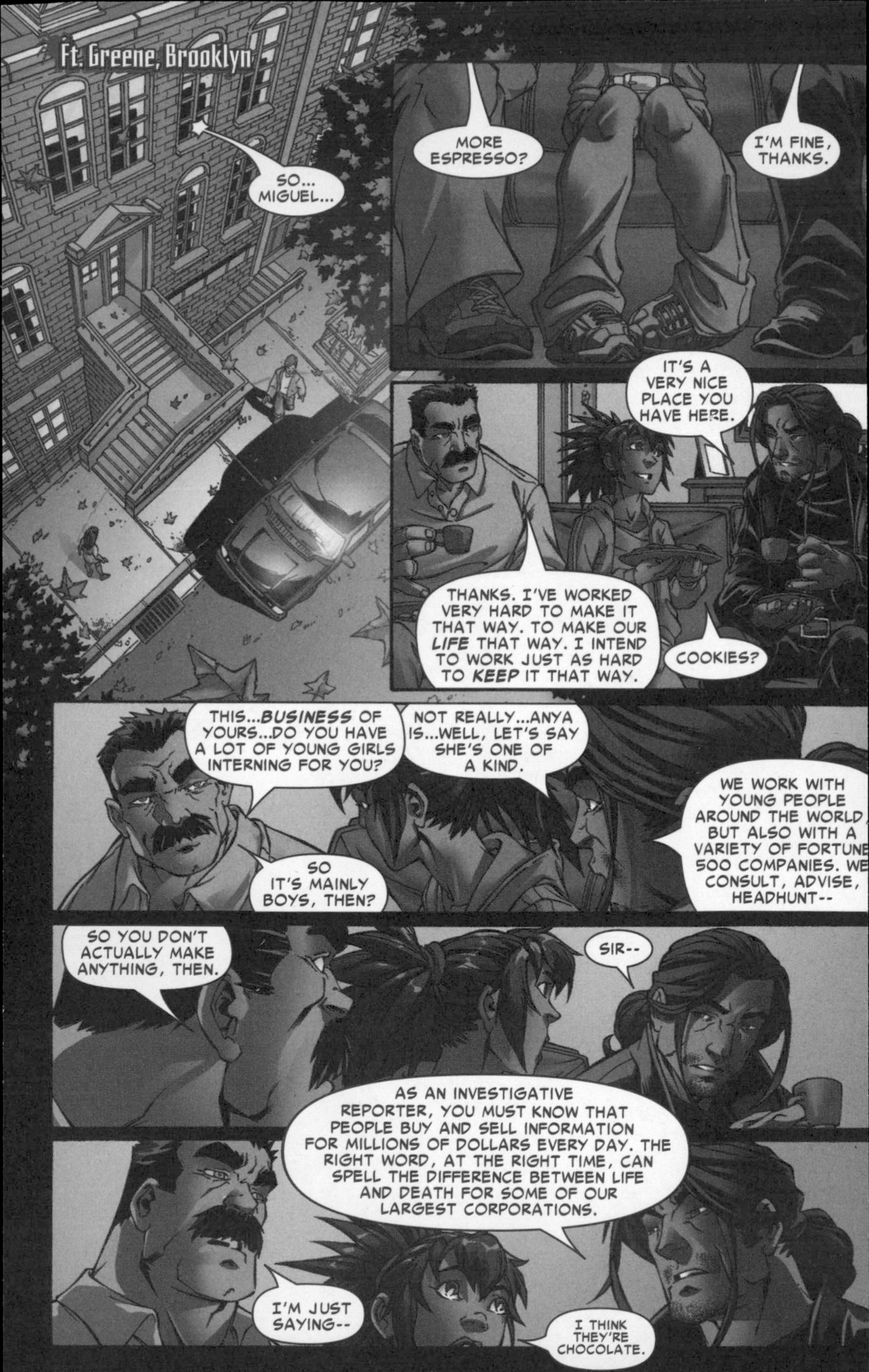
Ft. Greene, Brooklyn
SO... MIGUEL...
MORE ESPRESSO?
I'M FINE, THANKS.
IT'S A VERY NICE PLACE YOU HAVE HERE.
THANKS. I'VE WORKED VERY HARD TO MAKE IT THAT WAY. TO MAKE OUR *LIFE* THAT WAY. I INTEND TO WORK JUST AS HARD TO *KEEP* IT THAT WAY.
COOKIES?
THIS...*BUSINESS* OF YOURS...DO YOU HAVE A LOT OF YOUNG GIRLS INTERNING FOR YOU?
NOT REALLY...ANYA IS...WELL, LET'S SAY SHE'S ONE OF A KIND.
SO IT'S MAINLY BOYS, THEN?
WE WORK WITH YOUNG PEOPLE AROUND THE WORLD, BUT ALSO WITH A VARIETY OF FORTUNE 500 COMPANIES. WE CONSULT, ADVISE, HEADHUNT--
SO YOU DON'T ACTUALLY MAKE ANYTHING, THEN.
SIR--
AS AN INVESTIGATIVE REPORTER, YOU MUST KNOW THAT PEOPLE BUY AND SELL INFORMATION FOR MILLIONS OF DOLLARS EVERY DAY. THE RIGHT WORD, AT THE RIGHT TIME, CAN SPELL THE DIFFERENCE BETWEEN LIFE AND DEATH FOR SOME OF OUR LARGEST CORPORATIONS.
I'M JUST SAYING--
I THINK THEY'RE CHOCOLATE.

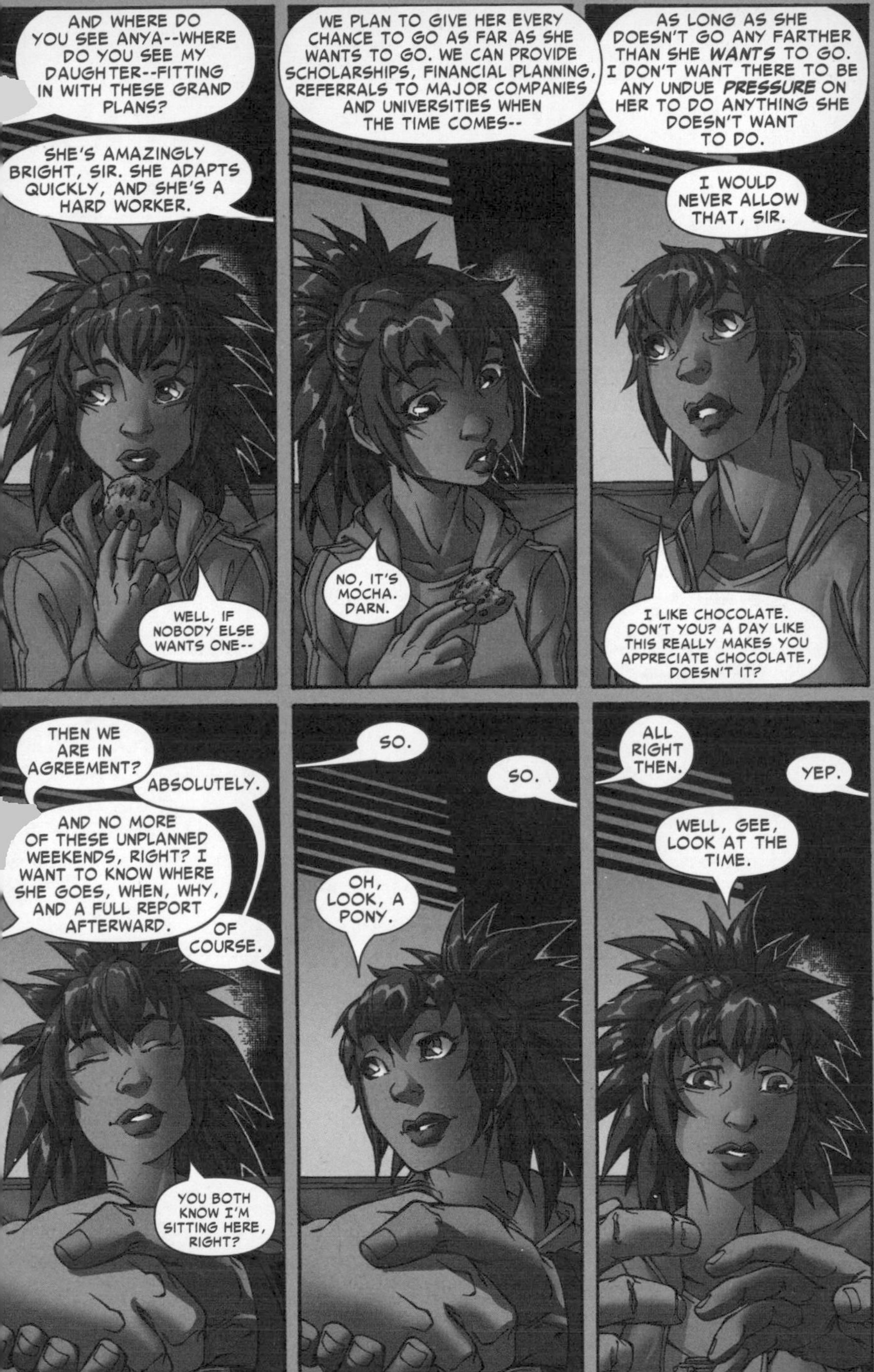
AND WHERE DO YOU SEE ANYA--WHERE DO YOU SEE MY DAUGHTER--FITTING IN WITH THESE GRAND PLANS?
SHE'S AMAZINGLY BRIGHT, SIR. SHE ADAPTS QUICKLY, AND SHE'S A HARD WORKER.
WELL, IF NOBODY ELSE WANTS ONE--
WE PLAN TO GIVE HER EVERY CHANCE TO GO AS FAR AS SHE WANTS TO GO. WE CAN PROVIDE SCHOLARSHIPS, FINANCIAL PLANNING, REFERRALS TO MAJOR COMPANIES AND UNIVERSITIES WHEN THE TIME COMES--
NO, IT'S MOCHA. DARN.
AS LONG AS SHE DOESN'T GO ANY FARTHER THAN SHE *WANTS* TO GO. I DON'T WANT THERE TO BE ANY UNDUE *PRESSURE* ON HER TO DO ANYTHING SHE DOESN'T WANT TO DO.
I WOULD NEVER ALLOW THAT, SIR.
I LIKE CHOCOLATE. DON'T YOU? A DAY LIKE THIS REALLY MAKES YOU APPRECIATE CHOCOLATE, DOESN'T IT?
THEN WE ARE IN AGREEMENT?
ABSOLUTELY.
AND NO MORE OF THESE UNPLANNED WEEKENDS, RIGHT? I WANT TO KNOW WHERE SHE GOES, WHEN, WHY, AND A FULL REPORT AFTERWARD.
OF COURSE.
YOU BOTH KNOW I'M SITTING HERE, RIGHT?
SO.
SO.
OH, LOOK, A PONY.
ALL RIGHT THEN.
YEP.
WELL, GEE, LOOK AT THE TIME.

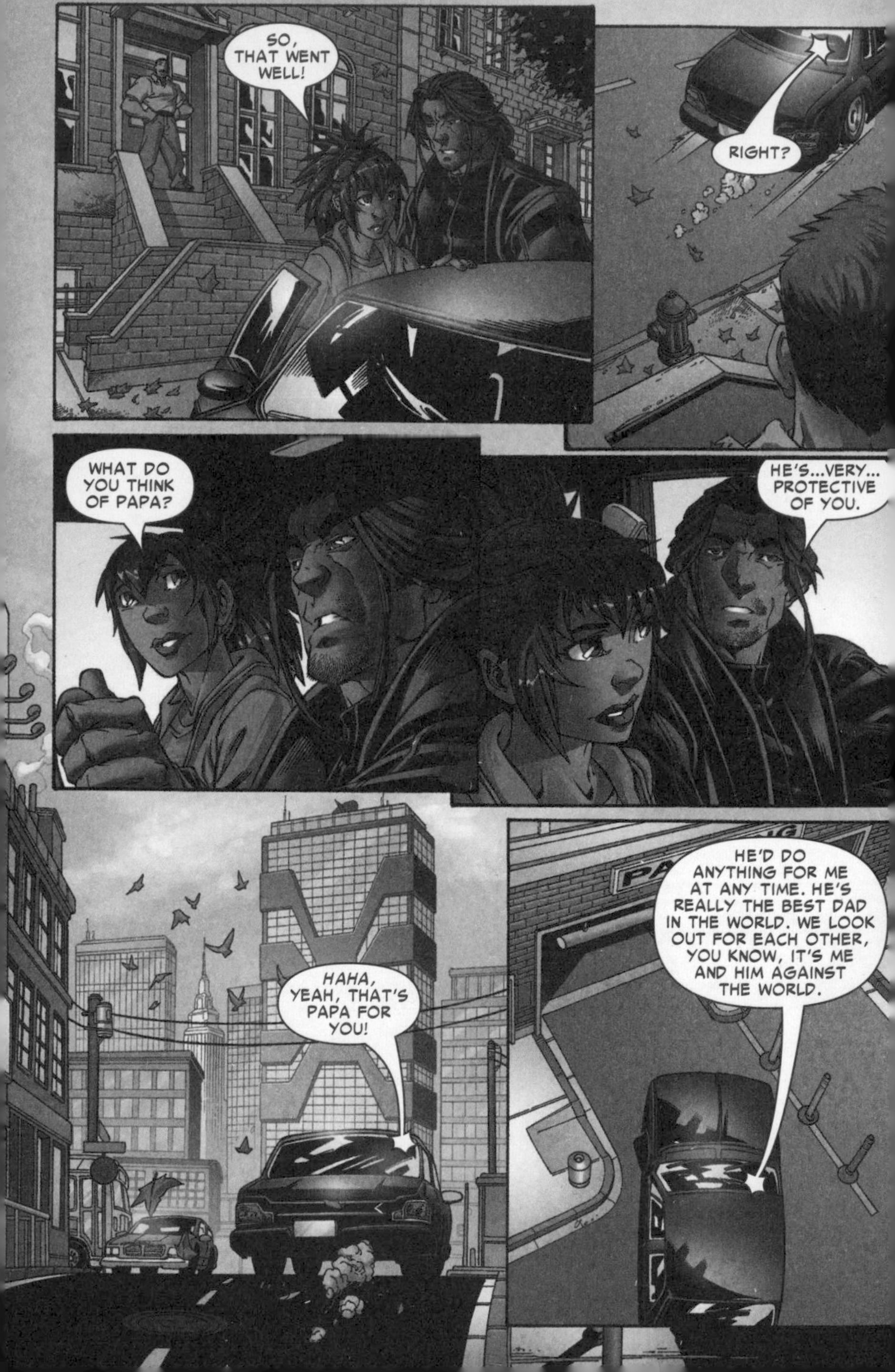
SO, THAT WENT WELL!
RIGHT?
WHAT DO YOU THINK OF PAPA?
HE'S...VERY... PROTECTIVE OF YOU.
HAHA, YEAH, THAT'S PAPA FOR YOU!
HE'D DO ANYTHING FOR ME AT ANY TIME. HE'S REALLY THE BEST DAD IN THE WORLD. WE LOOK OUT FOR EACH OTHER, YOU KNOW, IT'S ME AND HIM AGAINST THE WORLD.

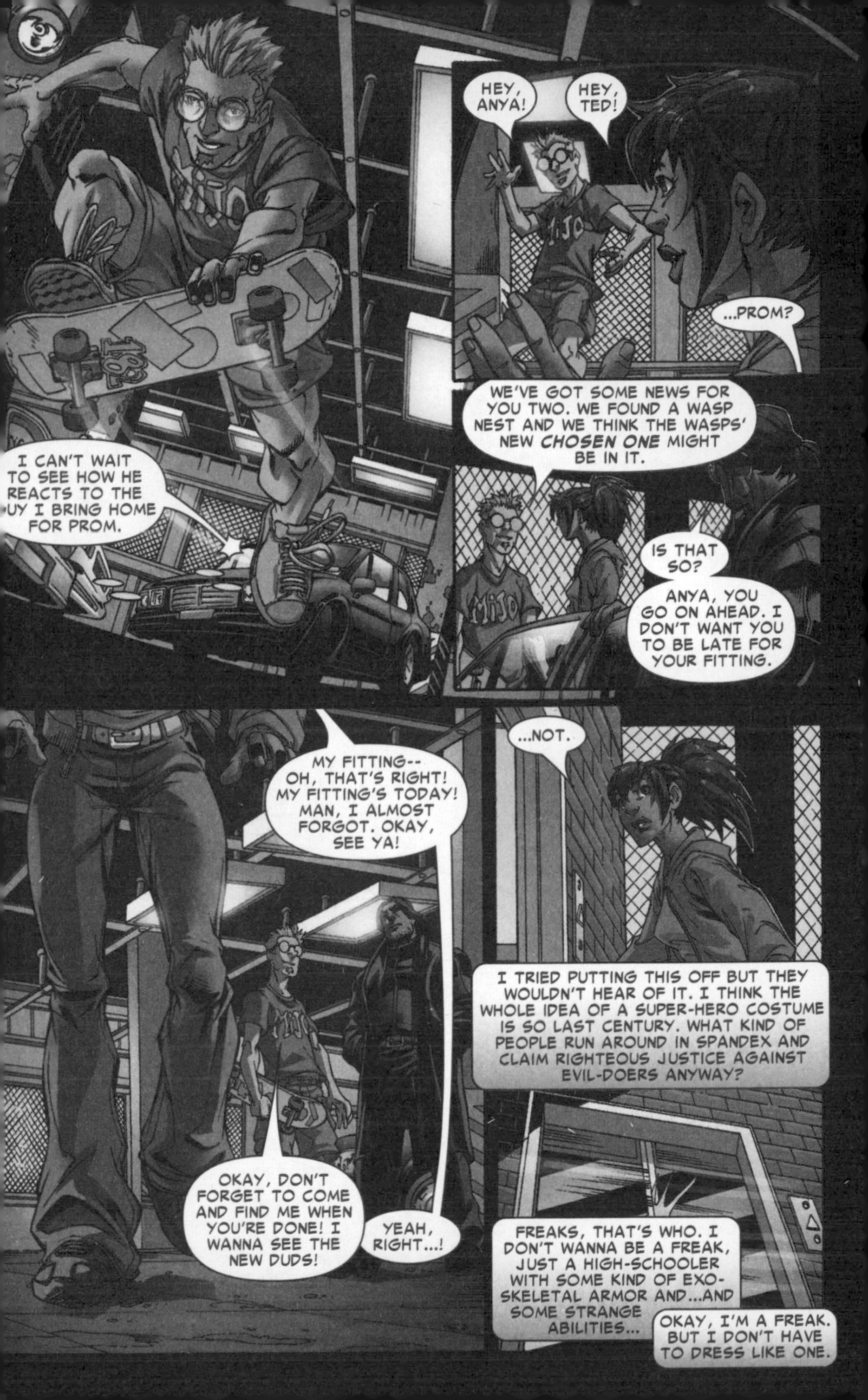
HEY, ANYA!
HEY, TED!
...PROM?
I CAN'T WAIT TO SEE HOW HE REACTS TO THE UY I BRING HOME FOR PROM.
WE'VE GOT SOME NEWS FOR YOU TWO. WE FOUND A WASP NEST AND WE THINK THE WASPS' NEW CHOSEN ONE MIGHT BE IN IT.
IS THAT SO?
ANYA, YOU GO ON AHEAD. I DON'T WANT YOU TO BE LATE FOR YOUR FITTING.
MY FITTING-- OH, THAT'S RIGHT! MY FITTING'S TODAY! MAN, I ALMOST FORGOT. OKAY, SEE YA!
OKAY, DON'T FORGET TO COME AND FIND ME WHEN YOU'RE DONE! I WANNA SEE THE NEW DUDS!
YEAH, RIGHT...!
...NOT.
I TRIED PUTTING THIS OFF BUT THEY WOULDN'T HEAR OF IT. I THINK THE WHOLE IDEA OF A SUPER-HERO COSTUME IS SO LAST CENTURY. WHAT KIND OF PEOPLE RUN AROUND IN SPANDEX AND CLAIM RIGHTEOUS JUSTICE AGAINST EVIL-DOERS ANYWAY?
FREAKS, THAT'S WHO. I DON'T WANNA BE A FREAK, JUST A HIGH-SCHOOLER WITH SOME KIND OF EXO-SKELETAL ARMOR AND...AND SOME STRANGE ABILITIES...
OKAY, I'M A FREAK. BUT I DON'T HAVE TO DRESS LIKE ONE.

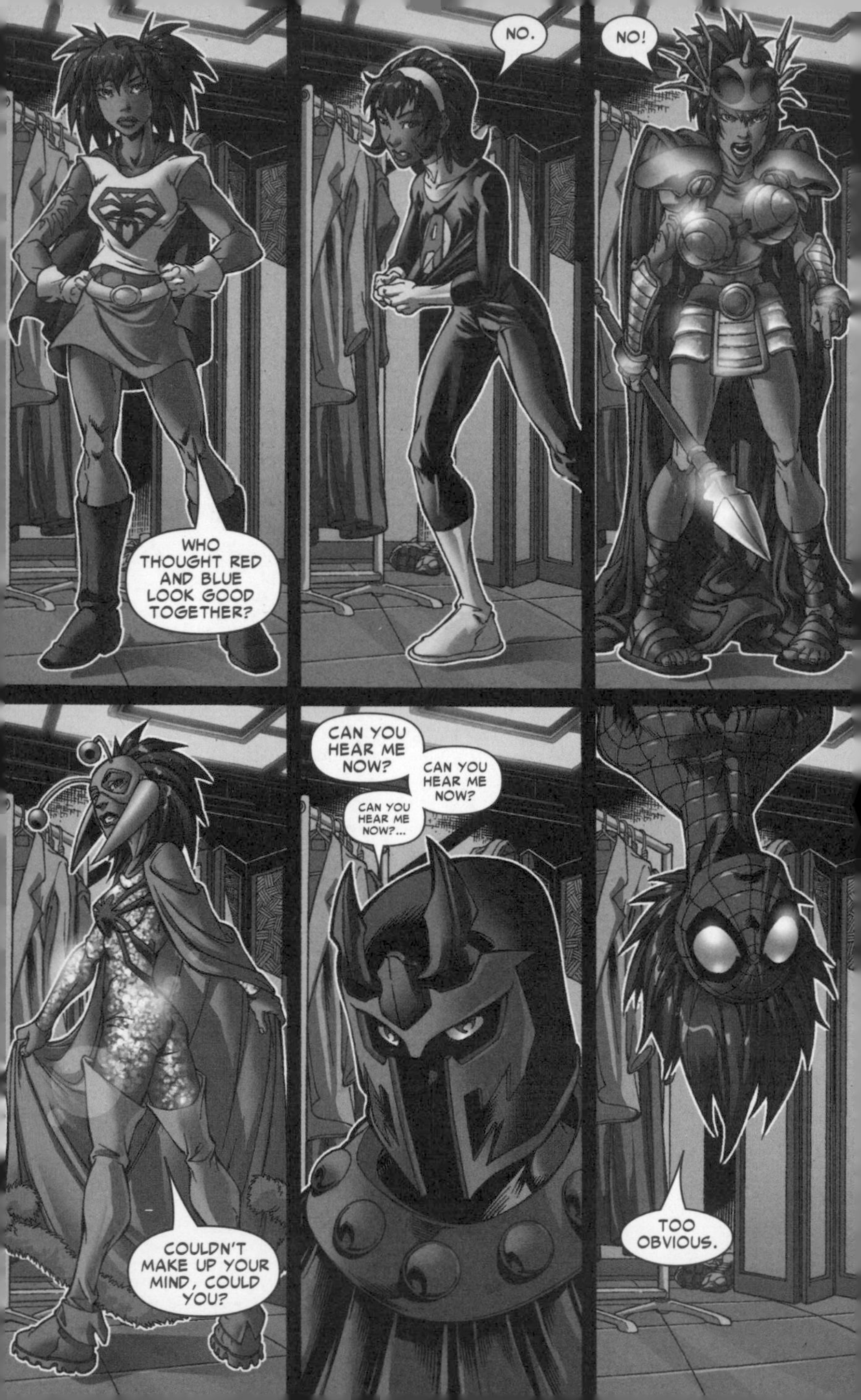
WHO THOUGHT RED AND BLUE LOOK GOOD TOGETHER?
NO.
NO!
COULDN'T MAKE UP YOUR MIND, COULD YOU?
CAN YOU HEAR ME NOW?
CAN YOU HEAR ME NOW?
CAN YOU HEAR ME NOW?...
TOO OBVIOUS.

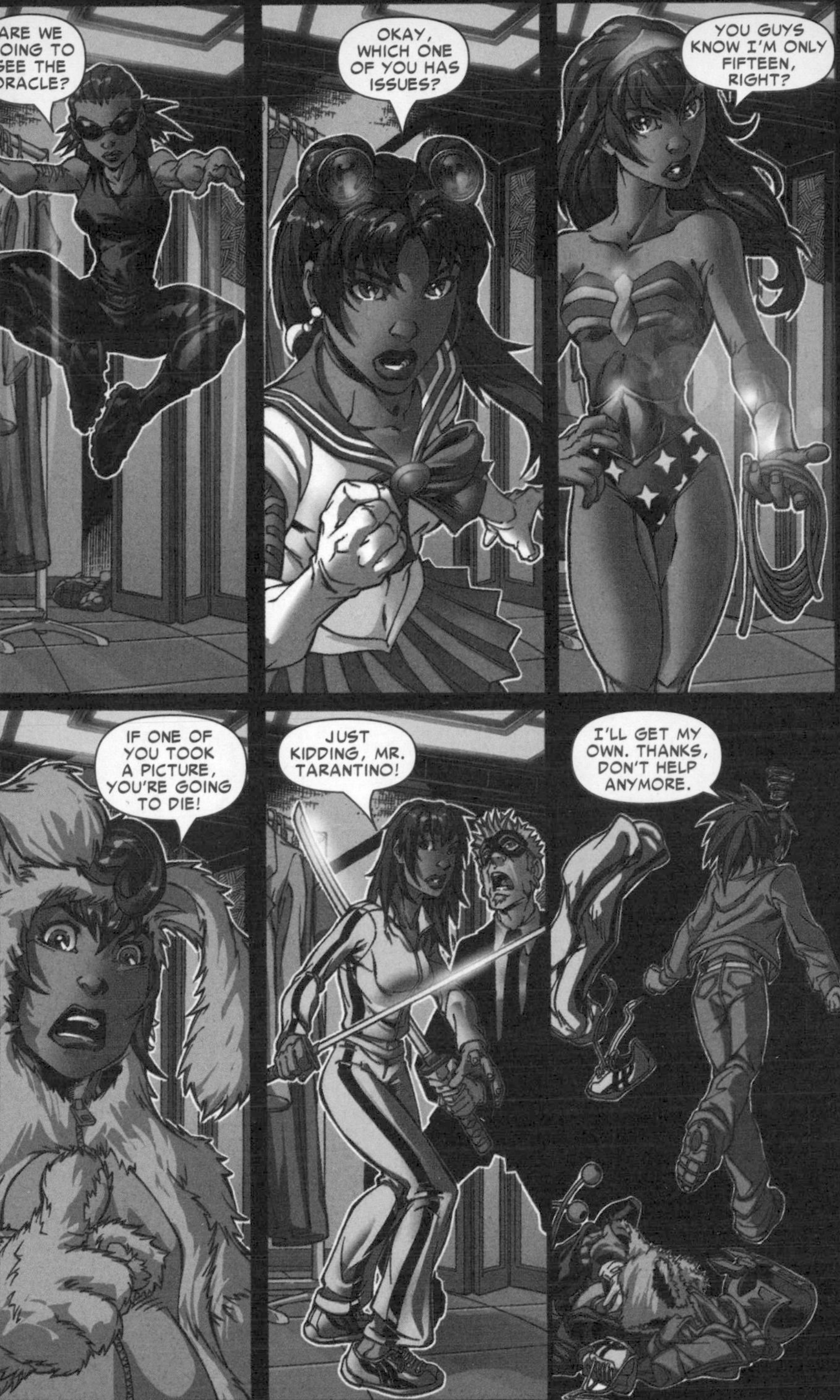
ARE WE GOING TO SEE THE ORACLE?
OKAY, WHICH ONE OF YOU HAS ISSUES?
YOU GUYS KNOW I'M ONLY FIFTEEN, RIGHT?
IF ONE OF YOU TOOK A PICTURE, YOU'RE GOING TO DIE!
JUST KIDDING, MR. TARANTINO!
I'LL GET MY OWN. THANKS, DON'T HELP ANYMORE.

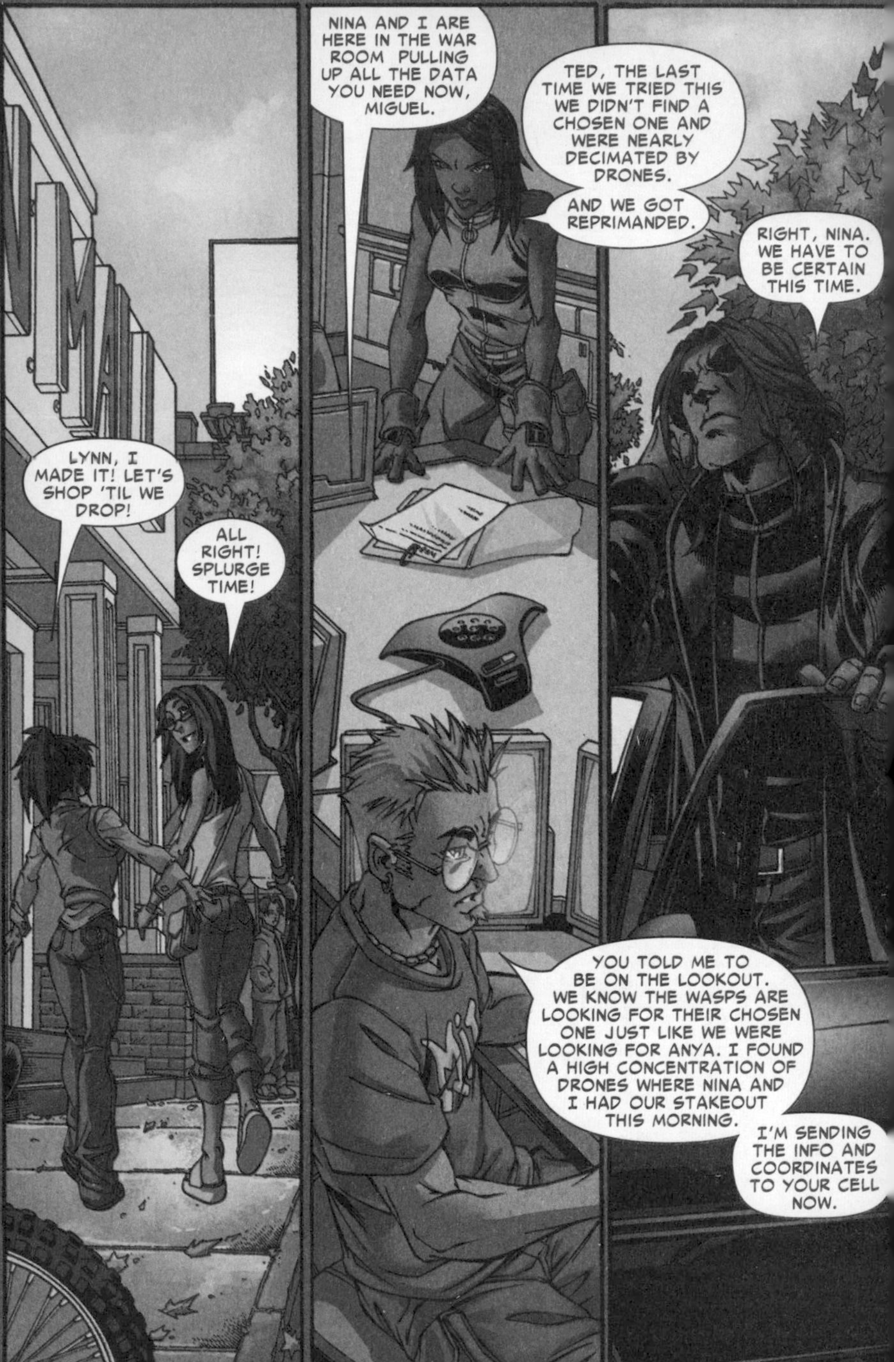
LYNN, I MADE IT! LET'S SHOP 'TIL WE DROP!
ALL RIGHT! SPLURGE TIME!
NINA AND I ARE HERE IN THE WAR ROOM PULLING UP ALL THE DATA YOU NEED NOW, MIGUEL.
TED, THE LAST TIME WE TRIED THIS WE DIDN'T FIND A CHOSEN ONE AND WERE NEARLY DECIMATED BY DRONES.
AND WE GOT REPRIMANDED.
RIGHT, NINA. WE HAVE TO BE CERTAIN THIS TIME.
YOU TOLD ME TO BE ON THE LOOKOUT. WE KNOW THE WASPS ARE LOOKING FOR THEIR CHOSEN ONE JUST LIKE WE WERE LOOKING FOR ANYA. I FOUND A HIGH CONCENTRATION OF DRONES WHERE NINA AND I HAD OUR STAKEOUT THIS MORNING.
I'M SENDING THE INFO AND COORDINATES TO YOUR CELL NOW.

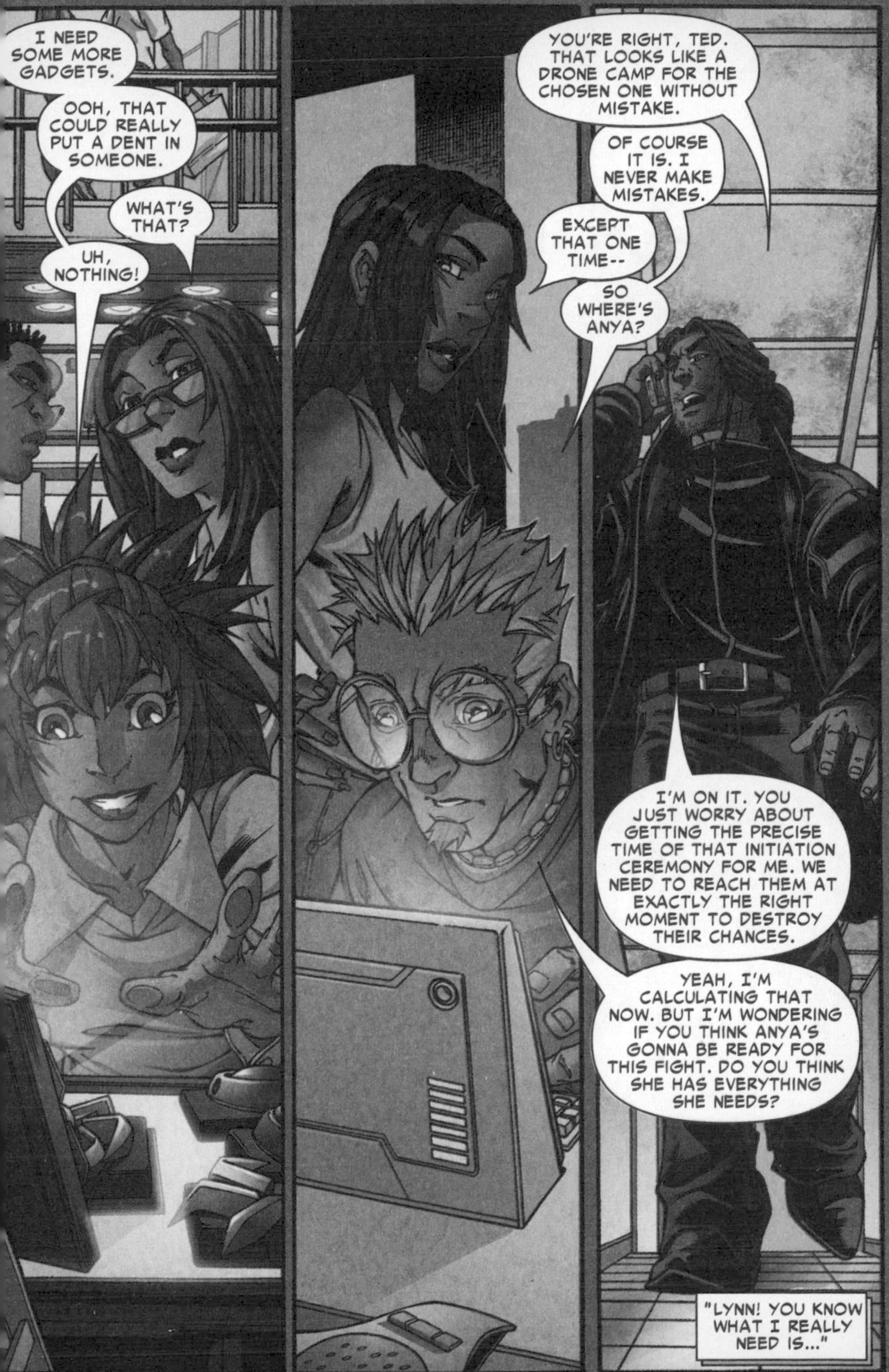
I NEED SOME MORE GADGETS.
OOH, THAT COULD REALLY PUT A DENT IN SOMEONE.
WHAT'S THAT?
UH, NOTHING!
YOU'RE RIGHT, TED. THAT LOOKS LIKE A DRONE CAMP FOR THE CHOSEN ONE WITHOUT MISTAKE.
OF COURSE IT IS. I NEVER MAKE MISTAKES.
EXCEPT THAT ONE TIME--
SO WHERE'S ANYA?
I'M ON IT. YOU JUST WORRY ABOUT GETTING THE PRECISE TIME OF THAT INITIATION CEREMONY FOR ME. WE NEED TO REACH THEM AT EXACTLY THE RIGHT MOMENT TO DESTROY THEIR CHANCES.
YEAH, I'M CALCULATING THAT NOW. BUT I'M WONDERING IF YOU THINK ANYA'S GONNA BE READY FOR THIS FIGHT. DO YOU THINK SHE HAS EVERYTHING SHE NEEDS?
"LYNN! YOU KNOW WHAT I REALLY NEED IS..."

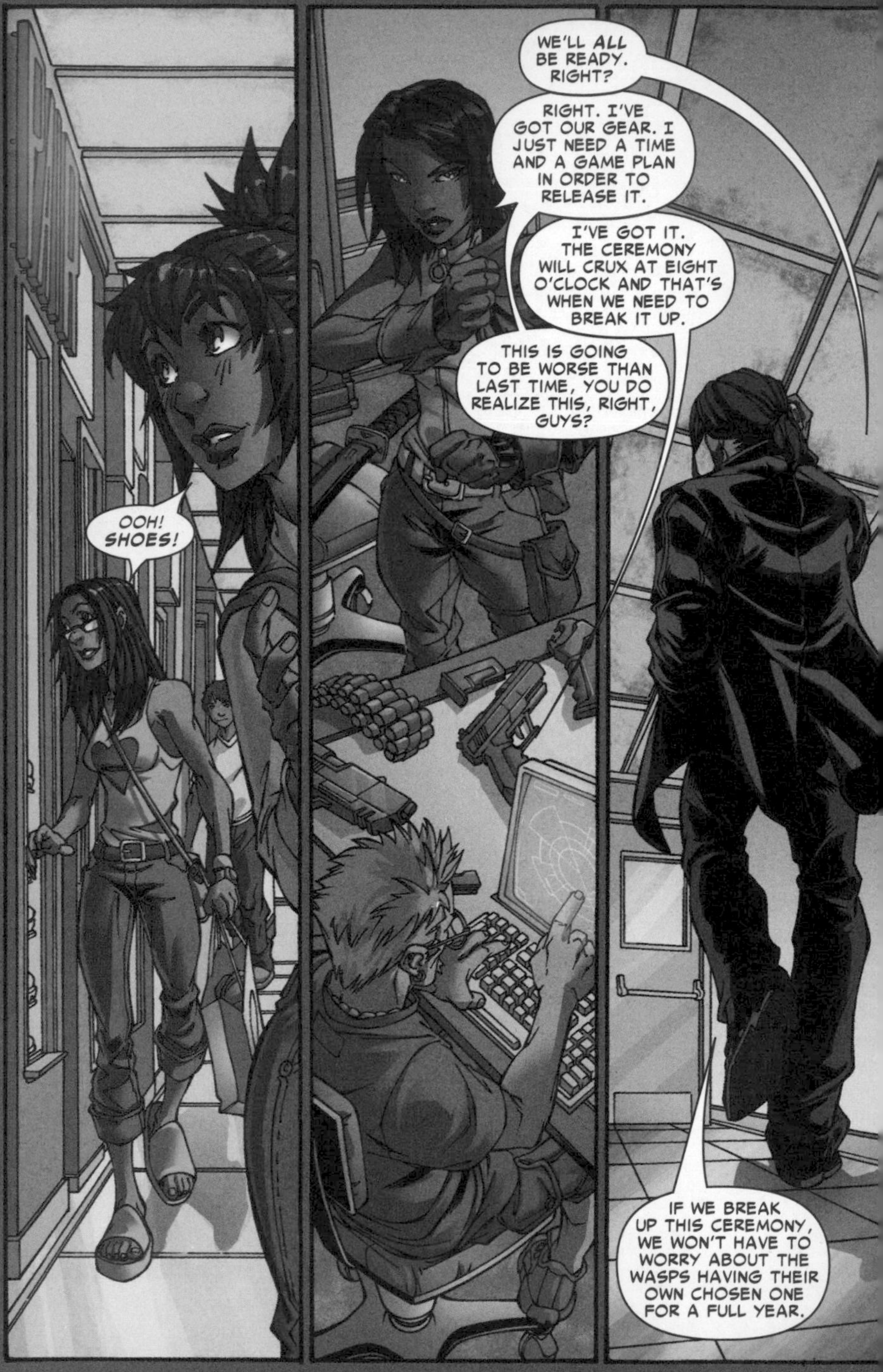
OOH! SHOES!
WE'LL ALL BE READY. RIGHT?
RIGHT. I'VE GOT OUR GEAR. I JUST NEED A TIME AND A GAME PLAN IN ORDER TO RELEASE IT.
I'VE GOT IT. THE CEREMONY WILL CRUX AT EIGHT O'CLOCK AND THAT'S WHEN WE NEED TO BREAK IT UP.
THIS IS GOING TO BE WORSE THAN LAST TIME, YOU DO REALIZE THIS, RIGHT, GUYS?
IF WE BREAK UP THIS CEREMONY, WE WON'T HAVE TO WORRY ABOUT THE WASPS HAVING THEIR OWN CHOSEN ONE FOR A FULL YEAR.

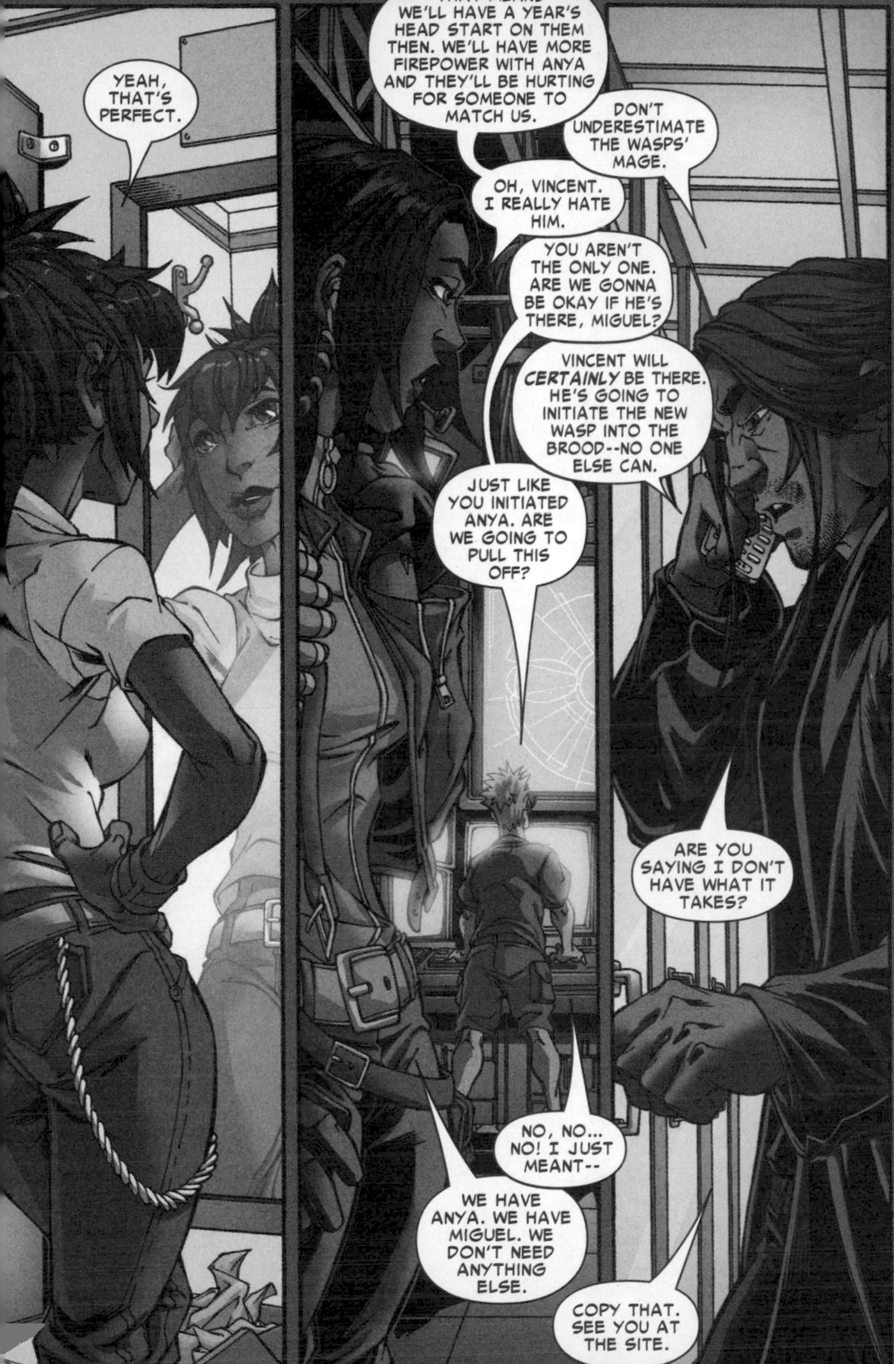
YEAH, THAT'S PERFECT.
THAT MEANS WE'LL HAVE A YEAR'S HEAD START ON THEM THEN. WE'LL HAVE MORE FIREPOWER WITH ANYA AND THEY'LL BE HURTING FOR SOMEONE TO MATCH US.
DON'T UNDERESTIMATE THE WASPS' MAGE.
OH, VINCENT. I REALLY HATE HIM.
YOU AREN'T THE ONLY ONE. ARE WE GONNA BE OKAY IF HE'S THERE, MIGUEL?
VINCENT WILL *CERTAINLY* BE THERE. HE'S GOING TO INITIATE THE NEW WASP INTO THE BROOD--NO ONE ELSE CAN.
JUST LIKE YOU INITIATED ANYA. ARE WE GOING TO PULL THIS OFF?
ARE YOU SAYING I DON'T HAVE WHAT IT TAKES?
NO, NO... NO! I JUST MEANT--
WE HAVE ANYA. WE HAVE MIGUEL. WE DON'T NEED ANYTHING ELSE.
COPY THAT. SEE YOU AT THE SITE.

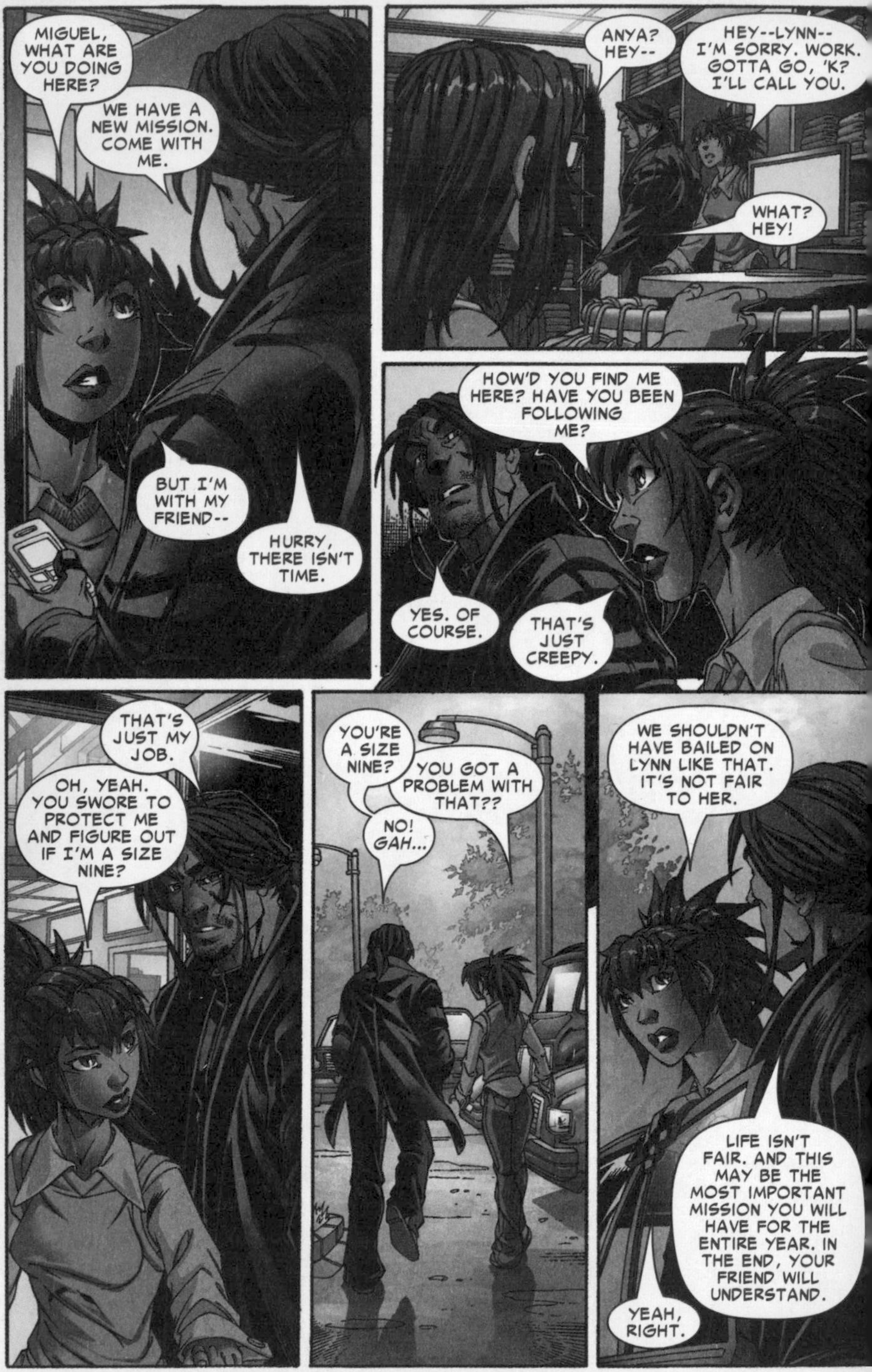
MIGUEL, WHAT ARE YOU DOING HERE?
WE HAVE A NEW MISSION. COME WITH ME.
BUT I'M WITH MY FRIEND--
HURRY, THERE ISN'T TIME.
ANYA? HEY--
HEY--LYNN-- I'M SORRY. WORK. GOTTA GO, 'K? I'LL CALL YOU.
WHAT? HEY!
HOW'D YOU FIND ME HERE? HAVE YOU BEEN FOLLOWING ME?
YES. OF COURSE.
THAT'S JUST CREEPY.
THAT'S JUST MY JOB.
OH, YEAH. YOU SWORE TO PROTECT ME AND FIGURE OUT IF I'M A SIZE NINE?
YOU'RE A SIZE NINE?
YOU GOT A PROBLEM WITH THAT??
NO! GAH...
WE SHOULDN'T HAVE BAILED ON LYNN LIKE THAT. IT'S NOT FAIR TO HER.
LIFE ISN'T FAIR. AND THIS MAY BE THE MOST IMPORTANT MISSION YOU WILL HAVE FOR THE ENTIRE YEAR. IN THE END, YOUR FRIEND WILL UNDERSTAND.
YEAH, RIGHT.

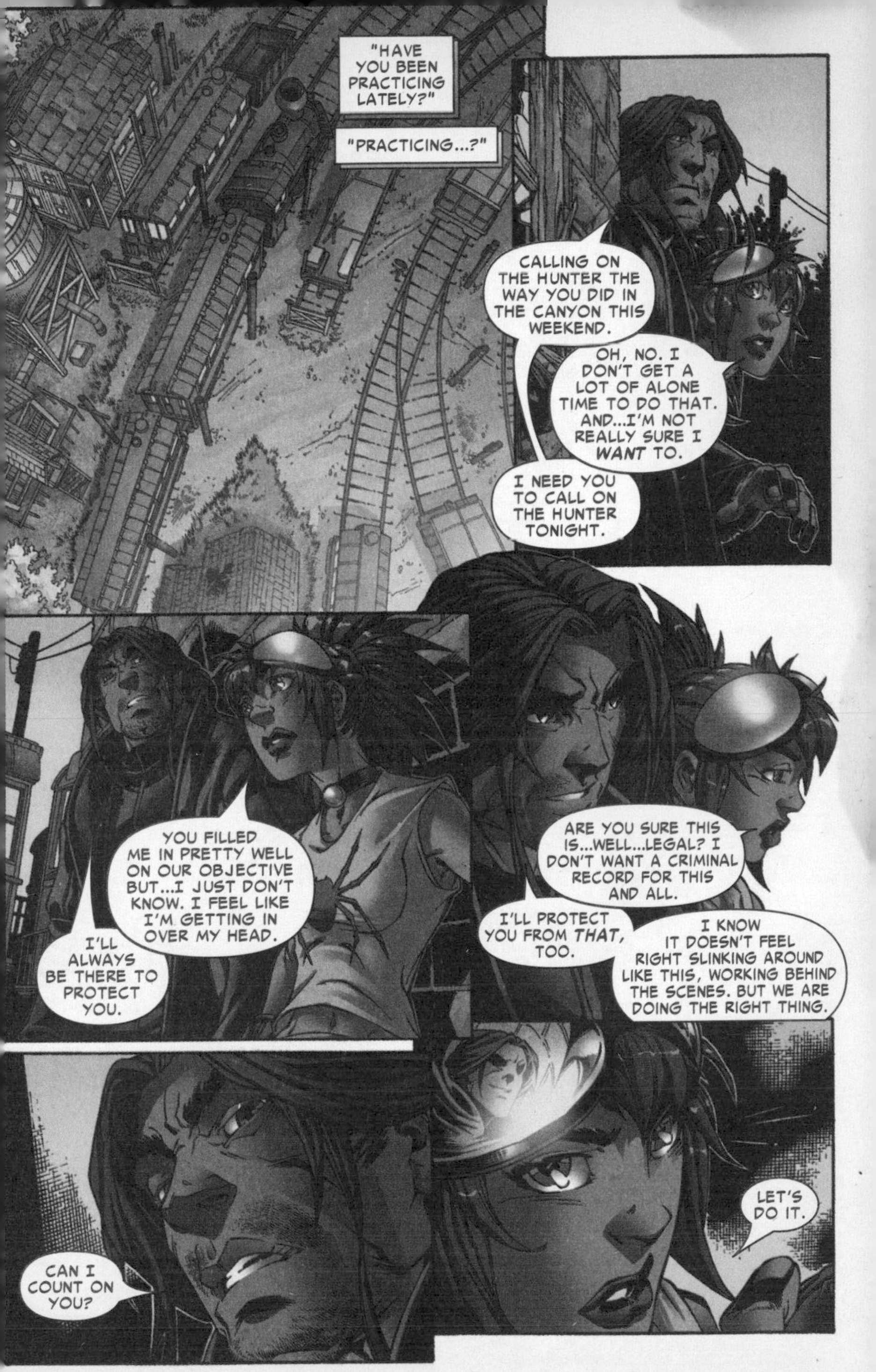
"HAVE YOU BEEN PRACTICING LATELY?"
"PRACTICING...?"
CALLING ON THE HUNTER THE WAY YOU DID IN THE CANYON THIS WEEKEND.
OH, NO. I DON'T GET A LOT OF ALONE TIME TO DO THAT. AND...I'M NOT REALLY SURE I *WANT* TO.
I NEED YOU TO CALL ON THE HUNTER TONIGHT.
YOU FILLED ME IN PRETTY WELL ON OUR OBJECTIVE BUT...I JUST DON'T KNOW. I FEEL LIKE I'M GETTING IN OVER MY HEAD.
I'LL ALWAYS BE THERE TO PROTECT YOU.
ARE YOU SURE THIS IS...WELL...LEGAL? I DON'T WANT A CRIMINAL RECORD FOR THIS AND ALL.
I'LL PROTECT YOU FROM *THAT*, TOO.
I KNOW IT DOESN'T FEEL RIGHT SLINKING AROUND LIKE THIS, WORKING BEHIND THE SCENES. BUT WE ARE DOING THE RIGHT THING.
CAN I COUNT ON YOU?
LET'S DO IT.

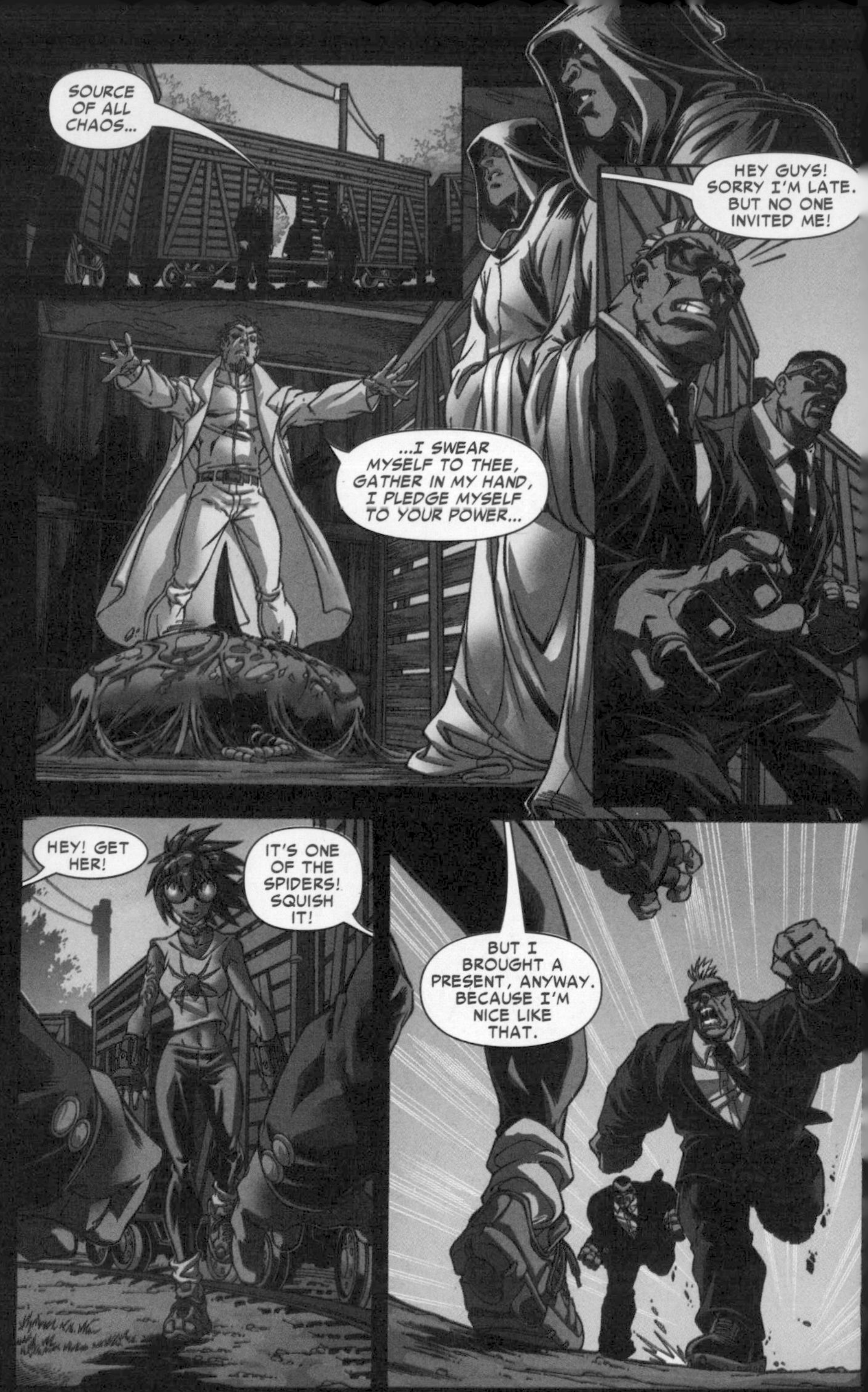
SOURCE OF ALL CHAOS...
...I SWEAR MYSELF TO THEE, GATHER IN MY HAND, I PLEDGE MYSELF TO YOUR POWER...
HEY GUYS! SORRY I'M LATE. BUT NO ONE INVITED ME!
HEY! GET HER!
IT'S ONE OF THE SPIDERS! SQUISH IT!
BUT I BROUGHT A PRESENT, ANYWAY. BECAUSE I'M NICE LIKE THAT.

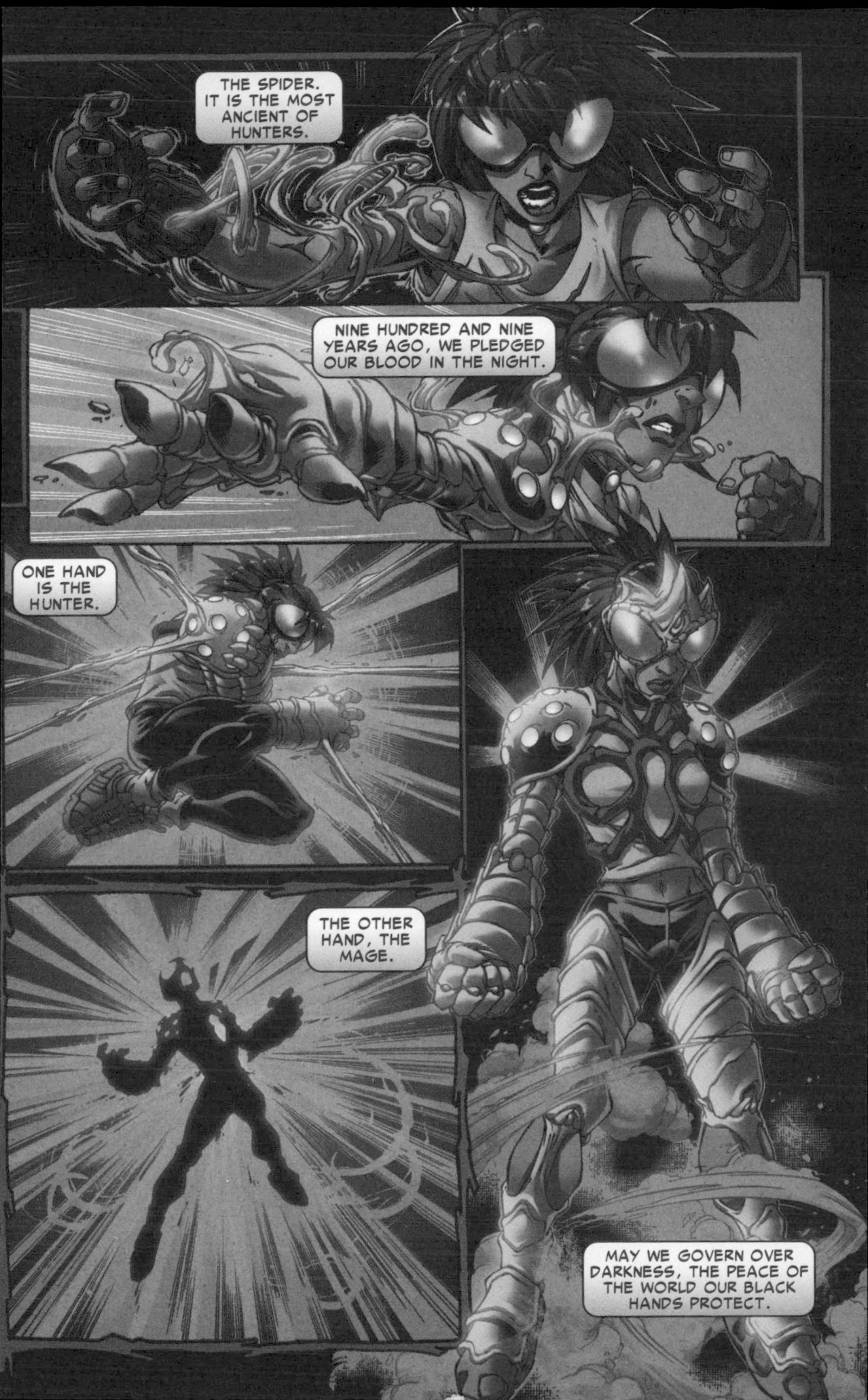
THE SPIDER. IT IS THE MOST ANCIENT OF HUNTERS.
NINE HUNDRED AND NINE YEARS AGO, WE PLEDGED OUR BLOOD IN THE NIGHT.
ONE HAND IS THE HUNTER.
THE OTHER HAND, THE MAGE.
MAY WE GOVERN OVER DARKNESS, THE PEACE OF THE WORLD OUR BLACK HANDS PROTECT.

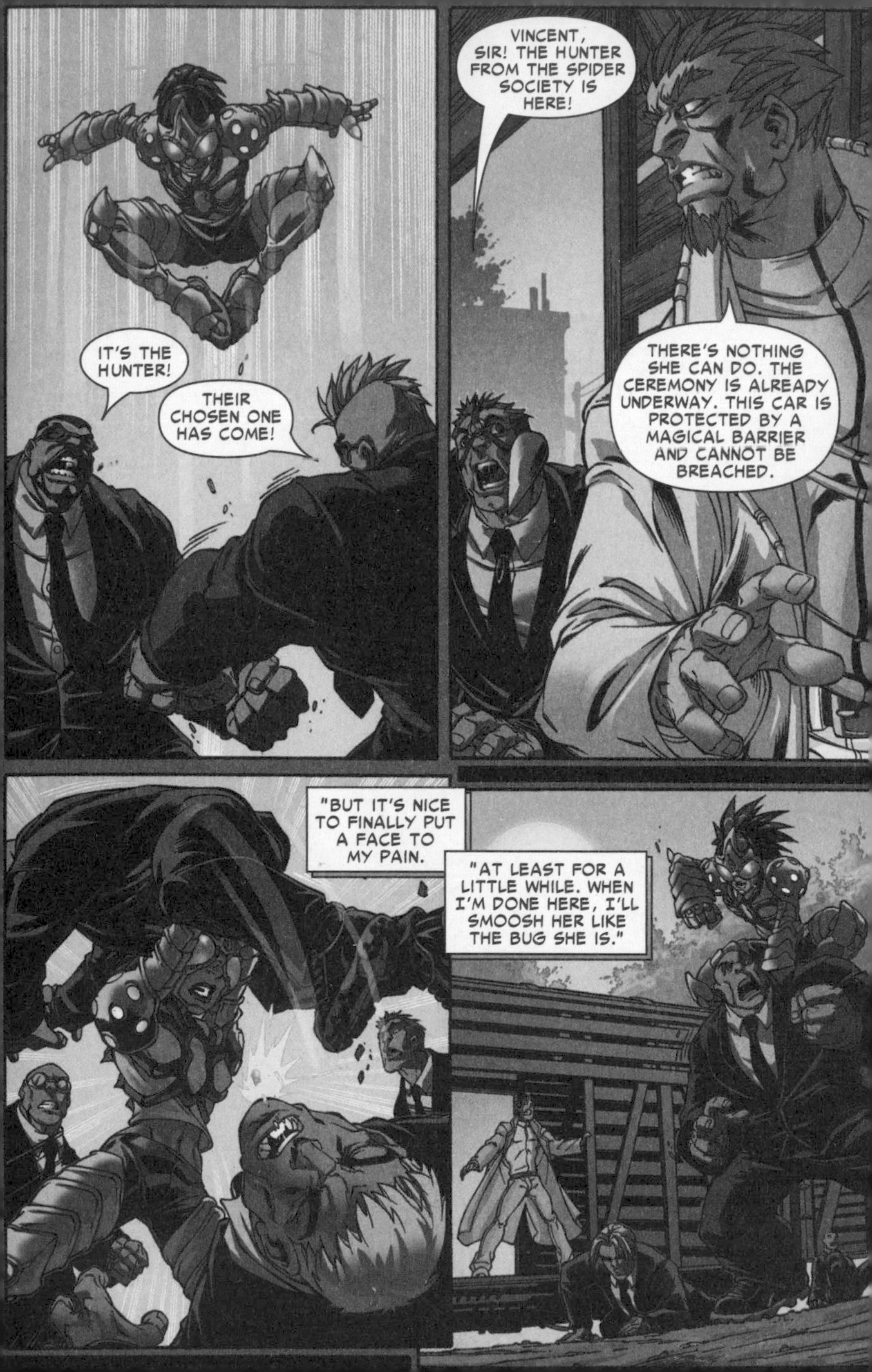
IT'S THE HUNTER!
THEIR CHOSEN ONE HAS COME!
VINCENT, SIR! THE HUNTER FROM THE SPIDER SOCIETY IS HERE!
THERE'S NOTHING SHE CAN DO. THE CEREMONY IS ALREADY UNDERWAY. THIS CAR IS PROTECTED BY A MAGICAL BARRIER AND CANNOT BE BREACHED.
"BUT IT'S NICE TO FINALLY PUT A FACE TO MY PAIN.
"AT LEAST FOR A LITTLE WHILE. WHEN I'M DONE HERE, I'LL SMOOSH HER LIKE THE BUG SHE IS."

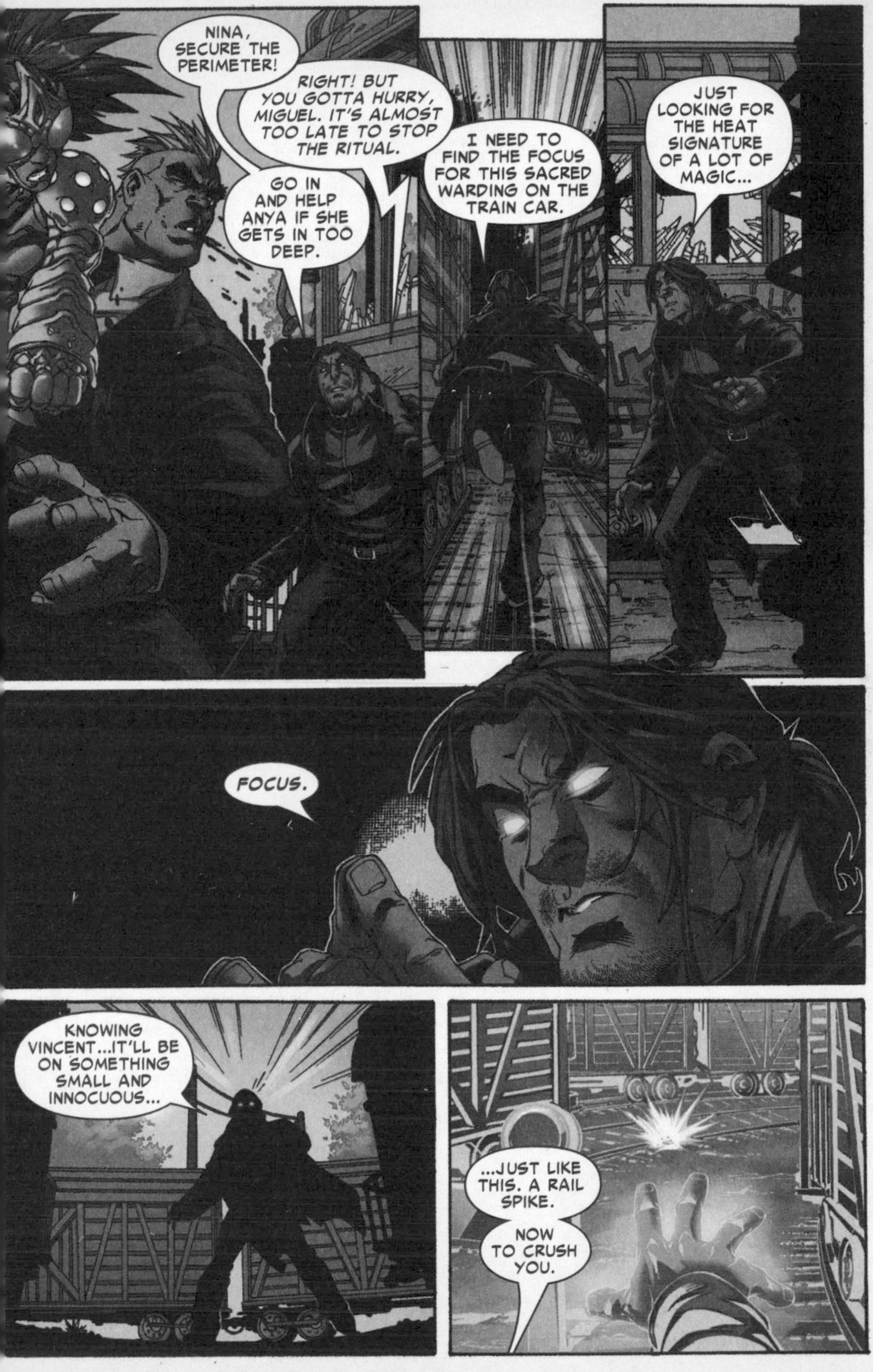
NINA, SECURE THE PERIMETER!
RIGHT! BUT YOU GOTTA HURRY, MIGUEL. IT'S ALMOST TOO LATE TO STOP THE RITUAL.
GO IN AND HELP ANYA IF SHE GETS IN TOO DEEP.
I NEED TO FIND THE FOCUS FOR THIS SACRED WARDING ON THE TRAIN CAR.
JUST LOOKING FOR THE HEAT SIGNATURE OF A LOT OF MAGIC...
FOCUS.
KNOWING VINCENT...IT'LL BE ON SOMETHING SMALL AND INNOCUOUS...
...JUST LIKE THIS. A RAIL SPIKE.
NOW TO CRUSH YOU.

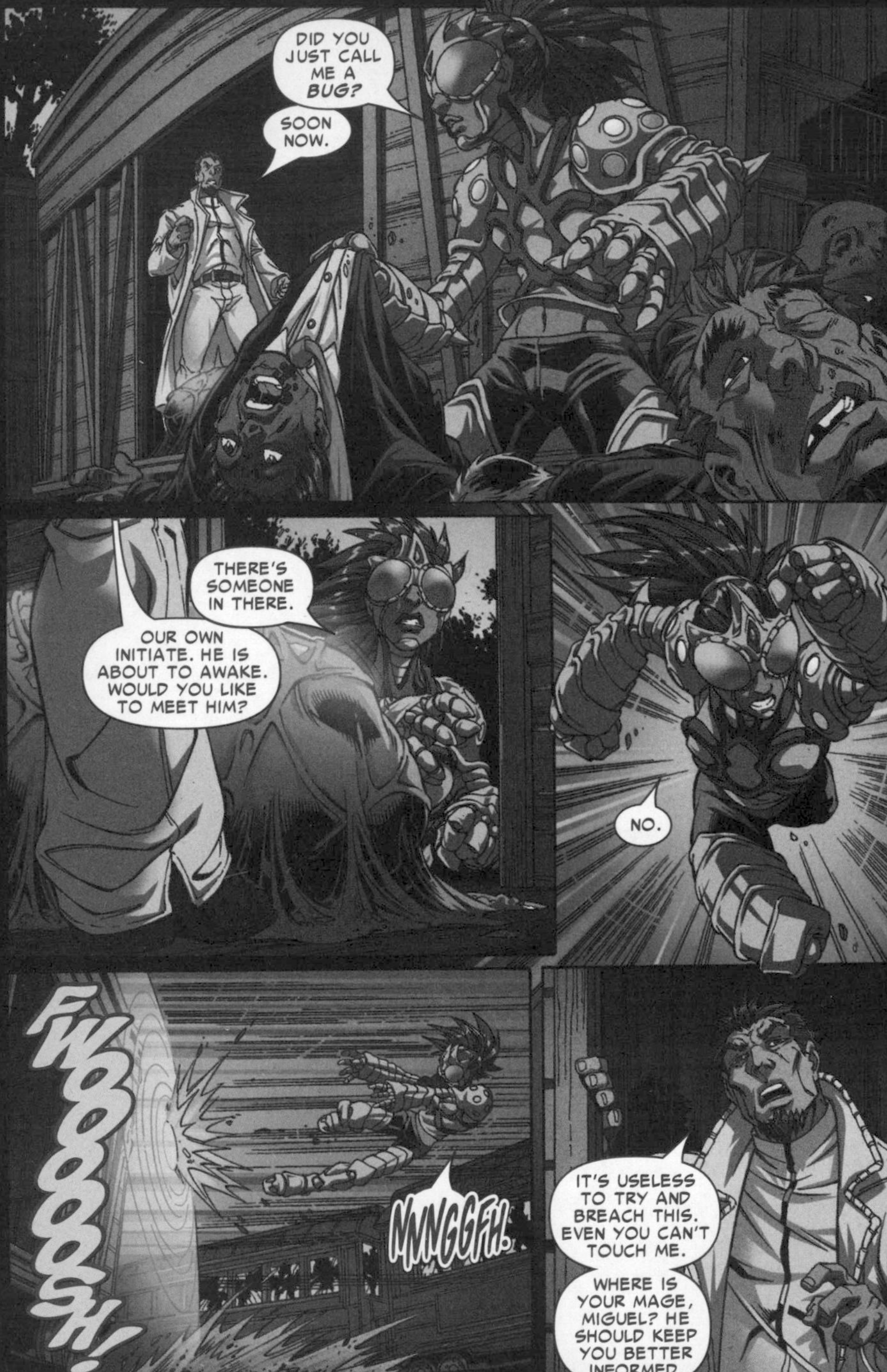
DID YOU JUST CALL ME A *BUG?*
SOON NOW.
THERE'S SOMEONE IN THERE.
OUR OWN INITIATE. HE IS ABOUT TO AWAKE. WOULD YOU LIKE TO MEET HIM?
NO.
FWOOOOOOSH!
NNNGGFH.
IT'S USELESS TO TRY AND BREACH THIS. EVEN YOU CAN'T TOUCH ME.
WHERE IS YOUR MAGE, MIGUEL? HE SHOULD KEEP YOU BETTER INFORMED.

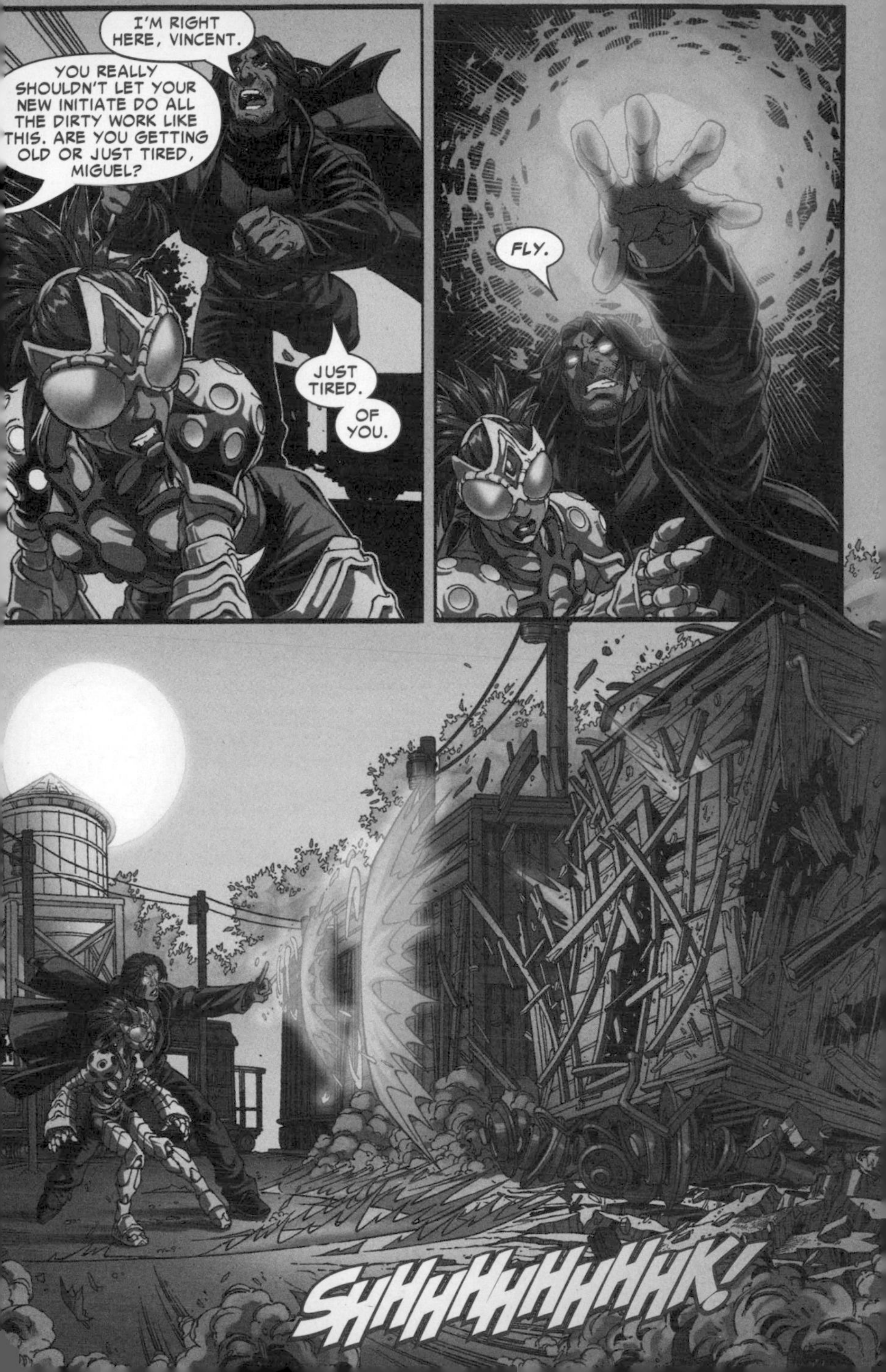
I'M RIGHT HERE, VINCENT.
YOU REALLY SHOULDN'T LET YOUR NEW INITIATE DO ALL THE DIRTY WORK LIKE THIS. ARE YOU GETTING OLD OR JUST TIRED, MIGUEL?
JUST TIRED.
OF YOU.
FLY.
SHHHHHHHHHHK!

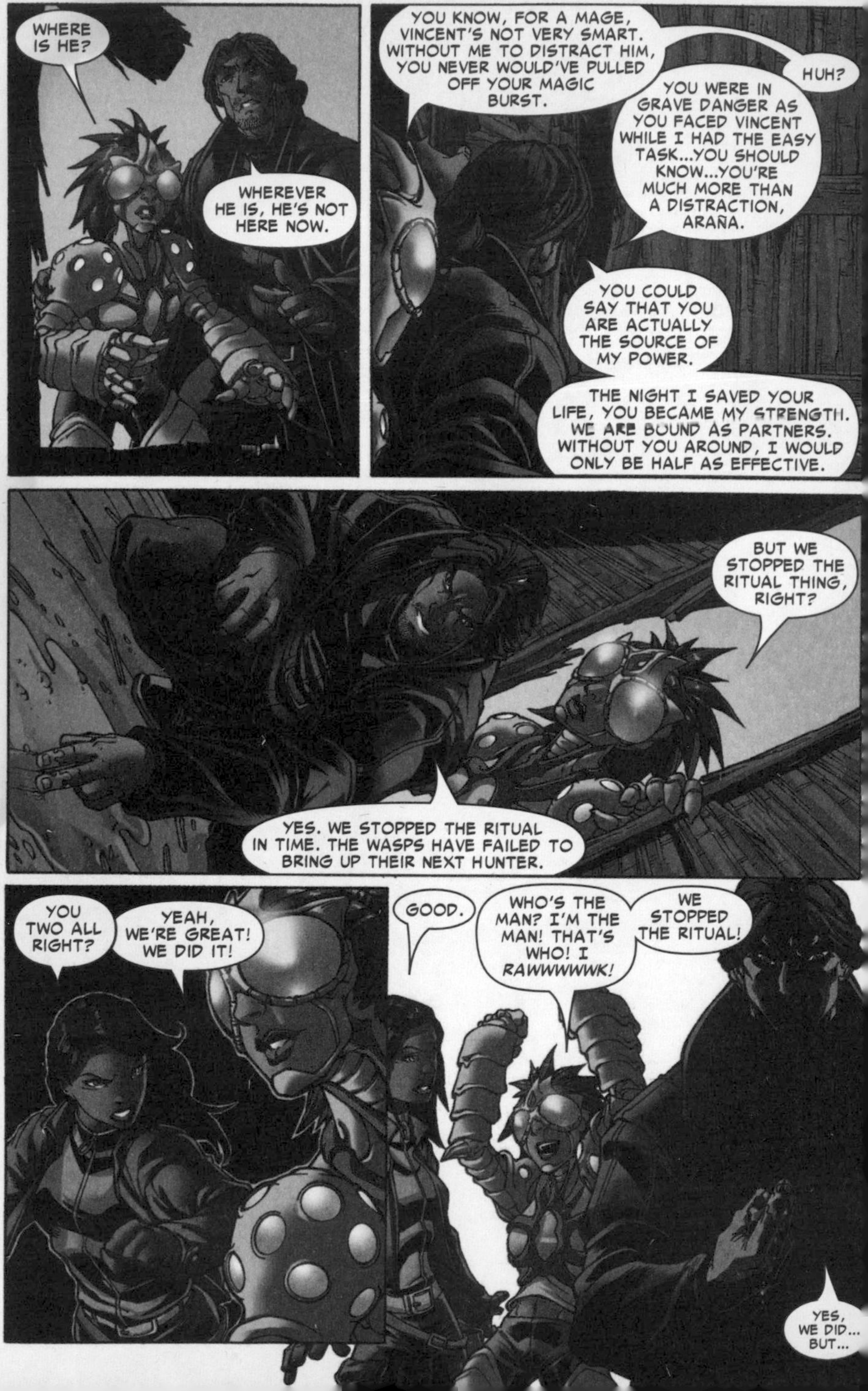
WHERE IS HE?
WHEREVER HE IS, HE'S NOT HERE NOW.
YOU KNOW, FOR A MAGE, VINCENT'S NOT VERY SMART. WITHOUT ME TO DISTRACT HIM, YOU NEVER WOULD'VE PULLED OFF YOUR MAGIC BURST.
HUH?
YOU WERE IN GRAVE DANGER AS YOU FACED VINCENT WHILE I HAD THE EASY TASK...YOU SHOULD KNOW...YOU'RE MUCH MORE THAN A DISTRACTION, ARAÑA.
YOU COULD SAY THAT YOU ARE ACTUALLY THE SOURCE OF MY POWER.
THE NIGHT I SAVED YOUR LIFE, YOU BECAME MY STRENGTH. WE ARE BOUND AS PARTNERS. WITHOUT YOU AROUND, I WOULD ONLY BE HALF AS EFFECTIVE.
BUT WE STOPPED THE RITUAL THING, RIGHT?
YES. WE STOPPED THE RITUAL IN TIME. THE WASPS HAVE FAILED TO BRING UP THEIR NEXT HUNTER.
YOU TWO ALL RIGHT?
YEAH, WE'RE GREAT! WE DID IT!
GOOD.
WHO'S THE MAN? I'M THE MAN! THAT'S WHO! I RAWWWWWK!
WE STOPPED THE RITUAL!
YES, WE DID... BUT...

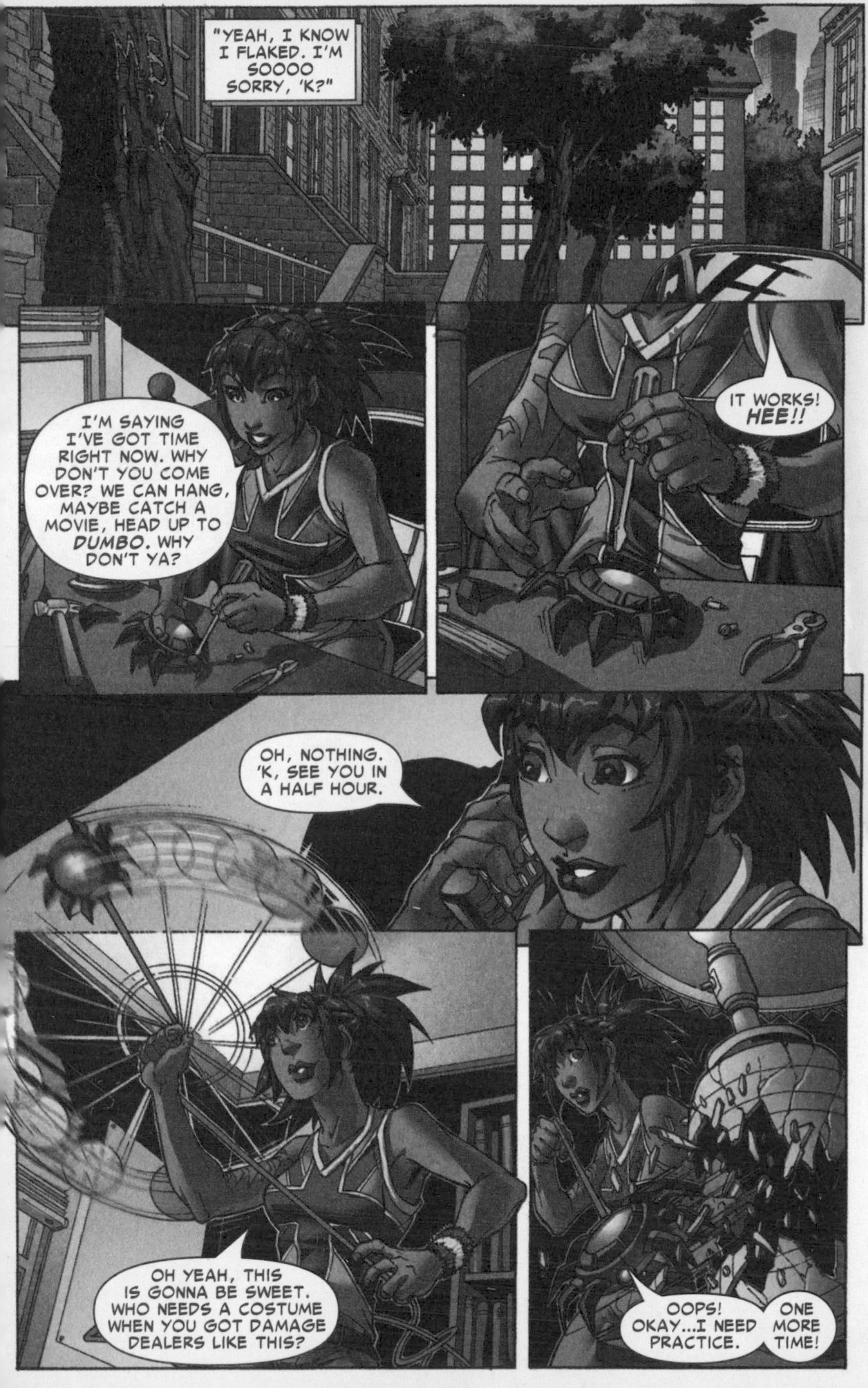
"YEAH, I KNOW I FLAKED. I'M SOOOO SORRY, 'K?"
I'M SAYING I'VE GOT TIME RIGHT NOW. WHY DON'T YOU COME OVER? WE CAN HANG, MAYBE CATCH A MOVIE, HEAD UP TO DUMBO. WHY DON'T YA?
IT WORKS! HEE!!
OH, NOTHING. 'K, SEE YOU IN A HALF HOUR.
OH YEAH, THIS IS GONNA BE SWEET. WHO NEEDS A COSTUME WHEN YOU GOT DAMAGE DEALERS LIKE THIS?
OOPS! OKAY...I NEED PRACTICE.
ONE MORE TIME!

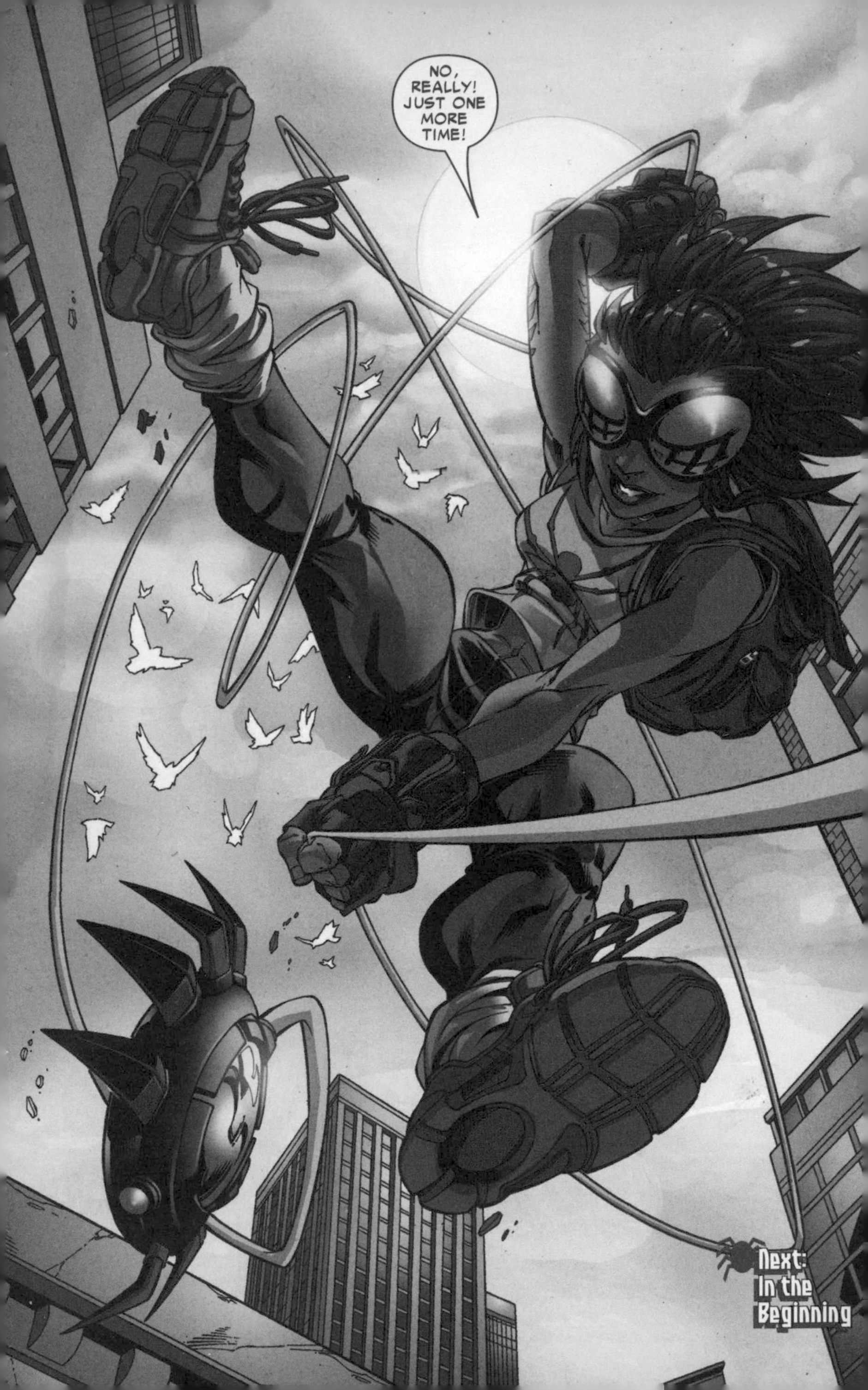
NO, REALLY! JUST ONE MORE TIME!
Next: In the Beginning